PEACEKEEPERS AT WAR

PEACEKEEPERS
AT WAR

Beirut 1983—
The Marine Commander
Tells His Story

Col. Timothy J. Geraghty, USMC (Ret.)

Potomac Books, Inc.
Washington, D.C.

Library of Congress Cataloging-in-Publication Data
Geraghty, Timothy J.
  Peacekeepers at war : Beirut 1983–the marine commander tells his story / Col. Timothy J. Geraghty, USMC (Ret.).
    p. cm.
  Includes bibliographical references and index.
  ISBN 978-1-59797-425-7 (hardcover : alk. paper)
  1. United States Marine Compound Bombing, Beirut, Lebanon, 1983—Personal narratives. 2. Lebanon—History—Israeli intervention, 1982–1984—Personal narratives, American. 3. United States. Marine Corps—History—Arab-Israeli conflict. 4. War on Terrorism, 2001—Causes. 5. Geraghty, Timothy J. I. Title.
  DS87.53.G45 2009
  956.9204'4—dc22

                                                                  2009031630

Potomac Books, Inc.
22841 Quicksilver Drive
Dulles, Virginia 20166

First Edition

10 9 8 7 6 5 4 3 2 1

Contents

Foreword

IT IS A SPECIAL HONOR FOR ME to write the foreword for this superb book, for it permits me to once again pay tribute to the valiant Marines, sailors, and soldiers of the 24th Marine Amphibious Unit whose courage, bravery, and enormous sacrifice, which was borne by them, their families, and loved ones, will live in the hearts and minds of the nation's Corps of Marines forever.

For the first time, *Peacekeepers at War* provides us with a well-researched and most accurate account of a long series of complex events and actions that led to assigning Marine units to the Multinational Peacekeeping Force (MNPF) in Lebanon in the 1982–84 time frame. Our author, Marine Col. Tim Geraghty, commanded the 24th Marine Amphibious Unit (24th MAU) during the toughest and most challenging times as the situation in Lebanon steadily deteriorated. He vividly describes the increasing dangers the USMNF faced and the various steps he took to provide appropriate security measures. In heart-wrenching detail, he codifies the 24th MAU's courageous response to the terrorist bombing of the battalion landing team (BLT) and its headquarters and the recovery operation, including assistance from our allies. Colonel Geraghty further describes the magnitude of the bomb delivered by the Iranian suicide truck driver that virtually assured massive casualties. This attack, of course, would contribute significantly to the terrorists' objective of getting the MNF to withdraw from Lebanon. Looking back, relatively few of us in the intelligence, law enforcement, or defense communities understood the full impact of this powerful bomb. Drawing on his extraordinary knowledge of intelligence and security operations, as well as his personal contacts maintained through the years and his experience in counterterrorist activities with the Central Intelligence Agency, Colonel Geraghty provides us with a unique analysis and leads us in a persuasive manner to his basic theme connecting the Beirut bombing with the multiple 9/11 attacks in the United States to the current war against terrorist activities. Our author's painstaking examination of linkages among various terrorist actors and operations for more than twenty-five years presents a most telling account. His "connecting the dots" reveals, inter alia, that the commander of the Iranian Islamic Revolutionary Guard Corps' contingent operable in Lebanon in 1983 has become Iran's minister of defense today. Other members of that Lebanon contingent have also risen to top tiers in that organization. Finally, Colonel Geraghty accurately points out that the experiences gained by the nations involved in the 1982–84 multinational peacekeeping mission caused major changes and a focus on training, education, and operations that have saved countless lives in fighting terrorism in the twenty-first century.

We selected Col. Tim Geraghty to command the 24th MAU because of his demonstrated leadership and performance for a long period in very demanding assignments. We first met on one of my tours in Vietnam, where he served as an infantry officer commanding one of our reconnaissance companies in 1966. When I was the S-3 of the 12th Marine Regiment, my people taught the Recon Marines how to call in artillery, air, and naval gunfire as part of an extremely successful concept called STINGRAY wherein these patrols behind enemy lines killed or captured thousands of enemy personnel. A most impressive young officer who did his homework and learned quickly, he was later assigned to the 3rd Marine Amphibious Force, Intelligence Division, where his knowledge and analytic talents contributed significantly to our efforts. Our paths have crossed many times since then. In early 1976, at the joint request of the Central Intelligence Agency and Headquarters, Marine Corps, appropriate contacts were made, and Colonel Geraghty was assigned to special operations focusing on counterterrorist activities. From a distance, I kept track of his performance through mutual friends, and his reputation was outstanding. In summary, Colonel Geraghty was considered uniquely qualified to command the MAU, and I still hold that opinion.

In January 1983, I visited Colonel Geraghty at his headquarters for detailed discussions on the various threats that his unit would face when deployed to Lebanon. We had carefully studied all-source intelligence on the region for the entire period of the Marines' 1982–84 commitment to Lebanon. We also kept track of events at the operational and tactical levels and had a standing threat analysis effort for the entire area. During my visit I emphasized the point that the main threat to our peacekeeping efforts and to the MNF would come from terrorist actions. Colonel Geraghty agreed and had already placed antiterrorism training and counterterrorist preparedness at the top of his priority list. We talked for several hours, reviewing much of the data we had studied and learned over the years. In my case, I had been deeply involved in special operations and special intelligence activities at all levels. Also, I was a member of the Holloway Commission, which reviewed the Iranian hostage rescue effort and U.S. counterterrorist activities in 1980. While commanding the Second Marine Division during this period, I also held a sensitive collateral assignment that involved, among other responsibilities, providing oversight of U.S. military counterterrorist operational planning for the Department of Defense in concert with the intelligence community. Colonel Geraghty was informed of our intent to provide additional special intelligence, surveillance, communications, and antiterrorist capabilities (as we had done for the earlier MAU deployments) to his command. We then covered special considerations when using these units and the need for all our people to be street-smart and to routinely play the "what if" game.

A Marine BLT has been deployed to the Mediterranean since 1948 on a continuous basis and normally rotates every six months. In 1971 we formally added an aviation element (called a composite squadron) and a logistics support group and renamed the organizations MAUs. These MAUs became the smallest of our Marine air-ground task forces (MAGTFs) with about eighteen hundred people. Next in size was the Marine amphibious brigade (MAB) with sixteen thousand to twenty thousand people, and the largest MAGTF (with forty-five thousand to fifty thousand Marines and sailors) was designated the Marine amphibious force (MAF). Since the end of the Vietnam conflict, the I MAF has been located at Camp Pendleton, California; the II MAF is based in the Carolinas (Cherry Point and Camp Lejeune in North Carolina and Beaufort, South Carolina); and the III MAF is located in Okinawa. In February 1988 the titles of all MAGTFs were changed by replacing "amphibious" with "expeditionary" to reflect the wide range of capabilities they possess.

As background, the II MAF conducted all its training and deployment activities as a MAGTF under a single commander and in concert with its navy counterparts at all levels. A Navy amphibious squadron (PHIBRON) was designated as the amphibious readiness group (ARG) counterpart for the MAU. Lt. Gen. John Miller was the overall II MAF commander responsible for organizing, training, equipping, and providing MAUs to the Sixth Fleet for operations in his area of interest.

Maj. Gen. Keith Smith, who sadly lost a son in the Beirut bombing, commanded the 2nd Marine Aircraft Wing, and Brig. Gen. Bob Winglass commanded the II MAF's logistics force, which was then called the 2nd Force Service Support Group. These three general officers were superb professionals with a wealth of knowledge and experience. Since we worked extremely well together and were close friends, our forces were known as the "Carolina MAGTF" with teamwork as our hallmark. Lieutenant General Miller, a wise and distinguished leader whom I had been privileged to serve with before, was physically located in Norfolk, Virginia. He also commanded all our Marine forces in the Atlantic and European areas. He therefore informally assigned me the task of overseeing the preparation of MAUs for deployment. As the commanding general of the 2nd Marine Division (the force ground combat element) and as the senior officer present, I had overall responsibility for the organization, training, equipping, and supporting the 24th MAU as well as all the other MAUs that served in Lebanon for the MNF mission. Therefore, I was responsible for the readiness and preparedness of the 24th MAU and not Colonel Geraghty. Further, I was directly responsible for the total performance of the BLT command by Lt. Col. Larry Gerlach, a distinguished combat veteran who had also been seriously wounded in Vietnam. We selected Larry for this command because of his overall background and experience as well as his demonstrated knack for handling complex challenges. I made these facts clear to the secretary of the navy and to the secretary of defense in the aftermath of the terrorist bombing of our BLT headquarters.

In addition to aviation and logistics units, the MAU's basic infantry battalion is normally reinforced with amphibious assault vehicles, armor, antiarmor, artillery, combat engineers, and reconnaissance and communication capabilities. This setup was the basic organization of our BLTs for many years, and they were structured in that manner for the Lebanon commitment. Fixed-winged attack and airlift/refueler aircraft were also assigned and kept in standby readiness status in the United States or forward deployed in the region of interest. Finally, an air alert regiment was assigned with the lead elements of a battalion on six hours' notice.

Because of the aforementioned threat from terrorist activities and the overall situation in Lebanon, additional II MAF capabilities were provided our MAUs. These assets included photographic imagery interpretation units, counterintelligence teams, air and naval gunfire liaison company detachments (specially trained

Marines to serve with allied forces and U.S. Army airborne units), defense systems security teams (provided by the National Security Agency), sensor control and management personnel (Marines skilled in seismic and acoustic surveillance), explosive ordnance demolition personnel, interrogator/translator teams, navy environmental preventive medicine units, additional combat and force engineer support, army target acquisition battery personnel, military police detachments, special communication facilities (for direct communications with national intelligence sources), detachments from the radio battalions (special intelligence support), and additional Marine scout and sniper experts. Additionally, all members of the ground combat element had two weeks of schooling on mines, booby traps, explosive devices, and related matters (conducted by our combat engineer battalion). Nevertheless, the Long Commission's investigation of the terrorist bombing of our headquarters concluded, among other things, "that our USMNF was not trained, organized, staffed or supported to deal effectively with the terrorist threat in Lebanon." It must be said that the II MAF made a super effort to get it right. In all fairness to the Long Commission, I believe the members were unaware of most of what we did and how we prepared units. My scheduled appearance to brief them and answer their questions was cancelled (after waiting eight hours to see them in the Pentagon), and the press of time apparently precluded a return visit. However, the Marine Corps, following the lead of our commandant, Gen. Paul X. Kelley, accepted the report, and we all learned from it.

It is not my intent to review the events leading up to the hideous terrorist attack or the steps taken in its aftermath. Colonel Geraghty has done that exceedingly well. Further, General Kelley's remarks before the Senate Armed Services Committee on October 31, 1983, were most accurate as well as comprehensive. What follows are some of my personal thoughts regarding this catastrophic event.

The USMNF peacekeepers were positioned at the Beirut International Airport (BIA), in part, because the State Department negotiators, with advice from the European Command and the international community involved, considered the airport to be relatively isolated from the rest of Beirut. Therefore, our Marine forces would be less likely to have confrontations with the various factions involved. Further, the Lebanese Armed Forces (LAF), which were expected to provide security for the entire U.S., French, British, and Italian peacekeeping forces, would have an easier task as they struggled to achieve peace and stability throughout the greater Beirut region. In fact, being located in the vicinity of the airport placed the Marines in the midst of a large Shiite Muslim population with ideological and religious relationships with Iran. To further complicate the situation, all Marine efforts to include occupying the high ground a few miles east of BIA for better security were disapproved for political reasons. The diplomats did not want to give the appearance we were supporting Israeli logistics efforts in the Shouf Mountains complex and therefore violate the neutrality posture that is essential to peacekeeping efforts.

In late 1982 the MNF peacekeeping effort appeared to be working, and considerable progress was noted. The LAF was becoming far more capable and extending its control. Political and economic actions were under way, and a lessening of civil strife was also noted. The USMNF was also conducting medical and dental support operations to the Lebanese people of all religious and factions. The MNF was demonstrating on a daily basis that it was truly interested in the welfare of all the Lebanese people and in observing strict neutrality in all situations. This interaction, of course, did not sit well with those who did not want Western influence, particularly American, in the region. Concurrently, Hezbollah was formally established in Lebanon in 1982 to exercise authority over radical Shiite groups and support Iranian objectives in the region. In addition to being supported by Iran, Hezbollah enjoys cooperation from Syria and others. Hezbollah preached a hatred of Western imperialism as represented by the United States and planned for a series of violent attacks against the nations providing the MNF. In April 1983, Hezbollah successfully conducted a suicide car bomb attack on the American embassy in Beirut.

Lebanon is known as a country of commerce, and the BIA was the symbol for this activity. There was therefore a major construction effort going on throughout the area, and the airport was extremely active. At least twenty big construction trucks were working there the day of the bombing, and our Marine forces had no authority, rightly or wrongly, to interfere with their operations. A nineteen-ton construction truck loaded with fuel-enhanced explosives (probably procured from the former Soviet Union) was used to attack our BLT Headquarters building and not, as frequently reported, a car bomb or a much smaller truck bomb. It is my judgment, based on forensic evidence and physics, that had the truck been stopped outside the building, more personnel would have been killed or injured because of blast pressure. It should be noted that terrorist techniques include remote explosive capability when feasible as well as over-watch procedures for damage assessment and propaganda purposes. We know from special sources that Hezbollah, which had never used this type of powerful explosive before, was completely surprised (and elated) at the results of the devastation. It was one of the largest nonnuclear explosions ever recorded. The attack on the French command post, within minutes of the BLT Headquarters bombing, certainly is evidence of a carefully planned and well-executed effort by Hezbollah with the full support of Iran and with elements of Syria serving as conduits. To my knowledge, there had never been a truck of that size used in terrorist bombings, and the only other truck bomb I am aware of was a pickup truck used in a 1972 Afghanistan incident. The reality that our USMNF peacekeeping force should have been prepared for this unexpected event does not square with the situation that morning. Those of us who have lived with and led warriors in combat or dangerous situations understand this fact. For this reason, the nation's Corps of Marines stood by Colonel Geraghty and Lieutenant Colonel Gerlach during the aftermath of the Beirut bombing and the subsequent investigations by the Long Commission, Congress, and others.

In closing I would like to again thank all those who provided such thoughtful support to the 24th MAU, their families, loved ones, friends, and all those serving in the greater Camp Lejeune Marine Corps complex. Hundreds of letters expressing their concern and support were received from all over the world. Care packages, foodstuffs, and several hundred thousand dollars were sent to aid our people. Our Camp Lejeune Officers' Wives' Club handled the complicated task of controlling and dispensing these donations in accordance with the appropriate regulations for conducting these activities. The city of Jacksonville, the home of Camp Lejeuene, became linked with the Marine Corps forever because of the residents' caring and support. The beautiful memorial erected in memory of our fallen comrades combined with the annual Beirut Memorial Observance Ceremony reminds us of their sacrifice. It also reminds us to be vigilant as we rededicate ourselves to defending against this hideous form of warfare. The legions of Marines and sailors throughout the country who provided mass casualty assistance for the bereaved families as they coped with this ordeal have my special gratitude. For all those who lost loved ones in this dastardly attack, your courage and understanding will be with me forever.

For the 24th MAU and the other MAUs that served in Lebanon during the tumultuous 1982–84 period, your courage, your sacrifices, your dedication to duty, and your eternal spirit are with us forever. Above all, your sacrifices were not in vain. It was only after the 1983 bombing of our BLT Headquarters that the United States officially recognized that terrorist activities are a form of warfare and that a comprehensive strategy must be devised to deal with this national security threat. Additionally, the magnificent performance of our fighting men and women in Afghanistan, Iraq, the Horn of Africa, the Philippines, and elsewhere around the globe may be traced to your legacy. Once again, I salute you for who you are, what you have done, and your sacrifices to make the world a better place. As always, take care of yourselves, take care of each other, God Bless, and Semper Fidelis.

AL GRAY, MARINE
TWENTY-NINTH COMMANDANT OF THE MARINE CORPS

Preface

ON OCTOBER 23, 1983, I was commanding officer of the 24th Marine Amphibious Unit (MAU) in Beirut. Early that Sunday morning, a suicide bomber drove a large truck through the southern perimeter of the Marine compound at the Beirut International Airport. Speeding past a sentry post, he detonated the truck's payload in the lobby of the headquarters building of the battalion landing team (BLT) of the 1st Battalion, 8th Marine Regiment. The BLT building was the barracks for more than 300 Marines, sailors, and soldiers.

The death toll at the Marine barracks would eventually reach 241 servicemen, plus an elderly Lebanese custodian. Forensics and explosives experts from the Federal Bureau of Investigation (FBI) determined that the compressed-gas-enhanced device caused the largest nonnuclear explosion on record. It resulted in the highest loss of life by the U.S. Marine Corps in a single day since D-Day on Iwo Jima in 1945.

Nearly simultaneously, a similar bombing killed fifty-eight French paratroopers at the French Multinational Force headquarters in another part of the city. The coordinated dual suicide attacks—which Iran and Syria supported, financed, and planned and Shiite proxies executed—achieved their prime objective. Four months later, the multinational force was withdrawn from Lebanon, forcing a change of U.S. national policy. The synchronized suicide attacks that Sunday morning resulted in the deaths of 299 U.S. and French peacekeepers and scores of wounded. The cost to Hezbollah was two suicide bombers.

The failure of the United States to retaliate against this act of war sent the wrong message to the terrorist state powerbrokers in Tehran and Damascus. Islamic extremists interpreted it as granting impunity to attack Western interests, which is what happened. Cascading acts of terrorism such as kidnappings, executions, torture, hijackings, and suicide bombing attacks provided their answer. Our timidity whetted the jihadists' appetite.

Somehow, we had lost our sense of justice by refusing to retaliate against Islamic extremists who committed acts of war and murdered U.S. citizens. It is no mystery that America's reluctance emboldened them to bring their bloodshed to the American shores.

Osama bin Laden drew inspiration from Hezbollah's dual suicide attacks against the multinational forces in Beirut in 1983. Al Qaeda's first simultaneous suicide attacks on two U.S. embassies in eastern Africa on August 7, 1998, were directly modeled on Hezbollah's 1983 attacks. Al Qaeda's coordinated suicide missions expanded the model three years later for four simultaneous airplane hijackings on September 11, 2001. The nineteen Islamic jihadists, who were armed only with box cutters, successfully hijacked four commercial planes to carry out their suicide mission. Their bravado spoke for itself in that they didn't even bother to have a backup plan.

The Beirut peacekeeping mission of 1982–84 was undoubtedly a noble undertaking that saved countless lives. The multinational force achieved some remarkable successes, but, in the end, the mission was "a bridge too far." Civilized rules of behavior and moral codes are anathema to Islamic extremists.

Since the 1983 suicide attacks against the peacekeepers, the world has witnessed the jihadists' mayhem on a global scale in New York; Washington, D.C.; London; Madrid; Tel Aviv; Bali; and many other locations. Their indiscriminate targeting of innocent civilians while spreading their incessant carnage is celebrated as a triumph for Allah. The civilized world rightfully rejects the butchery with repugnance.

In August 2009, Iranian president Mahmoud Ahmadinejad, recently reelected under dubious circumstances, selected Ahmad Vahidi to be his new defense minister. A former commander of the Iranian Revolutionary Guard Corps' Lebanon contingent in the 1980s and founder and first commander of the elite Quds Force, he is discussed in detail in chapter 13, "Iran, Syria, and Hezbollah." In addition to being on Interpol's most wanted list, Vahidi has a career pattern that spells danger for the West and America in particular.

Vahidi has worked in intelligence operations and in special operations abroad and was indicted as one of those responsible for conceiving, planning, financing, and executing the bombing of the Jewish community center in Buenos Aires in 1994. His previous primary responsibility was overseeing the research and development of weapons of mass destruction. Added to this development, the recent reports of Hezbollah operatives working with the Mexican drug lords to smuggle drugs and personnel into the United States should send up many red flags to the U.S. government. As defense minister, Vahidi has the background and experience to provide Tehran with a bloody roadmap for using Hezbollah terrorists for multiple (and likely simultaneous) attacks against the American homeland.

We are engaged in a generational battle today whose beginning we are closer to than its end. The suicide bombings in Beirut in 1983 were the first shots fired in the current global war on terrorism. To paraphrase Winston Churchill during the early dark days of World War II, "This is not the end. It is not even the beginning of the end. But it is, perhaps, the end of the beginning."

Acknowledgments

I HAVE BEEN ENCOURAGED BY MANY through the years to write my account of the 1983 peacekeeping mission in Beirut. My profound appreciation and respect goes to those peacekeepers who served with me during that tumultuous mission. I am proud and privileged to have seen up close their steadfast dedication to duty, their perseverance, and their mettle. I send my respect and humble gratitude to the many families and friends of those who paid the ultimate sacrifice for the cause of freedom. Not a day passes when I don't pray for them and remember their sacrifice.

I want to thank my friends in the archives at the Alfred M. Gray Research Center for their assistance and encouragement. Special recognition goes to Sara Holcomb, granddaughter of our Corps' seventeenth commandant, who volunteers her time at the research center.

I want to thank my agent, Julia Lord of Julia Lord Literary Management, for her encouragement and assistance. I want to express my gratitude to my editor, Hilary Claggett, at Potomac Books, for her invaluable help and support. Special thanks go to Don McKeon, Jr., whose father, Col. Don McKeon, Sr. (Ret.), was my 1st Reconnaissance Battalion commander in Vietnam in 1967. Don provided key suggestions and patience in preparation of the manuscript. I am indebted to my copyeditor, Vicki Chamlee, for her guidance and insight in helping to make my story professional and more readable.

Maureen Townsend was indispensable in helping me prepare the manuscript for the publisher. I was fortunate and appreciative of her assistance in meeting deadlines.

Special gratitude goes to my wife, Karen, and my son, Sean, for their boundless support and love. Karen helped many of the families whose loved ones never came home, and that love and compassion continues today.

Illustrations

MAP 1. Lebanon. *USMC Archives*

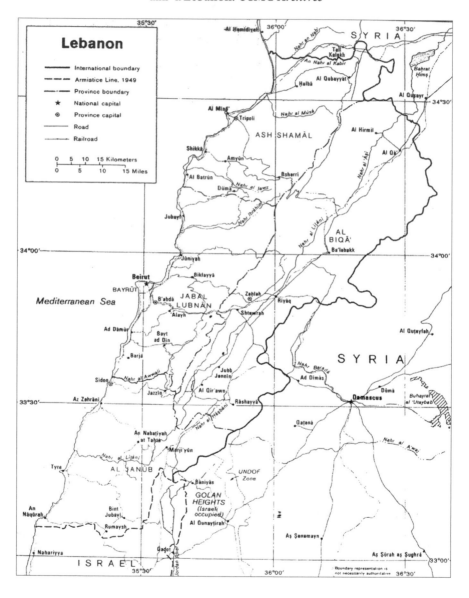

_1_

The Beginning

IT WAS JUNE 6, 1982, and I was busy overseeing the training, operations, and planning of the Second Marine Division at Camp Lejeune, North Carolina. We were deploying Marine units worldwide, and the pace of our activities placed heavy demands on everyone. The hectic routine was abruptly interrupted when we began receiving reports that the Israel Defense Forces (IDF) had just invaded southern Lebanon. In the years leading up to the invasion, the Palestinian Liberation Organization (PLO), under Yasser Arafat, had established a state within a state in Lebanon. It had been one of the main reasons for the outbreak of the Lebanese civil war in 1975. The PLO also used its positions in southern Lebanon to launch indiscriminate rocket and artillery attacks against northern Israeli civilian targets.

The Israelis' invasion was launched in response to the attempted assassination of Shlomo Argov, their ambassador in London. Ironically, this attack was carried out by a faction of Abu Nidal's organization, which was an archenemy of Arafat's PLO.

Thus began a series of events and counteractions that would eventually lead to the introduction of a multinational peacekeeping force (MNPF) to Lebanon—twice. It is a tale of conflict, commitment, mistakes, violence, and valor. It is an account of America undertaking a noble mission to assist a war-torn country whose own people were their own worst enemy. It is a story of the awakening of Islamic fanaticism, fanned and supported by ruthless external forces seeking power, influence, and subjugation. It is a story that continues today.

Code-named Peace for Galilee, the operation called for the IDF to swiftly deploy its armor and mechanized forces in a three-pronged attack against PLO military positions. The architect of the invasion, Defense Minister Ariel Sharon, told the Israeli government that it would be a limited incursion. It was believed that the thrust would be limited to the Litani River to provide a forty-kilometer artillery and rocket buffer zone to protect northern Israeli villages. However, as the IDF raced northward toward the capital, Beirut, it soon became clear that Sharon had more ambitious plans.

The Israel Defense Forces confronted fierce resistance from the Syrian Army and the Palestinian Liberation Army (PLA), which was based in and fully supported by Syria. The Syrian Army's strength in Lebanon was estimated to be about seventy thousand personnel. In a series of spectacular tactical moves, the Israeli Air Force struck Syrian surface-to-air missile (SAM) sites throughout the Bekaa Valley, wiping out nineteen SAM batteries without the loss of a single Israeli jet. In response, the Syrian Air Force launched its own jets to counter the Israeli attack and lost twenty-nine aircraft; the Israelis again suffered no losses. The Israelis established clear air superiority over southern Lebanon. On the ground, there were wide, sweeping armor battles involving the premier Syrian tank division led by top commanders and equipped with top-of-the-line, Soviet-supplied main battle tanks. Again, the brilliant Israeli tactics and combat leadership led to a decisive victory wherein the Syrians lost 150 tanks in the Bekaa Valley. After a series of failed cease-fires, with the Israelis and Syrians jockeying for positions, the beginning of July 1982 found the Israel Defense Forces well ensconced along the Beirut–Damascus highway and surrounding the PLO and its leadership in West Beirut.[1]

We were closely monitoring developments in Lebanon because the 32nd Marine Amphibious Unit (MAU), serving in the Mediterranean, was based out of Camp Lejeune and Cherry Point Air Station in North Carolina. When a crisis like this one develops, the MAU starts to update contingency plans, anticipating orders to evacuate American citizens from Lebanon. It also highlights a prime purpose of having Marine ready forces afloat 24/7 to carry out assorted missions in times of crisis. In late June, the 32nd MAU received orders to evacuate civilians from the port of Juniyah, about five miles north of Beirut. On June 24, large landing crafts, primarily U-boats (LCUs), loaded 580 evacuees and transferred

MAP 2. Beirut. *USMC Archives*

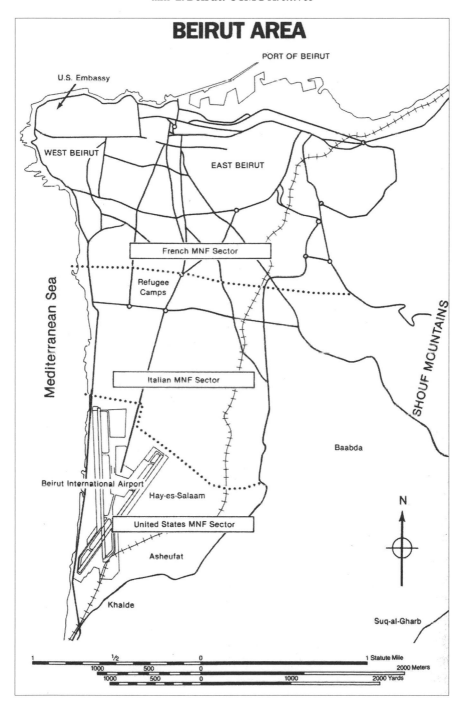

BEIRUT AREA

PORT OF BEIRUT

U.S. Embassy

WEST BEIRUT

EAST BEIRUT

French MNF Sector

Refugee
Camps

Mediterranean Sea

SHOUF MOUNTAINS

Italian MNF Sector

Baabda

Beirut International Airport

Hay-es-Salaam

N

United States MNF Sector

Asheufat

Khalde

Suq-al-Gharb

1	½	0	1 Statute Mile
1000	500	0	2000 Meters
1000	500	0	1000	2000 Yards

them to ships offshore, the USS *Nashville* (LPD-13) and the USS *Hermitage* (LSD-34), for an overnight trip to Larnaca, Cyprus. The mission was carried out without incident.[2]

The summer of 1982 involved intense peace negotiations and diplomatic activities, led by White House special envoy Philip Habib and Ambassador Morris Draper, to work out a peace settlement agreeable to all sides. The 32nd MAU remained offshore during this period while planning and working through the military and political committees that Ambassador Habib established. He also chaired their group sessions. On the military side, U.S., French, and Italian liaison teams discussed the political negotiations concerning plans for evacuating the PLO by sea and land and considered the kind of options available. Special Envoy Habib worked hard to find a way to evacuate the PLO without provocation.

Meanwhile, the Israelis were not standing still. Water, electricity, and supplies were cut off to West Beirut. Defense Minister Sharon ordered massive air and artillery barrages of West Beirut, where the PLO and its leadership were holed up. Arafat, whose use of women and children as shields for his PLO fighters was well known, adamantly refused to surrender. During one fourteen-hour Israeli bombardment, the Americans counted 220 bombing sorties and 44,000 artillery rounds. The bombardment of West Beirut lasted nine weeks. Whole neighborhoods were reduced to rubble, and civilian casualties soared into the hundreds, causing an international outcry. It took a personal call from President Ronald Reagan to Prime Minister Menachem Begin to stop the attack. President Reagan told him to cease the assault or our future relationship was endangered: "Menachem, this is a Holocaust." In his diary, President Reagan wrote that he used the word "Holocaust" deliberately. Twenty minutes later, Reagan wrote that night, "He called to tell me he'd ordered an end to the barrage and pleaded for our continued friendship." In a notable revelation, Begin also confided to the president that he had persuaded his cabinet to reduce the authority of Defense Minister Sharon, who had ordered the new attacks.[3]

The Habib-led negotiations revealed progress when the parties agreed that the PLO's evacuation would be conducted under the purview of a multinational force comprising U.S., French, and Italian troops. The PLO wanted the United Nations (UN) to be involved, which the Israelis rejected, period. After detailed negotiations over the security of the thousands of Palestinian civilians left behind, the United States gave a written statement guaranteeing their safety. The son of Lebanese Maronite Christian parents, Habib added his own personal assurances that U.S. forces would remain ashore for up to thirty days to ensure a long-term solution, a key part of the agreement.

At 5:00 a.m. on August 25, 1982, the 32nd MAU landed eight hundred Marines in Beirut under the command of Col. Jim Mead. Through the negotiations, they joined eight hundred French and four hundred Italian soldiers. This multinational force (MNF) carried out the evacuation of the PLO, the PLA, and Syrian Army without a major incident. It was widely viewed as a success beyond expectations. With tensions running high at times, the Marines conducted themselves with discipline and commitment.

The PLO's evacuation was completed on September 1. Secretary of Defense Caspar Weinberger, accompanied by Senator Charles Percy (R-IL), visited the MNF on September 3. On September 10, the 32nd MAU was ordered to return to the ships, which sailed for the U.S. Navy base in Naples. Either Secretary Weinberger was unaware of Habib's assurances that the United States would guarantee the safety of the PLO civilians left behind in the refugee camps or he chose to ignore them. Secretary of State George Shultz later recounted the many difficulties he had with Secretary Weinberger and the Department of Defense in getting the Marines deployed in the first place and his misgivings about their quick withdrawal.[4] Special Presidential Envoy Robert McFarlane claimed that the Arabs reacted with alarm to the Marines' withdrawal and pleaded with the United States not to leave the Palestinian civilians in such a vulnerable position. Beirut newspapers noted the Marines' premature departure with such somber and sarcastic headlines as "Last In, First Out." McFarlane went further, calling Weinberger criminally irresponsible for betraying Ambassador Habib's pledge without so much as placing a phone call to the secretary of state or the president first.[5]

This dispute was only the beginning of what would become the perfect storm involving the Department of State, the Department of Defense, and the National Security Council regarding our national policy in Lebanon. On September 14, while the MAU was still en route to Naples, early reports started coming in to our operations center that a massive, command-detonated bomb had exploded in President-elect Bashir Gemayel's headquarters in Beirut and killed him. This assassination triggered another series of moves that would further exacerbate the war. The State Department reiterated to the Israelis its demand not to send the IDF into Beirut. Prime Minister Begin sent word that the IDF was ordered to make "limited and precautionary" adjustments in the interests of security. On the same day, Ariel Sharon notified U.S. officials in Washington that the U.S. embassy in Beirut was "under fire" from PLO terrorists and offered the IDF to "rescue" U.S. citizens if requested. Washington had direct contact with our embassy, which stated that it was not under fire. We said no thanks to Sharon, who replied that the IDF had "occupied all key points in Beirut and by so doing, have prevented civil war." The Israelis, contrary to their assurances, had sent the Sharon-directed IDF into the heart of Beirut. Our negotiator, Ambassador Morris Draper, stated, "Begin has been manipulated again by Sharon."[6] What was interesting was that the Israelis' primary reason for occupying Beirut was to protect the Palestinian civilians in the Sabra and Shatila refugee camps, a duty the Israelis believed to be the MNF's responsibility for at least thirty days following the PLO's departure on September 1. This interpretation of the MNF's responsibility, particularly of the U.S. role, was exactly the same as Arafat's.

By Friday, September 17, the IDF had control of Beirut and had surrounded, but not entered, the refugee camps. On the morning of September 18, reports started leaking out that the Israelis had allowed the Christian Phalangist militia to enter the camps and that what followed was a massacre of staggering proportions. Estimates ranged that from 800 to 1,600 civilians were killed, mostly women, children, and older Muslim family members left behind after the PLO fighters' departure. The official Lebanese government count was just less than 2,000 deaths during the sixty-two-hour rampage. Throughout the night, Israeli jets and ground units provided illumination flares to assist in this gruesome operation. Television pictures showed piles of bodies while other reports said that the IDF was going house to house in West Beirut, arresting and detaining people. The United States, France, and Italy, meanwhile, were trying to sort everything out. Secretary of State George Shultz noted that "a mist of bitterness now hung over every American-Israeli official encounter."[7] The international outcry and anti-Israeli demonstrations all over the world grew as the sordid news of the massacre spread. More than 400,000 demonstrators in Tel Aviv chanted for Begin's and Sharon's resignations.

The United States had taken the Israelis for their word, and now our credibility with our allies was shattered. Several observers would later point to Sabra and Shatila as where the seeds of the Americans' failure in Lebanon were planted.

The most pressing requirement that had to be addressed was to avert another massacre. This time-compressed environment led to the multinational force's reconstitution and its presence mission. President Amin Gemayel, whom the National Assembly elected on September 21 to succeed his assassinated brother, requested a new multinational force, and all parties agreed within forty-eight hours following the discovery of the massacre. It took some days to recognize its extent and immensity after investigators and Red Cross workers moved through the camps. Accompanying these details was the clear evidence of Israeli complicity. It is my opinion that the collective guilt of all parties who felt some sense of responsibility for the massacre accelerated this process. "The brutal fact is, we are partially responsible," Secretary Shultz stated, adding, "we took the Israelis and the Lebanese at their word." Secretary Weinberger expressed his complete reluctance to redeploy the U.S. Multinational Force (USMNF) back to Lebanon: "Israel has gotten itself in a swamp and we should leave it at that." However, world opinion was crushing. Given the circumstances, the USMNF had little choice except to return to Beirut with all the attendant risks and uncertainties.[8]

On September 29, 1982, the 32nd MAU arrived in Beirut to join the twenty-two hundred French and Italian troops already in place. The Marines' mission was "to establish an environment which will permit the Lebanese Armed Forces to carry out their responsibilities in the Beirut area. When directed, USCINCEUR will introduce U.S. forces as part of a multinational force presence in the Beirut area to occupy and secure positions along a designated section of the line from south of the Beirut International Airport to a position in the vicinity of the Presidential Palace; be prepared to protect U.S. forces; and, on order, conduct retrograde operations as required." The agreement "expressly ruled out any combat responsibilities for the U.S. forces."[9]

Deciding where to locate the USMNF was a subject of intense negotiations between the United States and Israel. The United States wanted the Israelis to vacate the entire city of Beirut and Beirut International Airport (BIA). The Israelis wanted to retain control of the airport since it was adjacent to their main supply route (MSR) to their forward positions. It was finally agreed that the USMNF would carry out its mission as an interpositional force by being based at the airport. It was a logical political decision made without any tactical considerations. This location was tolerable at the time, but this decision would haunt us a year later when the civil war flared up, aided and abetted by Syria and Iran. What originally was a permissive environment had by then dramatically changed into a killing zone.

In preparation for their posting ashore, each Marine member of the USMNF was issued a white wallet-sized card with ten guidelines for rules of engagement (ROE):

Guidelines for ROE

1. When on post, mobile, or foot patrol, keep loaded magazine in weapon, bolt closed, weapon on safe, no round in the chamber.
2. Do not chamber a round unless told to do so by a commissioned officer unless you must act in immediate self-defense where deadly force is authorized.
3. Keep ammo for crew-served weapons readily available but not loaded. Weapon is on safe.
4. Call local forces to assist in self-defense effort. Notify headquarters.
5. Use only minimum degree of force to accomplish any mission.
6. Stop the use of force when it is no longer needed to accomplish the mission.
7. If you receive effective hostile fire, direct your fire at the source. If possible, use friendly snipers.
8. Respect civilian property; do not attack it unless absolutely necessary to protect friendly forces.
9. Protect innocent civilians from harm.
10. Respect and protect recognized medical agencies such as Red Cross, Red Crescent, etc.

Col. Jim Mead's 32nd MAU was relieved by Col. Tom Stokes's 24th MAU on October 30, 1982. The transition was seamless, morale was high, and all hands assumed their responsibilities enthusiastically. Colonel Stokes also honored the Ministry of Defense's request to help train the LAF. The government of Lebanon (GOL) introduced conscription, and young men from all over Lebanon answered the call to colors. The various religious groups—the Christians, Druze, Sunnis, and Shiites—were being trained and integrated into the Lebanese Army. Although the U.S. Army already had an ongoing training mission in effect, it was viewed that the Marines' additional training would quickly improve the LAF's combat capabilities.

The results of the training courses led to their expansion, particularly among the noncommissioned officers (NCOs). The religious integration of the LAF was a major goal of its commander, Gen. Ibrahim Tannous, who wanted to produce a true national army. The Marine training was contributing to that end.

The Israel Defense Forces were routinely experiencing ambushes along Sidon Road, their main supply route, that resulted in high casualties. The Marines' assigned position at BIA was adjacent to the MSR, which led to several ugly confrontations between the IDF and the Marines. Prior to our mission in Lebanon, the Marine-IDF relationship reflected a mutual respect between two warrior cultures. Many Israelis were U.S. citizens, had attended our service schools, and enjoyed a hard-earned reputation for winning decisive victories on the field of battle. The Marines were not alone in embracing the Israelis' demonstrated courage and sacrifice in defense of their homeland.

However, this relationship changed in Lebanon. The Israelis had a long-established policy of mercilessly responding to any attack against them, even minor ones. A sniper round from a village would cause the IDF to open up with .50-caliber machine gun fire from a convoy in many directions. This indiscriminate fire caused numerous civilian casualties, which did not endear the IDF to anyone. Another familiar tactic was "recon by fire," which essentially put sustained fire on anything that may appear to be a potential threat. If any vehicle was parked along Sidon Road, it earned a 105mm tank round.

The guidance stated that the Marines were to show no favoritism toward the Israelis, including any direct contact between the IDF commander and the MAU commander. The Marines felt that their best defense was their posture of neutrality as spelled out in the mission statement so that the Muslim perception vis-à-vis the Israelis and the Palestinians would be maintained. The Marines found the IDF to be arrogant, undisciplined, and sloppy in their appearance and conduct. The Sharon-directed IDF came to view the Marines as ungrateful, too conscious of appearances, and generally naive. The tensions became so serious that Colonel Stokes made the decision to meet face-to-face with the IDF commander, Brig. Gen. Amnon Lifkin, who had long been requesting a meeting. Both commanders realized that each side had come close to exchanging fire, and this pressure had to be defused immediately. The commanders met and reduced the tensions temporarily, but the problem would linger.[10]

On February 14, 1983, the 22nd MAU, again led by Col. Jim Mead, relieved the 24th MAU. (The former 32nd MAU had been redesignated the 22nd MAU.) In assuming the responsibilities again as commander, Task Force 62 (CTF 62), Mead encountered little change in the mission and the environment. The 22nd MAU had been reconstituted with new personnel but retained about half the members who had previously served tours in Lebanon.

A few days after the turnover, the weather turned ugly. The normally mild winter weather changed, with temperatures dropping to the low forties on the coast and with seventy-knot winds and heavy snow in the mountains, making it the worst weather in forty years. On February 20, President Gemayel requested MNF assistance in rescuing about two hundred Lebanese trapped in a blizzard near Dahr al Baydar, about twenty-five kilometers east of Beirut. The most severe casualties were painstakingly rounded up and evacuated by helicopter while other Marines distributed food and fuel supplies they had hauled in overland. The Italians and the French likewise conducted parallel rescue operations. In the end, the MNF won the gratitude of many Lebanese people for its extraordinary assistance.

The month of March reflected stalled diplomatic negotiations and the MAU's proactive moves to counter the increasing terrorist threats to its patrols. Daily patrols continued, but one foot patrol was halted at an Israeli checkpoint in Baabda. Later the same day, the Israelis challenged another Marine patrol just before it reentered Marine positions.

The patrols were also encountering IDF verbal harassment, which was becoming a persistent problem. Col. Jim Mead correctly realized that these confrontations could not continue. Why the Israel Defense Forces chose to reinstigate these types of conflicts with the Marines was puzzling. They served no purpose except to aggravate an already tenuous relationship. Colonel Mead contacted Ambassador Habib, who met with the new Israeli minister of defense, Moshe Arens, and told him that the Marine commander would personally lead the patrol through the Israeli checkpoint the next time it tried to stop a Marine. The confrontations reached such heights that they compelled the commandant of the Marine Corps (CMC), Gen. Robert Barrow, to write a letter on March 14 to Secretary of Defense Weinberger. Commandant Barrow demanded "that firm and strong action" be taken to stop Israeli forces from putting the Marines in "life threatening situations that are timed, orchestrated, and executed by obtuse Israeli political purposes." General Barrow was concerned not only with the harassment of the Marine patrols but also with the threats to Marine and army officers assigned to the United Nations Truce Supervisory Organization in Lebanon. The U.S. officers assigned to the United Nations worked primarily in southern Lebanon, and their duties required them to cross Israeli lines while carrying out their duties. Secretary Weinberger supported General Barrow's position and forwarded the letter to Secretary of State Shultz, who communicated its contents to Israeli foreign minister Yitzhak Shamir. This message led to a meeting of Mead; Deputy Chief of Mission Bob Pugh, the EUCOM liaison officer (LNO); and General Lifkin to exchange patrol information to avoid further confrontations. This action essentially resolved these confrontations.[11]

■

In early January 1983, Maj. Gen. Al Gray called me into his office at Camp Lejeune. I had been the division's assistant chief of staff for operations and plans (G-3) for eighteen months and thoroughly enjoyed working with the staffs and the commanders. After some preliminary discussion, General Gray told me it was time for command and offered me the choice of the 8th Marine Regiment or the 24th Marine Amphibious Unit. I thanked him for the opportunity and told him, without hesitation, that I preferred command of the 24th MAU. The command of an MAU, the smallest but formidable Marine air-ground task force (MAGTF), was the most sought-after assignment for a Marine colonel. Sailing and operating with an amphibious squadron brought together the significant capabilities of the U.S. Navy–Marine Corps team, which was ready to carry out whatever missions are assigned. He told me to think about it and let him know my final decision in the morning. I responded that I did not need more time to think about it; I had been in the Corps for more than twenty years and knew that circumstances can change quickly. I wanted my preference clear and known. He smiled and told me to get back to work.

On March 17, 1983, I assumed command of the 24th MAU from Colonel Stokes. The MAU was headed to the peacekeeping mission in Beirut, and I was thrilled to be part of the challenges that lay ahead.

—2—

Preparation and Deployment

I WAS BORN IN ST. LOUIS, MISSOURI, the fourth of seven children, to Howard and Virginia (Higgins) Geraghty. We children were taught early to help one another and work together. We were and remain a close-knit family. My father, himself the eldest of nine children, was born and raised in New York City. In the mid-1920s, my grandfather, John J. Geraghty, moved the entire family to St. Louis, where he managed and operated an aluminum manufacturing plant on the banks of the Mississippi River.

Dad worked for his father at the plant and helped it grow into a successful enterprise. During World War II, there was a great demand for aluminum chaff, strips of foil ejected in the air for reflecting radar waves and disrupting the enemy's radar detection capabilities.

Dad was not eligible for war service since he had five children, but his two younger brothers served in the Army. The youngest, Uncle Eddy, served with honor in the Pacific campaign while Uncle Bob served in France during the U.S. invasion of Europe in 1944. Wounded and captured by the Germans, Bob died in a prisoner of war (POW) hospital in January 1945. I have fond memories of my uncles and their service to our nation during the Big War.

Mom and Dad were married June 1, 1932, during the height of the Depression. All of us children agree that Mom was a living saint and not shy in providing abundant love, firm discipline, and encouragement. We all appreciated and recognized the blessing of having such loving and wonderful parents.

My education consisted of parochial school operated by the Franciscans, a military high school named Christian Brothers College High School, and St. Louis

University, operated by the Jesuits. I later acquired a master's degree in education from Pepperdine University while in the Marine Corps.

Upon graduation from St. Louis University in June 1959, I reported to the 25th Officer Candidate Course at Quantico, Virginia, the following September. I was commissioned a second lieutenant in December 1959. Upon completion of the Basic School, I was assigned to the First Marine Division at Camp Pendleton, California, as an infantry platoon commander (my first choice). Later, our unit deployed via amphibious shipping to the Third Marine Division in Okinawa for thirteen months. As a captain, I began serving with the 1st Reconnaissance Battalion in 1965 and deployed to Vietnam later that year. I served as Charlie Company's commander and extended my tour twice to serve with a special group of Marines and sailors deploying reconnaissance patrols throughout I Corps. One of these men was my acting first platoon commander, Gunnery Sgt. Jimmie E. Howard, who was awarded the Congressional Medal of Honor for extraordinary actions while leading a patrol during June 13–16, 1966. On October 20, 2001, the U.S. Navy commissioned a guided-missile destroyer, the USS *Jimmie E. Howard*, in honor of him.

It was during this period in I Corps that I met and worked closely with Maj. Al Gray, who had also extended his tour twice. We developed a lifelong friendship, which carried us to many climes and places. He later became the twenty-ninth commandant of the Marine Corps.

Following a short hospitalization upon my return from Vietnam to treat a severe case of hepatitis and to regain the thirty-plus pounds I had lost, I was promoted to major and ordered to the Second Marine Division at Camp Lejeune, North Carolina. The division was then deploying forces afloat to the Sixth Fleet in the Mediterranean Sea and to the Caribbean Sea. The day after I arrived, I was ordered to the 3rd Battalion, Second Marines as the operations officer (S-3) and left immediately for a North Atlantic Treaty Organization (NATO) Planning Conference in Thessaloníki, Greece. Battalion Landing Team (BLT) 3/2 would be conducting a combined landing in northern Greece with a Hellenic regimental combat team. The seven-month deployment, including the extended exercise and training with the Greeks, was professionally rewarding.

In 1969, I began a four-year tour at Quantico, Virginia. I was assigned as the ground reconnaissance officer at the Development Center, which happened to be one of the best billets in the Corps. Al Gray, now a lieutenant colonel and my immediate superior, encouraged and facilitated our mission. He was a strong proponent of reconnaissance operations, and his leadership and vision were instrumental in the development of new concepts, techniques, and equipment. Some of the projects included the lightweight laser target designator, which we combat tested in Vietnam; the Aqua Dart, a flat, motorized device to pull recon swimmers through the water; and free-fall parachuting. Fate smiled upon me when I received a call from Capt. Wes Fox, who was awaiting the next class at Amphibious Warfare School and looking for work. Wes, who later received the Congressional Medal of Honor for heroism in Vietnam, had a strong force reconnaissance background and was the most seasoned and experienced free-fall parachutist in the Corps. His contributions were extensive and professional. I made several trips to Vietnam to obtain combat evaluation and testing of new equipment and studies.

One of my favorite projects was helping test and evaluate a cold water wetsuit developed by the British Royal Navy. Capt. John Rawlins of the Royal Navy was the project officer while on an exchange tour with the U.S. Navy. His office was in a laboratory at Bethesda Naval Hospital. Captain Rawlins developed his considerable skills as one of the world's foremost experts in cold water exposure through the experiences of those Royal Air Force (RAF) fighter pilots whom the Luftwaffe had shot down over the English Channel during the Battle of Britain. Rawlins and I became good friends, and I introduced him to American barbeque, which he still enjoys. He later became an admiral and surgeon general of the Royal Navy. Upon his retirement, he became the Queen's physician and eventually was honored with a knighthood. Sir John is still going strong in the south of Great Britain and is truly a special friend who has dedicated his entire life to the cause of peace and the betterment of mankind.

In 1971, I became aide-de-camp to Lt. Gen. William G. Thrash, the commanding general of the Marine Corps Development and Education Command. General Thrash was an aviator and one of those revered leaders who had served his Corps and country in three wars: World War II, Korea, and Vietnam. In Korea, he was shot down over the Yalu River and remained a POW for two years. His leadership as the senior officer in the POW camp earned him the Legion of Merit. He was a mentor and remains a respected friend.

In 1972, I attended the Command and Staff College and subsequently returned to the Third Marine Division in Okinawa, where I was assigned as the S-3 of the

3rd Reconnaissance Battalion. In 1974, I was transferred to Honolulu, Hawaii, to become the inspector-instructor of 4th Force Reconnaissance Company.

Shortly after being promoted to lieutenant colonel, I received orders in 1976 to Headquarters Marine Corps (HQMC) in Washington, D.C., where I was initially assigned to the Manpower Plans and Policy Division. In early 1978, I was ordered to the Intelligence Division and informed that I was under consideration for a special assignment with the Central Intelligence Agency (CIA). Upon the CIA's approval, I spent the next three years in the Special Operations Group (SOG), where I came to know and respect some of our nation's finest patriots dedicating their lives daily for our national security.

Since my return to the Washington area, I had been dating Karen Peterschmidt. On December 13, 1979, we were married at St. Mary's Catholic Church in Alexandria, Virginia. My only regret is that I waited so long to marry her. I feel blessed to have her as my wife.

In early 1981, while on assignment in the Far East, I was notified that the Marine Corps had selected me for colonel. Upon my return, I was informed that I was being transferred to Camp Lejeune, North Carolina, where Major General Gray was assuming command of the Second Marine Division. When I reported for duty that summer, he informed me that I was being assigned as the division's G-3 and pinned the colonel's eagles on my collar shortly thereafter.

The normal operational tempo of the Second Marine Division was high paced, unrelenting, and challenging. General Gray briefed the division staff and commanders on his ambitious plans to truly integrate and strengthen the Navy–Marine Corps team. Our objective was to identify, at this earliest time, those Marines, sailors, crews, ships, and equipment so the team could train together with the same personnel and ships that were deploying. Because we were sending Marine units worldwide, it required focus and determination by a dedicated staff and resourceful commanders. The demands and stress also provided a fertile environment to learn and appreciate the value of teamwork, trust, and the responsibilities of command.

Each year, the secretary of defense invites a selected cross section of American civilians to witness the capabilities of the U.S. armed forces. Instituted in 1948 by Defense Secretary James Forrestal and officially known as the Joint Civilian Orientation Conference, it is the Pentagon's oldest orientation program for outsiders. All services are involved, and the guests get to see firsthand, up close, the military training and operations. The Second Marine Division hosted a group of more than twenty-five guests on May 26, 1982. We provided a static display of equipment, an air assault, and an amphibious landing securing multiple objectives ashore involving the Navy–Marine Corps team.

I escorted several individuals, one being Herman Wouk, the author of the classic novel *The Caine Mutiny*, whose more recent books, *Winds of War* and its sequel, *War and Remembrance*, were also bestsellers and later made into popular television miniseries. A pleasant gentleman with a fascinating curiosity, Mr. Wouk asked many perceptive questions about the armored vehicles, aircraft, equipment, and their capabilities. He explained that his two sons were reservists in the Israeli armed forces. I believe one was a naval officer and the other a helicopter pilot. In the course of our conversation, I mentioned my respect for his abundant talent as an author who could write a story that resonated so well with the public. I cited that one of the highest compliments to an author is when the readers enjoy the story so much that they are sad when it ends. His response surprised me. He told me he "wrote with his blood," anguishing over every detail and word and would rewrite passages countless times. He said he had taken up jogging in his sixties as a psychological balance in order to complete *War and Remembrance*. Mr. Wouk confided that he would never write another sequel, since writing it had taken such a heavy toll on him.

That evening at a large reception at the officer's club for all the guests, Mr. Wouk mixed with the attendees, speaking about how impressed he was by the Corps' demonstrated capabilities, and even took time to autograph some of his books. His humility, dignity, and quiet strength were evident. He has since been honored by the U.S. Congress as America's "Author Emeritus" in recognition for his literary contributions to our country and the world.

Upon my assumption of command of the 24th Marine Amphibious Unit on March 17, 1983, we reported for operations as Landing Force Sixth Fleet (LF6F) 2-83 to the commanding general of the Fleet Marine Forces, Atlantic (FMFLANT), on March 21. This started a familiar process, which normally lasts about forty-five days prior to deployment to the Mediterranean Sea for duty under the commander of the U.S. Sixth Fleet (COMSIXTHFLT).

The 24th Marine Amphibious Unit, like the previous MAUs, would become the landing force of the U.S. Sixth Fleet once it passed into the fleet's area of responsibility. In conjunction, Amphibious Squadron 8 (PHIBRON 8) becomes

Mediterranean Amphibious Ready Group (MARG) 2-83 and together provides the fleet with a ready amphibious force capable of carrying out a variety of missions in the Mediterranean area. A Marine landing force has been an integral part of the Sixth Fleet for more than thirty years. While trained as amphibious combat troops, Marines in the Mediterranean have participated in many humanitarian operations. From conducting rescues to distributing flood and earthquake relief to evacuating noncombatants from areas of danger, Marines and sailors remained ready to assist wherever needed.

The 24th MAU also was task organized as a Marine Air-Ground Task Force composed of four elements: command, ground combat, aviation combat, and combat service support. The 24th MAU command element provided a single headquarters for command and coordination of ground, air, and combat service support forces.

Battalion Landing Team 1/8 (1st Battalion, 8th Marine Regiment) was the ground combat element of the MAU and commanded by Lt. Col. Larry Gerlach. Respected by all hands, his demonstrated leadership was a matter of record. The ground element included artillery, tanks, amphibious assault vehicles (AAVs), reconnaissance, and combat engineer units. A former enlisted Marine, Larry earned his commission through the Naval Reserve Officers' Training Corps (ROTC) program at the University of Mississippi. During 1970–71, he served as an infantry battalion adviser in I Corps in Vietnam. He was a graduate of the U.S. Army's Advanced Infantry Officer's Course, the Airborne School, and the Command and Staff College at Quantico, Virginia.

Marine Medium Helicopter Squadron-162 (REIN) (HMM-162) was the air combat element of the MAU and commanded by Lt. Col. Larry Medlin, a Vietnam veteran and graduate of the U.S. Military Academy at West Point, New York. His extensive aviation skills complemented his leadership capabilities, which were well known and respected. He joined Marine Aircraft Group 26 (MAG 26) at New River, North Carolina, after graduating from the U.S. Army War College at Carlisle, Pennsylvania. The air element was configured with the new Super Sea Stallion heavy-lift CH-53Es, the Sea Knight CH-46Es for troop transport, the AH-1T Cobra attack helicopters, and the UH-1Ns for command and control. HMM-162 was capable of conducting multiple air operations to meet the peacekeeping mission's requirements.

The MAU Service Support Group 24 (MSSG-24) was commanded by Maj. Doug Redlich, who brought a solid record of accomplishments, leadership, and special skills that the MAU needed. This element was structured to provide landing support, supply maintenance, engineer support, military police, medical and dental support, and motor transport capabilities. Its performance, under Major Redlich's leadership, would be instrumental in saving numerous lives during the recovery operation following the Marine barracks bombing in 1983.

By the end of our deployment to Beirut in December 1983, each of these three commanders had displayed remarkable leadership skills, dedication to the mission, and selfless devotion to duty. I was fortunate to have had them in key leadership positions when the 24th MAU's mettle was tested.

The other half of the Navy–Marine Corps team (also called the Blue-Green Team) was Amphibious Squadron Eight (PHIBRON 8), commanded by an extraordinary leader, Commodore (Capt.) Morgan M. France, USN. (His position as commander of a squadron temporarily elevated his grade to commodore, ranking above captain and below rear admiral.) Known as Rick, he commanded the PHIBRON from aboard the flagship USS *Iwo Jima* (LPII-2). The four other ships that completed the PHIBRON were the USS *Austin* (LPD-4), the USS *Portland* (LSD-37), the USS *Harlan County* (LST-1196), and the USS *El Paso* (LKA-117). The Marines and sailors of the 24th MAU and the crews of PHIBRON 8 developed a close relationship, which reflected mutual appreciation and respect. Their teamwork and selfless dedication during the later post-bombing recovery operation would save countless lives.

During the workup, the 24th MAU conducted six amphibious rehearsals, includ-ing all-surface, heavy-surface/light-air, light-surface/heavy-air, and night-surface assaults. The final assault included a silent landing. Forward air controller (FAC) training with live fire and close air support (CAS) was conducted in conjunction with two of the landings.

Our pre-deployment training was suddenly interrupted on April 18 when reports started pouring in that our embassy in Beirut had been bombed. Any attack on a U.S. embassy or consulate anywhere has special meaning to U.S. Marines since we are tasked with providing security for all of them. A suicide terrorist driving a van, which was reportedly stolen from the embassy the year before and loaded with an estimated two thousand pounds of high explosives

(PETN), gunned his engine, raced past the Lebanese guards, and crashed into the embassy's lobby, detonating the payload. The massive blast devastated the reinforced lobby, causing the entire front of the seven-story building to collapse. U.S. ambassador Robert Dillon, in his penthouse office wearing a running suit and readying to work out, was lucky to survive. He was pinned under a collapsed wall but escaped serious injury. But sixty-three people were killed, including seventeen Americans, thirty-three Lebanese employees, and more than a dozen others in the building or passing by. The CIA Station in Beirut took the biggest hit. Seven CIA employees were killed, including the Chief of Station (COS) Ken Hass; his deputy, James Lewis; and Lewis's wife, who had started working at the embassy only that morning. They were working through the lunch hour, a reflection of their dedication to duty. Perhaps most damaging in national security terms was the death of Robert C. Ames, the CIA's national intelligence officer for the Near East, who was visiting Beirut. Some informed observers said it was a body blow to the agency.[1] During a memorial service at CIA Headquarters in Langley, Virginia, a few days later, Director William J. Casey eulogized Robert Ames, stating he was "the closest thing to an irreplaceable man." The devastation of the CIA station in Beirut led to William Buckley's assignment as the new chief of station.

Col. Jim Mead arrived shortly after the U.S. embassy attack and found French general Datin, in whose sector the embassy was located, already on the scene and guarding it with his French Marines. It wasn't the first or the last time the French would display their support, professionalism, and cooperation in carrying out the peacekeeping mission. In a gracious gesture, General Datin generously offered to place his men under the operational control of Colonel Mead, who gratefully accepted. As soon as the U.S. Marine reaction company arrived, it relieved the French and assumed responsibility.[2] On May 26, CMC Gen. Robert Barrow, making his final visits to Marines prior to his retirement on July 1, awarded General Datin the Legion of Merit on the president's behalf for Datin's assistance in the bombing's aftermath. Nine other French officers and medical personnel were also decorated by General Barrow for their services.[3]

Since the 24th MAU was the first MAU to deploy with both the new M198 howitzer and the CH-53E helicopter, extensive training was conducted with both of these systems during the workup. Noncombatant evacuation operations (NEO), in both a permissive and a nonpermissive environment, were conducted by both air and surface means. A mass casualty evacuation was performed by airlift in conjunction with one of the surface assaults. During the workup, BLT 1/8 and 24th MAU Headquarters were given a Marine Corps Combat Readiness Evaluation and received a combat ready rating. MSSG-24 participated in the workup, establishing a beach support area (BSA) on Onslow Beach to provide logistical support to the MAU and participated in the NEO operations. When the workup terminated, the general feeling was that the Blue-Green Team was blending well.

On April 28, I was in Norfolk, Virginia, the home port of the Atlantic Fleet and the Fleet Marine Forces, Atlantic, under the command of Lt. Gen. John Miller. On April 25, I had provided my pre-deployment briefing to the commanding general of the 2nd Force Service Support Group (2nd FSSG), Brig. Gen. Bob Winglass, and his staff at Camp Lejeune and that afternoon to the commanding general of the 2nd Marine Aircraft Wing (2nd MAW), Maj. Gen. Keith Smith, and his staff. The pre-deployment briefing by the deploying MAU's commander was one of the final checks by the major commands.

My briefing to Lieutenant General Miller and his staff was interrupted when I was informed that I had to take a phone call. I said to get the number and I would return the call, but I was told it was an emergency. After I excused myself, I took the call from my youngest brother, Tracy, who informed me that Dad had passed away that morning. My oldest brother had died suddenly two years earlier, and Dad's death struck me the same way. I was heartbroken, thinking of everything my father had done for his family. As I flew to Florida for the funeral, my thoughts lingered on how hard he had worked, putting seven of us through college, and with Mom, he had provided us such an ideal childhood. The previous year, they had celebrated their fiftieth anniversary. The funeral was solemn and emotional. My mother, with her ever-present rosary, was a tower of strength and devotion. I would have preferred to spend a few days with her, but I had to return to Camp Lejeune, North Carolina. We were sailing in ten days.

On May 2, my 24th MAU advance liaison party returned from a brief visit to Lebanon and gave orientation briefings to the 24th MAU staff. On May 9, two days before sailing, I made a final visit to Washington, D.C., for several briefings at HQMC and the Department of State (DOS). My staff flew to Fort Bragg, North Carolina, for a Lebanon briefing by the U.S. Army's Psychological Operations Battalion. All of us felt ready and anxious to go.

On May 13, my executive officer (EXO), Lt. Col. Bill Beebe, and the logistics officer, Maj. Bob Melton, departed for Beirut to coordinate details for the transition. The relief in place would occur when Commodore Rick France (PHIBRON 8) assumed the designation of commander, Task Force 61 (CTF 61), and I (24th MAU) simultaneously assumed the responsibilities of CTF 62, in Beirut.

During our transatlantic crossing, Rick France and I, along with our respective staffs, provided comprehensive orientation briefings for all hands. Some of the subjects covered were intelligence, Lebanese history and culture, terrorist threats covering Lebanese operations, geography, religious groups, multiple factions, and rules of engagement. This Lebanon briefing was taped and aired over PHIBRON 8 closed-circuit television for those who were unable to attend the live presentation. It became known among the Marines and ships' crews as "The Rick and Tim Show."

About halfway across the Atlantic, a young Marine suffered an acute attack of appendicitis. Since there was no anesthesiologist in the MARG, we had him medevaced for surgery to the aircraft carrier USS *Nimitz,* which was headed west, or homeward bound. We were lucky. I noted this serious medical deficiency in the MARG, as did Rick France, and recommended that the "possibility of obtaining necessary qualified medical personnel be explored to ensure availability to all MARG's transiting the Atlantic."

On May 17, 1983, while we were still en route to Lebanon and eight months after the redeployment of the second MNF, Israel and the government of Lebanon signed an agreement calling for the withdrawal of Israeli forces from the Shouf Mountains and for the institution of special measures in southern Lebanon to guarantee Israel's security. As the Long Commission later noted: "Israel, however, predicated its own withdrawal on the simultaneous withdrawal of Syrian and Palestinian Liberation Organization (PLO) forces from Lebanon, parties which had not been included in the negotiations. Syria refused to initiate withdrawal of its forces while the IDF remained in Lebanon. The stage was set for renewed violence."[4]

The agreement, calling for the withdrawal of all foreign forces from Lebanon, was not welcomed in all circles. Secretary of Defense Weinberger vigorously opposed it and cited a secret side letter, accepted by Secretary of State Shultz but unknown to President Gemayel of Lebanon, that stated Israel would not withdraw if Syria did not withdraw simultaneously. In Secretary Weinberger's view, "This agreement with its secret side letter gave President Hafez al-Assad of Syria veto power over any withdrawal and thus over Israel's ability to establish better relations with a key Arab neighbor, Lebanon."[5]

It should be noted that in any subsequent talks with President Assad, including both the negotiations for a cease-fire to end that September's Mountain War and the national reconciliation talks, the prime issue Syria opposed mightily was the withdrawal of Syrian forces from Lebanon. Syria effectively controlled half of Lebanon and had long coveted the fertile Bekaa Valley, from which it reportedly derived $1 billion in hashish exports alone. About the time this agreement was signed, Iran's Islamic Revolutionary Guard Corps (IRGC) had already moved into the Syrian-controlled valley to establish an operational and training base (which is still active today) and created Hezbollah (Party of God) as its proxy force to achieve its objectives. The day after the agreement was signed, Damascus declared that our chief Middle East envoy, Ambassador Philip Habib, was persona non grata because, as the Syrian Arab News Agency explained, "he is one of the most hostile American diplomats to the Arabs and their causes."[6] Two months later, under heavy Syrian pressure, Druze leader Walid Jumblatt announced the formation of the National Salvation Front, which opposed the May 17 agreement.

—3—

Taking over Responsibilities

LEBANON IS THE HISTORICAL HOME of the Phoenicians, who developed a maritime trading industry that flourished for more than two thousand years. By 1100 BC, the Phoenicians controlled the commercial sea-lanes and trade routes stretching from the Black Sea to Spain. Through this role, Lebanon became literally the bridge between East and West. In later centuries, Lebanon's mountains were a refuge for Christians, and the Crusaders established several strongholds there.

Approximately the size of Connecticut, Lebanon has a population of three million people and seventeen officially recognized religious sects. Following the Ottoman Empire's collapse after World War I, the League of Nations mandated five provinces that are part of present-day Lebanon to France. Lebanon's constitution, drawn up in 1926, specified a balance of political power among the various religious groups. There has been no official census taken since 1932, reflecting the political sensitivity in Lebanon over the religious balance; however, it is well known that the Muslim sects (Sunni and Shia) as a whole make up the majority and the Maronite Christians are in the minority. The country gained independence in 1943, and French troops withdrew in 1946.

The Muslim sects' majority claim was one of the primary causes leading to the civil strife in Lebanon during 1975–76. The civil war revealed the elements of Lebanese politics, with three armies, twenty-two militias, and more than forty political parties, most of which defined themselves by ethnic and religious loyalties. Among the main factions were the Maronite Christians, who had formal control of the Parliament and the government by virtue of the outdated 1932 census. During the 1982–84 multinational peacekeeping mission, the president, Amin Gemayel, and the Lebanese Armed Forces' commander, Gen. Ibrahim Tannous, were both Maronite Christians. Opposing factions viewed the LAF as an instrument to enforce Maronite interests since it was being trained and equipped by the United States. The Phalangists' political party is rooted in the Maronite community and was founded by Pierre Gemayel in the late 1930s. They dominated the well-armed and disciplined Lebanese Armed Forces, which had ten thousand troops and fifteen thousand reservists.

The Druze are an Islamic offshoot sect of 250,000 people who live mainly in the Shouf Mountains and Aley hills southeast of Beirut. Their once powerful position in Lebanon had been reduced by the more numerous Maronites. Their political party is the Progressive Socialist Party (PSP), and their four thousand–man militia was armed and controlled by Syria. Their leader was and remains Walid Jumblatt.

The Sunni Muslims, mainstream believers of Islam, made up about 30 percent of Lebanon's population. Their heavily armed militia, called the Mourabitoun, was created by PLO leader Yasser Arafat and much of the fighting was done by the Palestinians.

The Shiite Muslims were once considered the largest community in Lebanon with almost a million people. Their interests were guarded and enforced by the Amal militia, which was heavily armed by Syria. The Shiite community's predominant sponsor, however, shifted to Iran when the Islamic Revolutionary Guard Corps (IRGC) entered Lebanon in 1982. They helped create Hezbollah, which today operates a state within a state in Lebanon that is financed, trained, and supported by Iran.

The central government was based on Lebanese society's religious components in a framework called confessionalism. In this sectarian system, the president of the republic and the LAF's commander in chief were always Maronites, the prime minister a Sunni, and the speaker of the Chamber of Deputies a Shiite, and for every five non-Christian deputies, there must be six Christians. The founders of independent Lebanon recognized that sectarian cooperation was key and that sharing governmental posts among religious groups was the mechanism to facilitate compromise. However, political power traditionally resides with local leaders working through their sectarian and clan relationships with each of the sects—namely, the Maronite, Sunni, Druze, and so on. It was structured deliberately to keep the basic institutions of government—that is, the army, the judiciary, and others—weak to confirm the central government's dependency. This arrangement tended to pit major sects against one another, and when that occurred, the central government simply ceased functioning.

This inherent structure and the absence of any national identity that could unite all Lebanese led to the country's implosion, aided and abetted by Syria and Iran. Lebanon has always been and continues to be a battlefield where armed Lebanese factions simultaneously manipulate, and are manipulated by, the foreign forces surrounding them.

Lebanon's struggle has been marked by periods of political turmoil interspersed with prosperity built on Beirut's position as a regional center for finance and trade. Beirut earned the title of "Paris of the East," but the Arab-Israeli confrontation exposed the fragility of the Lebanese system. More than 100,000 Palestinian refugees fled to Lebanon in 1948 during the war with Israel, and over time a state within a state evolved. In July 1958, the threat of civil war between the Christian Maronites and the Syrian-supported Muslims created a crisis wherein President Camille Chamoun requested U.S. and British assistance. President Dwight D. Eisenhower responded by ordering a total of 14,000 U.S. Marines and U.S. Army Airborne troops to Lebanon. After a few weeks, the scheduled national elections were held, and the new president, Gen. Fuad Chehab, leader of the Lebanese Army, took office during September 1958. Things settled down, and U.S. forces departed after three months without any casualties. Twenty-four years later, another Marine unit would land on the same Red Beach, southwest of Beirut International Airport, with a different mission.

In 1971, a large influx of Palestinian fighters and their leadership entered Lebanon after being expelled from Jordan. This move was the result of Black September, when King Hussein of Jordan personally led his army to drive out the PLO after it attempted to set up a state within his kingdom. As a result, Arafat and the PLO established their own state within Lebanon and proceeded directly to use Lebanon as their base of operations against Israeli civilian targets across the border. Beirut the international playground became a battleground.

The civil war broke out on April 13, 1975, when shots were fired at a Maronite church where Christian Phalangist leader Pierre Gemayel was attending Mass. Four people, including one of Gemayel's bodyguards, were killed. Convinced the assassins were Palestinians, the Phalangists ambushed a busload of Palestinians traveling through East Beirut, killing twenty-seven passengers and wounding nineteen others. As the news spread, Lebanon erupted. Joined by the Druze and leftist Muslim factions, Palestinian forces battled the Phalangists, who were joined by Maronite militias as fighting spread throughout Lebanon.

In June 1976, the Christian president of Lebanon, Suleiman Franjieh, requested Syrian troops. In the fall the Arab League created an Arab Deterrent Force (ADF), which included the already present Syrian troops, to intervene.

In March 1978, Israel invaded Lebanon in response to a brutal PLO attack on a bus in northern Israel that had caused heavy casualties. While the Israelis occupied most of the area south of the Latani River, the UN Security Council passed Resolution 425, which called for their immediate withdrawal and created the UN Interim Force in Lebanon (UNIFIL) to restore peace.

But the PLO continued rocket attacks into northern Israel. After the attempted assassination of the Israeli ambassador to the United Kingdom, Defense Minister Ariel Sharon led the IDF's Operation Peace for Galilee invasion into Lebanon on June 6, 1982.

On May 21, 1983, the 24th MAU entered the Mediterranean and reported to the commander of the Sixth Fleet. The nineteen-man advance party was heli-lifted to Rota, Spain, and then traveled to Beirut. The Sixth Fleet Marine officer, Col. Jim Joy, who was an old friend, landed aboard the flagship USS *Iwo Jima* and presented an updated Beirut briefing to the officers of PHIBRON 8 and the 24th MAU. Shortly thereafter, I departed the flagship with my own advance party by helicopter and flew to nearby Souda Bay, Crete, for further transport via jet to Beirut. Upon arrival, I was met by Col. Jim Mead and started a series of briefings and meetings with the other multinational force commanders; General Tannous, the LAF's commanding general; and the diplomats.

The presence of the commandant of the Marine Corps gave import to the turnover. Despite being on a demanding schedule, General Barrow took the time to meet with Colonel Mead and me in private and provided his views on the current MAU's situation and positions. Months later, when the security environment was deteriorating at an alarming rate, I recalled time and again his prophetic comment that the human intelligence (HUMINT) had to be improved rapidly. It was an issue that was never resolved while we were there, despite the enormous efforts by the new CIA station chief, William Buckley, to rebuild the network. In the end, he gave his life trying to carry out his difficult, seemingly impossible duties in the service of our country. More than twenty-six years later, the dearth of HUMINT in the Middle East remains a major national security vulnerability. Many times, late into the night, I remember becoming blurry eyed while pouring over droves of intelligence data, yet I could not find out what was happening just across our concertina wire.

On May 29, all major elements of the 24th MAU landed ashore at first light and by noon had assumed their new positions while 22nd MAU elements began re-embarking aboard PHIBRON 2 shipping. The first motorized patrols from the 24th MAU commenced immediately. The advance party's coordination and liaison accomplished with the 22nd MAU significantly enhanced the turnover and reflected well on both units.

At 4:00 p.m. on May 30, I assumed full responsibility as commander of the U.S. Forces Ashore, Lebanon, and Commodore Rick France assumed full responsibility as the overall commander of U.S. Forces, Lebanon. Earlier in the day, Rick France and I, along with Col. Jim Mead and Commodore George Bess, commander of PHIBRON 2, held a joint news conference and answered many queries about the MNF and our mission. The same day, BLT 1/8 conducted the first foot patrols. The turnover and relief in place as Landing Force Sixth Fleet/U.S. contingent to Multinational Force, Lebanon, were effected smoothly and rapidly without interruption in the MNF operations. By sunset, PHIBRON 2 and the 22nd MAU were under way, sailing to the U.S. Naval Station at Rota, Spain, to wash down their vehicles and tracks before continuing the homeward voyage. Our challenges were just beginning.

I had made an early decision not to bring any of my dress uniforms ashore. I wanted to set a tone that the new MAU in town was serious about building on the solid relationships and operations that the 22nd MAU had so well established and nurtured. My rule was that when taking over the responsibilities of a new command, it was a good time to make changes to advance our objectives. I also enacted a policy that all hands were to wear full combat gear when on duty and when traveling throughout the greater Beirut area.

I also avoided the social scene and attended only those official functions deemed necessary. I further established a blanket no liberty policy in Lebanon for all hands. Commodore Rick France and I coordinated all the details with our policy regarding training, patrols, operations, and planning. This effort kept everyone on the same sheet of music and enhanced the coordination with our MNF partners.

Soon after my arrival, I was met by my executive officer, Lieutenant Colonel Beebe, who had earlier led the 24th MAU's advance party to Lebanon. I came to realize the superb job he did. Lieutenant Colonel Beebe gave me a note from Bill Buckley, with whom I had traveled and worked closely during my previous tour of duty with the agency. Buckley, who had arrived in Beirut shortly before 24th MAU came ashore, had told Lieutenant Colonel Beebe that he wanted me to contact him as soon as possible.

Lieutenant Colonel Beebe and I went over a long list of items that required immediate attention, among which were numerous invitations, media requests, and MNF priorities. When Col. Jim Mead and I discussed his final wrap-up notes and advice, he had advised that I accept the invitation to a farewell party for the departing British ambassador, Sir David Roberts, who had opened part of his embassy to U.S. diplomats immediately following the U.S. embassy's destruction that April. The chairman and president of Trans Mediterranean Airways (TMA) would host the party at his East Beirut residence in mid-June. Additionally, the USMNF was occupying TMA offices at the airport. I accepted that invitation and only that one; my staff sent regrets to the others.

When the 24th MAU went ashore, we moved into predetermined positions that the previous MAUs had already occupied. The 24th MAU Headquarters was located in a two-story reinforced concrete building that formerly housed the airport's firefighting school. BLT 1/8 and the attached units established their headquarters in the government of Lebanon's Aviation Administrative Bureau, a bombed-out four-story building that was considered one of the strongest in Beirut because of its reinforced-concrete construction. In more recent times, it had been occupied by the PLO, the Syrians, and later by the Israelis, who had converted it into a field hospital during their June 1982 invasion. The U.S. Marines had occupied the building since September 1982 when the MNF returned to Beirut with the presence mission. The 24th MAU Service Support Group occupied steel-reinforced concrete buildings directly north of the MAU Headquarters.

The rationale for selecting BIA and, more specifically, the building housing BLT 1/8's headquarters, came under intense scrutiny following the bombings.

Tactical considerations and the MNF's security were not particularly high priorities given the permissive environment at the time of their selection in September 1982. The dramatic transformation of the security environment throughout Beirut during the late summer of 1983, however, forced the MNF to take action that moved us farther away from the purpose and required neutrality of the peacekeeping mission.

MAP 3. U.S. Multinational Force Compound, Beirut International Airport. *USMC Archives*

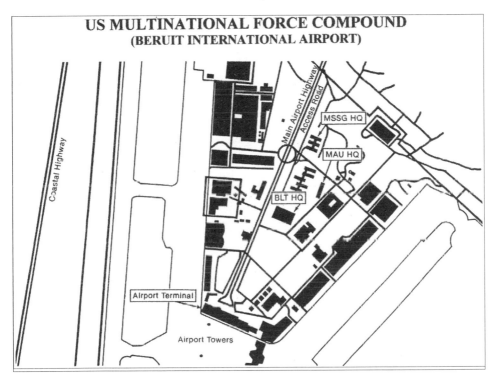

—4—

Relationships and Training

IN EARLY JUNE, BILL BUCKLEY called to tell me he wanted me to meet someone and that he'd pick me up at my office. He also said to be in civilian clothes. (It was the only occasion I wore civilian clothes while ashore.) It was Sunday evening when he arrived at my command post (CP) at BIA, and we had a few laughs about how both of us ended up in Beirut, brought together again by a series of events that neither of us could have forecast.

Bill drove. As we made our way through the streets of Beirut at dusk, he gave me an update on the current situation and his assessment. As usual, it was professional and informative. Bill was never one to shy away from new challenges; indeed, he sought them. I joked with him that his driving was as crappy as ever but was more suitable for Beirut than Northern Virginia, where we'd last seen each other. His response was hilarious and unprintable.

We pulled up to a high-rise building in East Beirut, where we were meeting Simon Quassis, the chief of Lebanese Intelligence, for dinner and discussions. Lebanese Army soldiers and several young, hard-eyed men in civilian clothes carrying submachine guns provided ample security. I assumed, and Bill confirmed, they were part of the intelligence chief's personal security detail.

When we entered the lobby, some members of the security detail quickly led us to an elevator that took us to the top floor. As the elevator doors opened, we found ourselves in a majestic penthouse restaurant with a panoramic view of Beirut. I was impressed. We were led to a large dining table where the director of intelligence sat. Having just arrived in Beirut days earlier, I was still slowly taking everything in. What struck me as I looked around was that the whole place was totally empty except for security personnel, waiters, and staff.

After exchanging pleasantries, it was apparent that Director Quassis was aware of my background. He spoke excellent English and was most accommodating in answering my questions. He and Bill provided me with their current assessment and an analysis of the threats facing the multinational force and the Lebanese government. Bill reiterated that he confronted a significant challenge in building a new intelligence team in Beirut. We finished the pleasant dinner, and I thanked the director for his time and information. Bill delivered me back to my CP, and we agreed to stay in touch and periodically meet to try to stay ahead of the threat curve. It would become a daunting challenge.

I wanted a fresh look at the security at all Marine positions, and we had a full list of tasks that we tackled with determination and enthusiasm. As part of our security reassessments, we sent an MAU engineering team to survey the British embassy, the Durrafourd Building (part of the U.S. embassy compound), and other locations and to provide recommendations for future fortifications. It became an ongoing process as we continually reviewed and improved the security of the multiple sites, particularly as the violence escalated in the late summer of 1983.

We were conducting four to seven foot patrols daily in the area surrounding the airport. The number, route, and times of the patrols did not follow a fixed or predictable pattern. The patrol leaders determined their routes and submitted them to the BLT's headquarters for approval, although the patrol leaders had the authority to vary the patrol routes after notifying the BLT. Their routes were published at least a week in advance and distributed to all concerned. Position reports were called in as each patrol reached a numbered reference point. The patrol was normally a reinforced squad consisting of thirteen to fifteen lightly armed Marines.

Two mobile patrols were also conducted daily throughout the greater Beirut area. The routes and times of these patrols varied as well, with the route determination made and published in the same manner as those of the foot patrols. The patrol leader reported his location through a series of lettered reference points and colored phase lines. A lieutenant from the Lebanese Armed Forces accompanied each mobile patrol, and beginning June 24, a four-man fire team from the LAF accompanied selected foot patrols.

MAP 4. U.S. Multinational Force Area, Beirut. *USMC Archives*

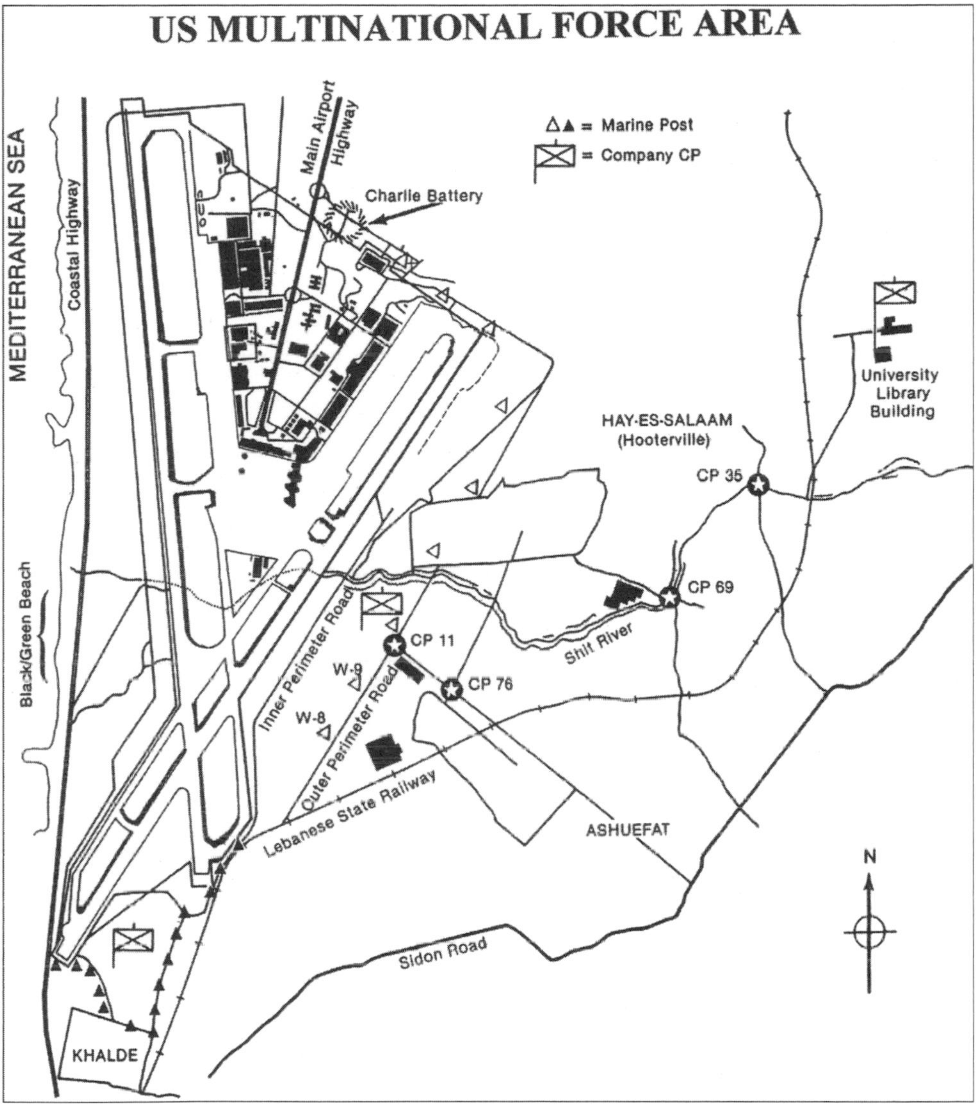

US MULTINATIONAL FORCE AREA

△▲ = Marine Post

⊠ = Company CP

Main Airport Highway

Charlie Battery

MEDITERRANEAN SEA

Coastal Highway

University Library Building

HAY-ES-SALAAM (Hooterville)

CP 35

Black/Green Beach

CP 69

Inner Perimeter Road

Shit River

CP 11

W-9

Outer Perimeter Road

W-8

CP 76

Lebanese State Railway

ASHUEFAT

N

Sidon Road

KHALDE

The BLT manned seven joint checkpoints with the LAF. The size of these checkpoints varied from a fire team to a squad. (Depending on the time and location, each checkpoint had four to fifteen fully armed Marines, reinforced with LAF soldiers. The size, reinforcement, and improved capabilities of each checkpoint increased as the civil war escalated. By September 1983, some of these checkpoints were beginning to resemble combat outposts. Our Italian partners to our north underwent a similar transformation.) The Marines' principal function, in both the patrols and the checkpoints, was to provide both a visible presence in support of the LAF and stability for the government of Lebanon. After the suicide truck bombs on October 23, 1983, this interpretation of the presence mission, which was constant throughout most of our tour, was the point of considerable criticism directed at me because it supposedly exposed my command to needless attacks. This interpretation of our mission was never raised as an issue during the many VIP and congressional delegation visits.

On a quiet evening in mid-June, I departed my CP at dusk to attend departing British ambassador Sir David Roberts's farewell party. I wore combat gear, as did my driver, Cpl. Michael Cavallaro, and the security detail. We had been provided with explicit directions to the East Beirut residence of the host, Munir Abu-Haidar, president and chairman of Trans Mediterranean Airways. My plan was to make a quick visit, pay my respects and appreciation to the ambassador for his support following our embassy bombing, thank the host for his hospitality, and depart. As I was to learn, things are not that simple in Beirut.

As we approached the residence, LAF checkpoints were evident and abundant. I was escorted to the row-house type residence, which was nice but not that impressive. Security guards in civilian clothes, with their ubiquitous submachine guns, were everywhere. By now, it was dark, so I was escorted to an elevator in the lobby, put inside alone, and proceeded to the penthouse. When the elevator doors opened into the main room, I looked upon a penthouse scene that could easily have been one on Park Avenue or the Champs-Elysées. Soft music was playing, and the men were in tuxedos, the ladies in gowns and cocktail dresses, and attachés and MNF attendees in their military dress uniforms. All eyes were on me when I entered, and I must have looked as if I wondered whether I had gotten off on the wrong floor. At least my camouflaged utilities were pressed. Mr. Abu-Haidar, the host, welcomed me since I had never met him before. He and his American wife were very gracious hosts, and everyone seemed to be amused that the new Marine commander had arrived in his combat uniform. The furnishings, paintings, tapestries, food, and clothing reflected the high society of Beirut, and the party was memorable. I saw U.S. ambassador Robert Dillon, who represented the United States so well during this dynamic period in Lebanon. I paid my respects to Sir David, thanking him for his generous support following the bombing, and expressed my appreciation to the gracious hosts for their hospitality.

As I returned to my CP that night, a nagging thought kept creeping into my head. Not far from this luxurious party and company that I had just attended were the Palestinian refugee camps, Sabra and Shatila, where the grotesque massacre of hundreds of Palestinian civilians had sparked the return of the Marines and the presence mission. By coincidence, I had had a peek at the opposite ends of Beirut society.

The first of our VIP visitors had begun arriving within a few days of our arrival. A congressional delegation, which included Representatives Thomas Foglietta (D-PA), Peter Kostmayer (D-PA), and Theodore Weiss (D-NY), visited on June 2. Commodore Rick France (CTF 61) and I (CTF 62) briefed the delegation and gave the members a tour of the area at BIA and the Lebanese Science University. This routine—the briefings and tour—was slightly modified as the situation grew more dangerous. A few days later, Rear Adm. Jerry Tuttle, USN, visited us. Admiral Tuttle's group (CTF 60) included the Carrier Battle Group over the horizon, and it would provide air support if required. Because of his significant responsibilities, Rick France and I gave him an in-depth briefing and tour of our positions. CTF 60 remained on station throughout our tour, and Rick and I made certain that Admiral Tuttle was kept abreast of the fast and furious changes. He and his staff visited us throughout our tenure, and they were always available and professional.

On June 9, the commander of the Sixth Fleet, Vice Adm. William Rowden, USN, and his party, which included Mrs. Rowden, visited since he was nearing the end of his tour of duty. In addition to the tour of our positions, Admiral Rowden was awarded the National Order of the Cedar by LAF commander General Tannous.

We continued to tap all sources that could provide us with some insight and current information about the local culture that could help us in carrying out the mission. To this end, on June 14, Foreign Service Officer (FSO) Ryan Crocker from the U.S. embassy provided an informative briefing on the political situation to the PHIBRON 8 and 24th MAU officers. Crocker had been wounded in the embassy bombing less than two months earlier, but that did not affect his sense of duty. His reputation as a talented Arabist marked him as an FSO to watch. He was also the embassy official inside the Shatila refugee camp on September 18, 1982, reporting firsthand the carnage there. Later, Crocker became ambassador to Lebanon, Kuwait, Syria, Pakistan, and Iraq. His dedication, abundant talent, and selfless service in diplomatic hot spots reveal him to be a special American serving his country with distinction.

On June 18, I met with Col. Larry Williams, USMC, and gave him a briefing and tour of MAU positions throughout greater Beirut. Larry was the commanding officer of the 11th Marines at Camp Lejeune before being selected as the EUCOM's representative in Lebanon. His duties involved being the military liaison in Lebanon for Gen. Bernard Rogers, the commander in chief of the U.S. European Command (USCINCEUR). He had access to our plans and operations, and we made an extra effort to keep him current with the changes.

■

We inherited some robust training programs that previous MAUs had started. The cross training was well received by the French, Italian, and British MNF partners, but none was more enthusiastic than the Lebanese Armed Forces. General Tannous was the chief proponent of Marine training for his army, especially the elite 1st Air Assault Battalion.

We conducted a demonstration amphibious landing at Green Beach that was observed by a group of 105 officers and NCOs from the French 31st Brigade, under the command of Brig. Gen. Jean-Claude Coulon. Mass casualty drills were held continuously to enhance our readiness posture. Parachute operations, special patrol insertion-extraction rig training, rappelling, familiarization firing of each country's weapons, and explosive ordnance disposal (EOD) training honed skills and improved readiness.

Our mobile training teams provided basic infantry and air assault techniques to the LAF's 3rd Company, 1st Air Assault Battalion. The demanding curriculum ran for four weeks, and an exceptionally talented officer, Maj. George Converse, was the MAU's operations officer overseeing the training. He handled the myriad demanding tasks with insight, leadership, and humor. George proved indispensable as the MAU moved into troubled waters.

Upon our arrival in Beirut, the flight operations of Marine Medium Helicopter Squadron-162 were critical and extensive. Two aircraft were on continuous medical evacuation alert while two AH-2T Cobra gunships remained on strip alert. Daily operational flights consisted of personnel transfers, logistical flights, command and control aircraft, VIP transport, and long-range logistical flights to Larnaca, Cyprus, and flights to Tel Aviv in support of diplomatic negotiations. HMM-162 operationally supported the training of U.S., British, French, Italian, and Lebanese armed forces by providing helo support for parachute operations, recon inserts, helo familiarization, and air assaults. In June alone, they conducted four priority medevacs from Landing Site (LS) Red to the USS *Iwo Jima*.

The staff had developed a comprehensive intelligence and security awareness program to support our role as the U.S. contingent to the MNF. It included information security training for all 24th MAU personnel, preparation of intelligence summaries and intelligence reports, submission requests for imagery support, and an exchange of releasable intelligence data among all elements of the MNF. Under the able leadership of the intelligence officer (S-2), Capt. Kevin McCarthy, the 24th MAU established a joint coordinated intelligence collection and reporting procedure with CTF 61 and the U.S. Defense Attaché Office in Beirut. All source intelligence briefings, which included the Radio Battalion Detachment and satellite communications (SATCOM), were held on a regular basis. Classes in security and antiterrorist countermeasures were routinely conducted.

We also built on and strengthened our relations with the French, British, and Italian liaison sections. Along with Lebanese security, we investigated a labyrinth of tunnels beneath BIA, where one passageway terminated in the basement of the BLT's headquarters. We eventually blocked it with a series of obstacles and posted a Marine sentry 24/7; it became sentry post 9. Shortly thereafter I accepted an invitation to be Gen. Franco Angioni's guest in the Italian sector. He briefed the members of my staff on operations in his sector, which was located directly north of the American sector at the airport. After lunch, he led us on a tour that eventually led to the maze of tunnels beneath his sector near the sports arena. The underground network revealed storage areas, classrooms, and endless tunnels. It was soon evident that the Palestinian Liberation Organization, like the Vietnamese, used these extensive tunnel networks to support their training and operations. They also provided ideal cover for clandestine arms smuggling operations, which had been immense and lucrative.

One of many reports we sent to higher headquarters was a weekly Situation Report (SITREP). The report's final section included the commander's comments, and I would provide my assessment of the current situation and address any other germane subjects. The mid-June SITREP mentioned that the MAU remained alert in response to threats to the Durrafourd Building, where the U.S. embassy staff worked, and to possible assassination attempts. I presented to the Multinational Force Military Committee a proposal to combine the Marine foot patrols with Lebanese Army fire teams. I noted that the area that the foot patrols covered had grown increasingly hostile and that the addition of LAF soldiers might help to alleviate the threat. The proposal was approved, and joint patrols commenced on June 24.

I also included a comment that increased command attention was directed to weapons safety at all levels after an accidental discharge by a Marine occupying a line position at BIA. In what could only be described as bizarre, the round struck, not one, but two LAF soldiers jogging together along the perimeter road. They were immediately rushed to a Lebanese Army hospital for treatment. I quickly went to see General Tannous to explain and defuse a potentially ugly incident. When I was led into his office, hat in hand, he was cordial and informed me he knew about the incident. I offered my apology for the unfortunate occurrence, but he waived it off and said that both soldiers were doing well and should have a swift recovery. What surprised me was that the gist of the conversation was General Tannous's amazement that a single M-16 rifle round could penetrate four legs. From his standpoint, that was the end of the incident. I later visited the two soldiers in the hospital, and they were in good spirits and, fortunately, mending. The Marine involved was disciplined.

In the early morning hours of June 23, Marine positions at BIA were peppered with scattered small arms fire, which was a result of the Israel Defense Forces responding to some rocket-propelled grenades (RPGs) landing near their positions. The Israelis were continuing to take casualties, and their disproportionate responses reflected their exasperation and frustration. It was understandable but also a menace to anyone who happened to be in the vicinity when they responded. A later incident involved IDF .50-caliber heavy machine gun fire impacting Marine positions. We did not suffer any casualties, luckily. I contacted the U.S. European Command representative and the Israeli officers to protest the dangers of these tactics. EUCOM later notified us that the IDF regretted the incident and would seek to avoid similar incidents in the future.

The escalating tensions since the U.S. embassy bombing in April, along with the stagnation of diplomatic and political progress, generated rumors of a possible expansion of our mission. There had been some hints, so we initiated planning to consider options for that possibility. The LAF, under General Tannous's command, was preparing for the day when the Israel Defense Force would depart and it could occupy the IDF's vacated strategic positions. In planning for the possible U.S. Multinational Force's expansion, our own choices were limited. We had to stay west of the IDF's main supply route. The LAF wanted to assume the same positions in the mountains east of and overlooking Beirut for the same reason the Israelis had—that is, for their strategic location. For the USMNF to move in and occupy those positions would have meant a change of mission and a dramatic increase in force levels. The United States wanted to avoid this possibility for good reasons, so occupying the foothills south of BIA was one of the few options available.

An MAU can also serve as a forward element of a Marine Amphibious Brigade (MAB). I thought this scenario would be likely if our mission was expanded. Along with BLT 1/8 commander Lt. Col. Larry Gerlach and members of our respective staffs, we reconnoitered sites in the foothills along Sidon Road located south of the airport.

I supported the idea of reducing the concentration of the USMNF at BIA. The expansion plan was hotly debated back in Washington, but it would eventually be rejected. From day one, I had been uncomfortable with the USMNF's static location in the middle of an active international airport, a tactical choice that defied any military logic. Although I understood the rationale for its selection, the longer we remained there, and the more the violence accelerated, the more my uneasiness grew.

—5—

Peacekeepers in Action

THE BEGINNING OF JULY saw the pace of our activities accelerate in operations, training, flight operations, and official visitors. The BLT commenced inserting some of the security foot patrols by helicopter in order to provide the squads additional training in helicopter-borne operations. Each squad would be inserted in one of several landing zones (LZs) surrounding the airfield and the Lebanese Science University and then patrol a predesignated route to return to BIA. Live-fire immediate-action drills (for rapid response to provocations such as ambushes) were also conducted for all units that were providing personnel and vehicles for the mobile patrols. We coordinated training with the Italian contingent so that when the patrol passed the Italian live-fire range in its sector, one vehicle at a time drove through the range and a simulated ambush. The Marines dismounted, returned fire at the dummy attackers, recovered a simulated casualty, and withdrew while maintaining covering fire. This realistic training provided the Marines with a confidence-building exercise.

On the Fourth of July, we held an Independence Day celebration aboard our flagship, the USS *Iwo Jima*. We heli-lifted the guests, who included fellow MNF commanders, embassy officials, and Gen. Ibrahim Tannous. The quiet ceremony included a cake cutting with all the guests enjoying the cake and ice cream. Ashore, we had a picnic and cookout, including the requisite hot dogs and hamburgers, for all hands. Some of the Marines would later comment that the real fireworks did not begin for another two months, when the Israelis withdrew from the greater Beirut area and triggered the September War.

On July 5, Secretary of State George Shultz and his party of twenty-five people visited Beirut. Rick France and I met with the secretary for discussions while Mrs. Shultz, accompanied by Mrs. Bob Pugh, the wife of Deputy Chief of Mission Bob Pugh, toured the MAU compound and had a meals ready to eat (MRE) lunch with the Marines. A gracious lady who took the Marines under her care, particularly those assigned to the 24th MAU's external security force (ESF) after the U.S. embassy bombing, Bonnie Pugh visited the MNF, baked cookies for the personnel, and assisted in any way she could. Bonnie epitomized those gallant ladies who raise their families, many times in adverse circumstances; accompany their husbands to far-flung places around the globe; and persevere through the rough patches of life. Her positive attitude and outgoing personality were always evident and welcome, and she earned a special place of honor with the Marines in Lebanon. In the late 1980s, her husband became ambassador to Chad. On September 19, 1989, while headed to the States to help plan her daughter's wedding, she and 169 others were killed when a bomb exploded on UTA Flight 772 from Brazzaville to Paris. In what had to be a salute to Bonnie, her daughter's wedding proceeded on schedule.

On July 6, we were visited by Vice Adm. M. Staser Holcomb, the deputy commander in chief of U.S. Naval Forces, Europe, who received a joint CTF 61 and 62 briefing and a tour of MAU positions followed by a visual reconnaissance of Beirut in the command helicopter. The 24th MAU hosted Gen. Sir John Stanier, chief of the General Staff of the Royal Army, on July 9. Following the briefing, he was also given a helicopter orientation of Beirut. Vice Adm. Edward H. Martin, the new commander of the Sixth Fleet, paid the first of many visits to Beirut, which would consume an inordinate amount of his schedule in the tumultuous months ahead. He was a Navy fighter pilot who had been shot down over North Vietnam during the war and held as a POW for more than five years. Maj. Gen. Keith Smith, commanding general of the 2nd Marine Aircraft Wing, whose son, Vincent, was a captain serving as the BLT 1/8 air liaison officer (and later perished in the suicide attack), also visited along with Brig. Gen. Bob Winglass of the 2nd Force Service Support Group. Brig. Gen. Ernie Cook (deputy J-3, USCINCEUR), Brig. Gen. E. Heinz (J-2, USCINCEUR), and two congressional delegations also came to Beirut to view the peacekeeping mission firsthand. Besides the briefings and tours, the congressional delegations (CODELS) were also provided an opportunity to visit with their constituents if that could be arranged.

On July 30, Chairman of the Joint Chiefs of Staff (JCS) Gen. John Vessey and his party visited, accompanied by Vice Admiral Martin (COMSIXTHFLT). Rick France and I provided an expanded briefing, a tour of MNF positions, and a visual recon by helicopter over Beirut. General Vessey met with U.S. Army officials of the Office of Military Cooperation (OMC), embassy officials, and the other multinational force commanders. Commodore Rick France hosted a dinner in his honor aboard the USS *Austin*.

On July 18, Lt. Col. Harry Slacum arrived to relieve Lt. Col. Bill Beebe as the 24th MAU's executive officer. Bill was returning to the States to take command of a helicopter squadron. Harry assumed his responsibilities quickly and would develop into a key leader in handling multiple, critical tasks during the chaos and aftermath of the terrorist attack.

We continued to conduct a wide variety of combined training with the members of the MNF and LAF. The success of previous training evolutions with these forces resulted in both enthusiastic participation and the scheduling of increased cross-training opportunities. In order to acquaint members of the MNF with foreign weapons systems, we conducted a series of briefings and static displays. Officers attended Fire Support Coordination Exercises (FSCX) while cross training French, Italian, and U.K. forces on our tube-launched, optically tracked, wire-guided (TOW) Dragon antitank (AT) weapons while the Marines were briefed and trained on their MILAN AT systems.

Also during July, the 24th MAU concluded training with the LAF's 3rd Company, 1st Air Assault Battalion. The training of this religion-integrated unit consisted of demonstrating basic infantry skills and air assault techniques along with providing an evaluation report of the company's performance. This unit acquitted itself quite well during the war in September following the Israelis' withdrawal.

I attended the 3rd Company's graduation ceremony with Lt. Col. Larry Gerlach, whose men helped train them. I presented graduation certificates to the honor graduates, or the top 30 graduating soldiers from a class of 280. I recall that the honor graduates represented all religious factions of the LAF: the Christians, Shia, Sunni, and Druze. During some later fierce battles, they held together as a credible national army, fulfilling General Tannous's dream.

Our foot and mobile point patrols with the LAF put us in day-to-day contact with Lebanese civilians. Most of the people would wave, give a thumbs-up sign, smile in return, or say hello or "Hey, Joe." The adjacent village Hay-al-Sellum (called Hooterville by the Marines) was a crowded and poor complex suburb of Beirut, being predominantly Shiite Muslim. Incidents of children throwing rocks and of young men with hard looks making gestures had occurred but were relatively few. Pictures of Iranian leader Ayatollah Ruhollah Khomeini were often displayed but so were the pictures of many other Muslim religious, political, and military figures. The patrols were told to remain alert, watch, and report hostile behavior.

More typical were hundreds of unreported contacts that would build good-will and create an atmosphere of cooperation and helpfulness. Some examples included a Navy corpsman helping a sixty-two-year-old woman who was burned by scalding water. Our dental detachment treated children at a local orphanage, and the Marines from our service support group built and installed playground equipment for a children's park.

The relatively tranquil environment since our arrival was suddenly shattered on July 22 when BIA was attacked. The Druze Progressive Socialist Party, under the leadership of Walid Jumblatt and totally supported by Syria, rained about a dozen 122mm Katyusha rockets and 102mm mortar shells on Marine positions. A Lebanese civilian was killed and seven wounded while three LAF soldiers, a U.S. Navy sailor, and two Marines were also wounded.

Anti-American conduct escalated after this attack. Shortly afterward, three gunmen opened fire with semiautomatic weapons through the airport fence at a group of Marines jogging on the airport's perimeter road. No Marine was hit, but we later learned that this attack was meant as a warning for the Marines not to get involved in LAF training and operations. The assailants were identified as Shia Muslim supporters of Amal, which is also supported by Syria.

As a result of these attacks, we formalized our response procedures and implemented a graduated escalation response (see appendix A). In my SITREP commander's comments at the end of the week, I noted, "The wounding of the two Marines and one Sailor from the USMNF typifies the daily threat to the USMNF. Caught between a multitude of factions and long-standing conflicts, the Marines must maintain a fine balance."

As one of the multinational forces involved in the peacekeeping effort in Lebanon, the USMNF maintained a cordial but separate relationship with the other MNF members. There was no combined headquarters, and none of the contingents reported to another contingent or to the Lebanese Armed Forces in an operational manner. Each was under the specific control of its own government and adhered to its government's rules of engagement established as each interpreted the role of its forces ashore. Each member was asked to assist the government of Lebanon individually, and its specific relationship was solely a bilateral matter between the GOL and itself.

Each force sent representatives to weekly political, military, and intelligence meetings, which served as forums for exchanging information in these areas. A central communications link at the Presidential Palace with officers from the British, French, U.S., and Italian contingents provided a liaison for the Lebanese government to the headquarters of each MNF. These liaison officers were colocated in a room in the palace and monitored individual communications nets to their respective combat information centers. Each force manned this post differently, and the only requirement was that it had to be manned by an officer. The 24th MAU rotated this duty weekly between BLT 1/8, MSSG-24, and the MAU Headquarters.

The USMNF also provided a liaison officer and radio watch to each of the other three forces. An attempt was made to have an officer fluent in Italian and French assigned to the posts, but the 24th MAU had only been successful in finding qualified French speakers. Where necessary, we provided skilled Interrogator/Translator Team (ITT) personnel to assist. These officers provided close and continuous contact with the other members of the MNF that proved quite valuable.

As part of training and equipping the Lebanese Armed Forces, the Pentagon made the decision that they should receive the newest 155mm howitzer, the M-198. Its range and accuracy added a significant upgrade to the LAF's artillery capabilities. I decided it was time that I visit the training site and evaluate how the training was progressing.

It was a typical hot day when my driver, Corporal Cavallaro, and I, along with the security detail, headed for the distant site. The training base was located deep in the Christian-controlled mountain sector east of Beirut. BLT 1/8's Charlie Battery was tasked to train about 140 LAF soldiers who would man the two recently formed M-198 batteries. As we made our way through the Christian-controlled mountain villages and streets, I enjoyed the cool air and the quaint beauty of the surroundings. The small shops, restaurants, and dress shops easily resembled those of a small town in southern France.

When we arrived at the training site, the senior Marine instructor and his LAF counterpart greeted me. They gave me a detailed briefing on their status and progress and a tour of the facility. They were conducting a basic cannoneer school with instruction about artillery mechanics and the procedures for operating a fire direction center (FDC). I found them focused and enthusiastic, and all indicators appeared that the training program was progressing well. While making the final rounds at the site, I asked the LAF escort officer about the cluster of buildings that appeared to be a fortress on top of the highest mountain. He explained it was an abbey dating back to the thirteenth century and asked if I wanted to visit it. I could not refuse, and up we went.

Upon our arrival at the monastery, the LAF officer went inside while I waited outside. The buildings and surroundings resembled an era of antiquity, and the majestic scenery was breathtaking. One would not have to be a tactician to realize the location's strategic importance. Looking east, I could see all the way to the Bekaa Valley, which Syrian troops controlled, and to the west, the Mediterranean Sea. I was thinking, given the choice, I would relocate the U.S. Multinational Force to this site in a minute. Soon the LAF officer returned with the abbot who ruled the monastery.

The abbot led me on a limited tour, careful not to intrude in those areas of the abbey that were cloistered. I felt like a student in a graduate course of the history of the Middle Ages taught by a scholar. He showed me the monks' living quarters, each of which had a stone bed with a hay mattress and a stone table on a stone floor, period. His eloquence in describing the area's history going back before the Crusades was spellbinding and educational. What I found most intriguing was the library's ancient books and manuscripts, which the monks studied and translated between their prayers. I recall the majority of the precious documents were in Latin, Hebrew, Arabic, French, and English.

When it was time to depart, I expressed my appreciation to the abbott for the tour and his personal hospitality. I also wished him and the monks safety and security in the cloudy days ahead. On the return trip to Beirut, I had a strange feeling that I had spent part of the day in a Middle Eastern time capsule reflecting the beauty, turmoil, and tragedy of Lebanon today.

■

In early August, BLT 1/8 rotated the line companies to new positions in order to maintain the alert status of all hands on the front lines. During the rotation, Company B intercepted a patrol of eleven Israel Defense Force soldiers within our perimeter and escorted them back to Sidon Road without incident. Whether the patrol had become disoriented or was testing Company B's perimeter during the line companies' turnover could not be determined. Details of the incident were passed to the EUCOM liaison officer for appropriate action.

On August 6, the U.S. Army's Field Artillery School's Target Acquisition Battery (FASTAB) deployed two counter-mortar/counter-artillery (AN/TPQ-36) radars to Beirut in direct support of the 24th MAU. The mission of the FASTAB detachment was to support the USMNF by providing data to us on incoming mortar, artillery, and rocket rounds. The detachment was under the operational control of CTF 62 and, along with our Marine radars, improved the MAU's target acquisition capability.

The FASTAB detachment was put to work immediately. On the night of August 8, two more 122mm Katyusha rockets impacted at the airport. These rounds indicated that the earlier attack two weeks prior was no longer an aberration and signaled more attacks were likely.

On the tenth, another Katyusha landed between the MAU and BLT headquarters at 5:25 a.m. A Marine first lieutenant was wounded by shrapnel, but this incident was just a prelude for the day's action. An hour later, a rocket barrage aimed at the Lebanese Air Force's flight line and camps directly north of BIA. Within an hour, twenty-seven 122mm rockets rained around the airport; however, this time our FASTAB Marine radars pinpointed the launch sites. In order to get the hostile rocket battery to cease fire, our 81mm mortar platoon fired four illumination rounds directly above the suspected firing sites. The rocket barrage halted within ten minutes.

During the attack, two AH-1T Cobra helicopter gunships had been launched over Green Beach, prepared to respond to any request for fire. CTF 61 (PHIBRON 8) placed all ships at general quarters and moved naval gunfire support into position to fire if needed.

The 24th MAU sustained no casualties during this exchange, but major fire-fights between the LAF and various Muslim militias continued throughout the next two days and nights. Continuous mortar and rocket rounds landed north of BIA and had several spillover impacts at Rock Base, HMM-162's ashore terminal at Landing Site Red, and in the northern portion of the perimeter. It became clear during this attack that the Marines at the airport were caught between the hostile batteries' line of fire and their target, the Lebanese Armed Forces.

The fighting in the hills and within the city gradually increased in intensity for the next two weeks, with isolated rounds landing in Marine positions and near the American ambassador's residence. The LAF continued to have some violent clashes with the pro-Khomeini Amal militia in West Beirut and the southern suburbs, which were located directly across the concertina wire in front of our positions. Incidents of minor harassment of our patrols increased, and the Italians, French, and British contingents also received small arms and mortar fire within their positions.

I expanded my views of the current situation and the developing dilemmas in my weekly SITREP's commander's comments:

This week's events illustrated the deteriorating security situation here in Beirut. Direct attacks against the LAF are increasing and are placing the USMNF in a position where the demonstration of its neutrality is becoming more difficult. I have considered very carefully the steps to take in order to respond to the incoming fire, while at the same time limit the engagement. The Druze interpretation of our actions is always nebulous but I feel that our actions this week were appropriate and achieved the desired result. Intelligence information has since confirmed that they were surprised by our actions and ceased fire to avoid becoming decisively engaged. I feel, however, that if it serves their interest, they will directly attack the Marine positions at the airport, and 81mm mortar illumination rounds may not be sufficient to deter them the next time. Our information also indicates that they are unsure of how to deal with the AH-1T Cobra, and its presence offshore currently serves as somewhat of a deterrent. All of these deterrents are transitory, however, and once they feel they have the capability to deal with each threat, I believe they will become emboldened to take one more step. I am prepared to deal with each of their steps and am confident that our response will be proper and restrained, yet send them the appropriate signals. If they fail to understand the signals, I am prepared to deal with that as well.

I should like to point out the superb performance of the Marines and Sailors of the USMNF during the small disturbances this week. I was extremely proud of all hands and found them to display poise, courage, and a good deal of humor in a most irritating situation.

During a break between the rocket and artillery attacks, I hosted Bill Buckley. In an earlier meeting, I had told Bill he had a standing invitation to visit us anytime to get a briefing on our operations, tour our positions, and meet the peacekeepers. He received the VIP treatment he deserved, including getting an aerial reconnaissance of greater Beirut and the surrounding countryside. From the command helicopter, I pointed out some locations in the Shouf Mountains where the hostile rockets and artillery were originating. As he viewed this site and looked at our positions at the airport, he wryly commented that I had picked a wonderful tactical location for my men. Bill was a highly decorated U.S. Army veteran of the Korean War, and we usually engaged in the good-natured bantering that's common between soldiers and Marines. In a more serious tone, he asked, how did we end up in the airport location? At the end of his visit, we agreed to step up our personal dialogue and meetings as necessary.

On August 16, the new commandant of the Marine Corps, Gen. P. X. Kelley, and his party arrived for a visit. It was the first of his three visits to Beirut. The new sergeant major of the Corps, Robert Cleary, accompanied General Kelley and met with the staff NCOs and Marines as well as the other peacekeepers. The CMC visited Commodore Rick France on the flagship *Iwo Jima* and other ships offshore and toured the MAU positions at and around BIA. He paid a call on the diplomats at the U.S. embassy and paid a personal visit to General Tannous. After the latter visit, it was obvious that Generals Kelley and Tannous had struck a special rapport.

A few days later, on the twentieth, Secretary of the Navy (SECNAV) John Lehman paid us a visit. Adm. Ed Martin (COMSIXTHFLT) escorted him. Admiral Martin took an active role in supporting the peacekeeping mission, and the sailors and Marines of the multinational force came to respect him highly. Secretary Lehman visited the PHIBRON 8 ships and crews as well as our positions ashore. Rick France and I gave him a comprehensive update of our current status, and he expressed great interest in our mission and the evolving situation. He, too, later returned to Lebanon.

As part of the coordination for the pending but unannounced Israeli withdrawal, Special Presidential Envoy Robert McFarlane and I overflew the Israeli-held territory south of Ad Damur to the Awali River in late August. The flight had to be coordinated through diplomatic and military channels with both Lebanon and Israel. But all of the preliminary discussions and work that should have gone into supporting the IDF's withdrawal was ignored since the force withdrew on its own schedule before allowing the LAF to assume its vacated strategic positions in the Shouf Mountains. This regretful decision by Israeli leaders predictably accelerated the resumption of the Lebanese civil war, culminating in the dual suicide truck attacks on the multinational peacekeeping force six weeks later.

—6—

The Predictable War

IN LATE AUGUST, THE ENVIRONMENT definitely changed. The sporadic shelling and intermittent exchanges of small arms fire increased with accuracy and intensity. There was ample evidence that we were heading into troubled waters. Our restraint in responding to the provocations was measured and precise. Our rules of engagement stated that we were not to initiate any of the exchanges, and when we were forced to respond, our response should be structured on trying to terminate it at the lowest possible level and in the shortest period of time so that it did not escalate into a larger fracas. Although this technique was quite successful in most cases, the ante was continually being raised.

In anticipation of these contingencies, Commodore Rick France and I oversaw a mass casualty evacuation drill on August 27 that involved U.S. and British contingents ashore being evacuated to our flagship USS *Iwo Jima* for simulated treatment. Rick and I discussed several scenarios that could trigger the plan's activation. One was a noncombatant evacuation operation involving the evacuation of the U.S. embassy and all U.S. citizens if the situation really deteriorated. The exercise went well and proved fortuitous in that seven weeks later, this training undoubtedly saved scores of lives following the suicide truck bombing.

The Israelis had announced on July 20 their intention to withdraw their forces south to the Awali River. They were continuing to suffer significant casualties from guerrilla-style attacks along their MSR, Sidon Road, and in their forward areas along the Beirut–Damascus highway. In anticipation of this pending but unspecified date of withdrawal, the Lebanese Armed Forces launched a multi-battalion sweep operation in the early afternoon hours of August 28 westward through the Shia-dominated southern suburbs. Fighting erupted and quickly spread in the densely populated residential districts. The battle against the LAF was led by the Shia Amal and other radical Shiites while Syrian-supported Druze and Sunni militias joined the fray. The fighting was vicious and primitive, spreading throughout the Shia suburbs and causing all of West Beirut to explode.

The inevitable happened, and the fighting spilled over into Marine positions adjacent to the village of Hay-al-Sellum. Checkpoints 35 and 69, jointly manned by Marines and the LAF, engaged the attackers in a fierce two-hour gun battle. This fighting marked the first time the U.S. peacekeepers directly engaged the attacking Muslim militias. Surprisingly, none of the Marines were injured, but the intensity of the conflict did not bode well for the future. As one Marine reported, the small arms fire was as great as that on a 200-yard rapid-fire string of the Marine Corps' rifle qualification course.

During the ensuing period, it was estimated that more than a hundred rounds of 82mm mortars, 122mm mortars, and 122mm rockets were fired into BIA. Artillery and rocket rounds also impacted around USMNF positions at checkpoints 35 and 69 and near Bravo Company's position at the Lebanese Science University. Hundreds of rounds, including rocket-propelled grenades, exploded outside this area. Whether the USMNF was the specific target in these attacks quickly became a moot point. The proximity of LAF soldiers was not an issue since these were direct attacks on Marine positions.

The Marines responded to these attacks in accordance with a series of preplanned levels of return fire. In small arms exchanges, they fired in self-defense on their identified attackers in accordance with the rules of engagement. They ceased firing when the attacker's fire was no longer directed at them.

As the firing around BIA escalated on August 29, the impact of mortar rounds became concentrated on Marine positions on the line. The 81mm mortar platoon returned six illumination rounds over suspected firing sites. At 9:45 a.m., an Alpha Company platoon command post received a large barrage of 82mm rounds, killing 2nd Lt. Donald G. Losey and Staff Sgt. Alexander M. Ortega, Jr., and wounding three others.

Minutes later, a Druze 122mm rocket position increased shelling of the LAF camp in BIA's northern portion, and we also learned that another Druze artillery battery was preparing to fire on it. At this time, rockets were pouring in, one every fifteen seconds. Our Marine 81mm mortar platoon fired illumination rounds over the hostile artillery positions, and Charlie Battery added 155mm howitzer illumination rounds over the Druze rocket battery. Shortly thereafter, 5-inch/.54-caliber illumination rounds from the USS *Belknap* (CG 26) offshore fired over the rocket positions. When the Druze battery failed to cease fire, our M-198 155mm howitzer battery fired in anger for the first time. With pinpoint accuracy, Charlie Battery fired 155mm high-explosive, point-detonating (HE-PD) rounds on the Druze position, reportedly killing or wounding fifteen. It was unknown if any Syrian advisers were among the casualties.

The process used to identify the hostile firing positions was thorough and used all available sources to establish precise locations. Principal sources included the integrated observation station, visual sightings from the BLT Headquarters' roof, sightings from observers on the line, visual observation from aerial observers in Huey and Cobra gunships, electronic imagery from counter-mortar (AN/TPQ-36) radars, and intercepts of Druze and Muslim radio transmissions by the Marine Radio Battalion Detachment. This compilation of data and intelligence enabled us to fire with a high degree of confidence. Simultaneously, Alpha Company was engaged in a fierce firefight with Shiite militia from Hay-al-Sellum. A Cobra gunship fired rockets to suppress a hostile machine gun bunker. During this exchange, the gunship received hits from ground fire and made an emergency landing on the *Iwo Jima*. A local cease-fire followed shortly thereafter, but at the end of the day, the 24th MAU had suffered our first combat casualties—two killed in action (KIA) and fourteen wounded in action (WIA). The French suffered four KIAs and several WIAs.

Our earlier use of firing parachute flares above the Muslim militia's positions (as opposed to using HE rounds) carried the implied message that "we know where you are, so knock it off." Although this technique worked for quite a while, it eventually succumbed to the direct, sustained provocations. By the second day, the LAF had committed thirteen thousand soldiers supported by tanks and artillery. Firefights and shelling occurred throughout the city and continued through the night.

At 6:55 a.m. on August 30, the intensity of the fighting picked up at checkpoint 69. A firefight ensued, and the Marines responded with M60 machine gun fire, which caused the hostile fire to cease. Bravo Company also became involved in a firefight at the same time, and fighting increased in northern Beirut near the Durrafourd Building and British embassy, where we had the Marine external security force positioned. (Having U.S. Marines guard a British embassy was, according to the British ambassador, a historical first. After the U.S. embassy's destruction the previous April and the obvious need for beefed-up security, the USMNF had established the ESF for this purpose.) Concern was raised for the safety of the seventy-nine lightly armed U.S. Army soldiers assigned to the U.S. Office of Military Cooperation (USOMC). The Druze were threatening to attack the Cadmos Hotel, where the soldiers were billeted and protected by a company of LAF soldiers. Negotiations were intense between the Druze, the Amal militia, and U.S. embassy officials to secure their safe evacuation.

As the mayhem continued to grow and become more widespread, I dispatched a seventeen-man detail from BLT 1/8's Dragon Platoon by helicopter to reinforce security at the U.S. ambassador's residence in Yarze, which was located in the foothills east of Beirut. Shelling of the airport restarted with rounds landing in the UN Educational, Scientific, and Cultural Organization (UNESCO) compound and at Charlie Battery. A CH-46 helicopter was caught on the ground at Landing Site Red when the shelling recommenced and eventually made it out, but the windshield took a small arms round in the process. Bravo Company at the university came under intense shelling with rounds impacting around the library. Charlie Battery fired 155mm illumination rounds at a gun position believed to be firing at Bravo Company, and the shelling ceased. Two Cobra gunships, orbiting "feet wet" (over the sea) off Green Beach, reported taking small arms and .50-caliber machine gun fire but could not identify the targets in the darkness. Simultaneously, several rockets impacted near the Italian naval gunfire ship ITS *Sagittario* while transiting the LPH operations area. During the next eight hours, checkpoints 76, 35, and 69 and all the line companies reported small arms and mortar fire directed toward their positions.

Alpha Company again became engaged in a fierce firefight with Shia militia from Hay-al-Sellum. The tactics, the small arms, machine guns, and RPGs employed against the Marines and the LAF indicated that this confrontation was likely the first with Iran's Islamic Revolutionary Guard Corps trainers and advisers. We would see them again a couple of weeks later at the battle for Suq-el-Garb.

Another challenging development was the issue that Marine positions were occasionally the target of incoming artillery from areas under the control of Christian forces. Since the Christian Lebanese Forces (LF) militia and the LAF artillery were collocated at certain sites, it was difficult to determine from which the fire came. These events reflected the desire of selected Lebanese elements to deepen the Marines' involvement in their nation's plight. Their purpose was clear to me: they wanted to provoke us into unleashing our massive firepower against the Druze and Muslim militias.

At dawn on the thirtieth, vicious fighting continued throughout the city and its southern suburbs. Massive shelling occurred in all MNF sectors but appeared heaviest in the northern portion of the city and its port area. In what was to become a familiar ploy, when the Syrian-supported Druze and Muslim militias were fighting the LAF, indirect artillery, rocket, and mortar fire rained down on Marine positions at the airport, which caused its closure. The heaviest shelling came from the Syrian-occupied upper Metn Mountains northeast of Beirut and from the Druze batteries in the Shouf Mountains directly east of the capital.

The shelling at BIA, with air bursts occurring over the runway's northern end, caused shrapnel to fall around Charlie Battery and our helicopter Landing Site Red. Two hostile artillery positions firing at the French headquarters area were identified by our Air-Naval Gunfire Liaison Company (ANGLICO) teams. Discussions with the French leadership indicated that while they were not requesting that we return fire, they would not oppose such action. We responded with 155mm illumination rounds over these positions, and the firing ceased for about an hour. It was later determined that one area was an LAF battery firing at an Amal position located near the French headquarters while the other was a Druze battery. Some of these rounds landed only fifty meters from Charlie Battery's howitzers. The indiscriminate shelling continued for a fourth day, causing scores of casualties among civilians, the French, and the Italians.

Shortly after midnight on the thirty-first, a local cease-fire was negotiated, and twenty-six of the U.S. Army soldiers were allowed to move by van from the Cadmos Hotel to the Durrafourd Building. The process was interrupted when an RPG round landed behind the van during the trip. Fifty-three of the U.S. Army soldiers remained in the Cadmos, and the fighting renewed. Artillery and Katyusha 122mm rockets continued to slam around the British embassy, and a building directly behind it took a direct hit. The fighting continued unabated through the rest of the morning.

As a result of the incessant violence, the 24th MAU had postponed all patrols and activated plans to reinforce the USMNF. The USS *Eisenhower* (CVN-69) Carrier Battle Group moved closer to shore from over the horizon, as did the French aircraft carrier *Foch* and several Italian naval gunfire ships. We coordinated with the U.S. embassy and planned for possible evacuation of U.S. citizens. Evacuation sites were examined, plans were reviewed and updated, and a noncombatant evacuation communications net was established, linking the American embassy in Beirut and the task force commanders: Admiral Tuttle (60), Commodore Rick France (61), and I (62). Additionally, Rick France and I received a Joint Chiefs of Staff message from Vice Admiral Martin, COMSIXTHFLT, to transfer 500,000 rounds of ammunition from the 24th MAU's contingency supply to the LAF at Juniyah Naval Base, north of Beirut. Using PHIBRON 8 landing craft and HMM-162 helicopters, it was conducted without incident. The peacekeeping mission was indeed getting foggy with the prospects for a peaceful settlement looking increasingly remote.

The deepening engagements were a result of a two-pronged sweep of the northern Beirut area by the 4th and 8th brigades of the LAF. Also, the LAF had changed its tactics and commenced direct attacks on the hostile artillery and rocket positions in the eastern hills. In response to this offensive, the Druze PSP commenced firing on the Ministry of Defense (MOD), which took direct hits, endangering the lives of our MAU liaison team and U.S. Army personnel of the USOMC. The 24th MAU's Charlie Battery fired several rounds from two howitzers at the suspected firing position, which was the same position on which we had fired illumination rounds the previous night.

Fighting gradually tapered off around sunset on September 1. An eerie silence settled over the city. The fighting during this period had been the most explosive that had occurred since our arrival, but it also represented a significant positive step for the LAF. Almost all the LAF units were committed, and considering their religious integration and level of training, they performed surprisingly well. Their continued strong performance during the Mountain War was, in my opinion, one of the primary reasons that the leadership in Tehran and Damascus decided to move into the shadows and use terrorism after conventional attacks failed.

In the midst of all the activities and negotiations, we conducted a memorial service on September 2 to pay respects to Second Lieutenant Losey and Staff Sergeant Ortega. My SITREP comments up the chain of command stated:

> Keeping the peace became considerably more difficult this week as the ante was raised to the personal level. The Marines and Sailors stood firm, did not flinch, and shipped home their dead with quiet resolve to see the job through. Our Intelligence Section displayed their professionalism throughout the week as the major problem was trying to find out who was doing what to whom and why. The when was readily apparent. They were our best supporting arm. The Navy-Marine Corps Team was tight, and evidenced the finest degree of coordination and effectiveness I have ever seen. Our support to the Lebanese people will continue and restraint will continue to determine the pace.

It was clear to anyone looking at this situation that the Israeli forces' withdrawal required close coordination and a high degree of cooperation between the LAF and IDF. There was a flurry of diplomatic and military activity to persuade the IDF to delay its withdrawal. President Gemayel authorized General Tannous to negotiate directly with Israel and obtain an agreement for the IDF to remain in place until the LAF was ready to take over from the IDF. The critical issue during these talks was to avoid, at all costs, creating a void when the IDF withdrew from its strategic positions. All MNF commanders and our respective diplomats shared this concern. The Israelis assured General Tannous that he would be notified when a date was set.

During a meeting General Tannous hosted on September 2, the Israelis notified Tannous the withdrawal would begin immediately, starting the next night. They would not delay. Shocked and humiliated, Tannous felt betrayed.

The following morning, Israeli defense minister Moshe Arens met with U.S. ambassador Richard Fairbanks, who requested a postponement, but his appeal was rejected. That night, all could hear the rumble of Israeli tanks, personnel carriers, and heavy vehicles heading south. Their departure started the predictable race by the LAF, Druze, Amal Shiites, the Syrians, and Phalangists to fill the huge vacuum. These events triggered the beginning of the Mountain War, which accelerated Lebanon's downward spiral.[1]

The Israel Defense Force's uncoordinated withdrawal also put the multi-national peacekeeping force, especially the U.S. contingent, directly in the cross-hairs of the Muslim militias. Our static positions on the flat plains below the Israelis' vacated positions in the Shouf Mountains highlighted our vulnerabilities in carrying out the peacekeeping mission. The rhetorical question I posed was, Who would be left holding the bag after the IDF departed? The answer came soon enough and to no one's surprise.

The LAF Mechanized Brigade at BIA and its perceived line of departure (LOD) was adjacent to and extending into Charlie Company's position at the southern end of the airport. As the LAF began assembling its troops, BIA and Charlie Company, in particular, came under fire, which increased proportionately with the number of massed LAF soldiers. The LAF then mounted the main axis of its assault through Charlie Company's positions and into the adjoining town of Khaldeh. The returning fire from Druze and other Muslim positions was intense and accurate. The Marines identified those targets firing directly at them and returned fire with small arms, machine guns, and mortars. Among the targets identified were Druze PSP fighters who were moving antitank recoilless rifles into position to fire at LAF armored vehicles and Marine bunkers.

Offshore, aboard the USS *Austin*, Cobra gunships were placed on five-minute alert. An M60 tank moved forward, using its main gun to suppress hostile targets. At this time, the LAF moved a column of more than sixty mechanized vehicles south along the coast road and attacked southward into Khaldeh with the 4th Brigade.

Our responses were necessary, measured, and appropriate but were likely perceived by competing Muslim sects as offensive support to the LAF assault. The USMNF was caught in the middle of the assault, and there was little we could do to influence events. It would not be the last time that I felt we were being used.

In the Shouf Mountains to our east, the combat among the militias grew fierce, but none more so than that between the Druze PSP and the Christian Lebanese Forces. The Druze PSP, supported by Syria, was reinforced by Syrian-based Palestinians and other Lebanese opposition groups. Their attack was westward on an axis of the Beirut–Damascus highway. The LF militia attempted to defend a key crossroads village named Bhamdoun but were overwhelmed by the superior PSP Druze forces and their Syrian tanks, heavy artillery, RPGs, and sound tactics. As a result, the LAF deployed a brigade to defend the ridgeline that overlooked Beirut and the Beirut International Airport. The firing at BIA, all Marine positions, and Green Beach continued unabated. Small arms, RPGs, artillery, and rockets were impacting throughout our area, and the Marines responded. The 81mm mortar platoon fired illumination rounds over one suspected firing position. When this action failed to reduce the incoming, the Marines fired several HE adjusted rounds to silence the target. My weekly SITREP to higher headquarters read: "The stakes are becoming very high. Our contribution to peace in Lebanon since 22 July stands at 4 killed and 28 wounded."

During this period, the MAU spent most of the time in Condition One, our highest alert status. On September 6, once again, Rick and I received orders to provide a major resupply of artillery ammunition from the 24th MAU's contingency supply to the LAF at Juniyah Naval Base. Operation Rubber Wall ensured the successful transfer of the required ammunition, but it also revealed that the LAF was firing more than two thousand rounds of heavy artillery in each twenty-four-hour period. This report also provided insight about the ferocity of the ongoing battles. For the sake of perspective, Lebanese intelligence estimated that the hostile artillery raining on the LAF in the Shouf Mountains and on East Beirut (Christian section) during the heaviest fighting was at times coming at a rate of twelve hundred rounds an hour. Neighborhoods in East Beirut ended up resembling those in bombed-out Berlin in 1945.

The incessant pounding that the Marines received at BIA from the artillery and rocket launch sites in the surrounding hills did confirm an earlier matter: I had made the right decision to relocate the Marines, sailors, and soldiers into any hardened sites available rather than leaving them exposed in the open or in tents. Lives were saved and casualties were minimized. Although this decision would be severely criticized during the investigations following the suicide truck bombing, it was made where there were no other options.

Beginning September 6 and continuing for the next three days, BIA came under heavy rocket, artillery, and mortar attacks. Two more Marines were KIA and several wounded when rocket barrages slammed on Marine positions. Pinpointing the precise location of the firing battery was difficult, so at dawn, the forward air controller and the Cobras were launched in an attempt to locate them.

The following day, Admiral Tuttle (Task Force 60) launched the first F-14 tactical aerial reconnaissance pod system (TARPS) mission to gather intelligence, including the location of the militia's firing sites. These aircraft, catapulted from the *Ike*, provided valuable intelligence, which we shared with our allies. The French were flying their own photoreconnaissance missions over the Shouf Mountains, identifying artillery and rocket emplacements that had fired on the French sector.

Lt. Gen. John Miller, commanding general of the Fleet Marine Forces, Atlantic, and Maj. Gen. Al Gray, Second Marine Division commander, visited us on September 7. Rick France and I presented an updated briefing as sporadic shelling rained down on BIA. I escorted them around Marine positions and visited each of the MNF commanders and the U.S. ambassador.

While on a tour of Marine positions at BIA, we received a rocket attack that landed too close for comfort. One rocket landed about a hundred yards away, sending shrapnel flying. One piece hit my driver, Cpl. Michael Cavallaro, in his helmet. A second one followed, impacting nearby, and we got the generals out of there immediately.

On that day, we received three barrages of Katyusha 122mm rockets at Marine positions at BIA from Druze and Syrian sites in the Shouf Mountains. We responded with Charlie Battery's 155mm HE rounds, coordinated with 5-inch/.54-caliber HE rounds from the USS *Bowen* (FF-1029), which silenced the Druze emplacements. This support marked the first time both that naval gunfire was fired to defend the Marines ashore in Lebanon and that a U.S. Navy ship fired HE rounds in the Mediterranean since World War II. However, slowly and inevitably, we were slipping further away from our peacekeeping presence mission while providing self-defense against multiple hostile acts. The opposition had the lead in this play.

I also escorted Generals Miller and Gray to the MOD to visit with General Tannous in his office, where he provided a private briefing and gave his assessment of the current situation. In the middle of this meeting, one of the Marines with the security detail came into the office and whispered in my ear that I had to take a phone call. I gave him an irate look and quietly asked, "Who is it?" The Marine replied, "Silver Screen Six, sir." I asked again, "Who is that?" He replied, "Sir, you have to take this call." Generals Tannous, Miller, and Gray glared at me as I left the office. I picked up the phone and said, "Colonel Geraghty." A voice answered, "Colonel, this is the White House. Stand by for the President." Silver Screen Six was President Reagan's call sign.

President Reagan assured me that he would provide "whatever support it takes to stop the attacks" on my positions. He added, "Tell the Marines the entire nation is proud of you and the outstanding job you are doing against difficult odds." I pledged to the president that the Navy–Marine Corps team would hang tough and carry out our mission. I told him, on behalf of all the Marines, sailors, and soldiers serving in Lebanon, that we truly appreciated his support and leadership. I ended with, "Semper Fi, Mr. President."

I returned to General Tannous's office as he and Generals Miller and Gray were finishing their discussions. Later, I told Miller and Gray about my conversation with the president and the gist of his remarks. After I finished, General Miller, who was known for his dry sense of humor, asked me, with a deadpan face and a glint in his eye, whether I had any other phone calls that I would like to report.

My weekly SITREP's commander's comments section reflected my thoughts:

The increasing involvement in direct and more frequent combat actions has tasked the 24th MAU assets to their fullest. All hands are at quick step and the forced march pace is beginning to tell . . . 24th MAU has added a new page to the discussion on maneuver warfare, i.e. stakes are being raised weekly and our contribution to peace in Lebanon since 22 July stands at 4 killed and 28 wounded. Phibron 8 also added 1 wounded. We will stand our ground, however, and accomplish the mission we were sent here to do. Morale is high and while many of the Marines do not fully understand the complexities of the effort, all realize its importance to the nation. The call from the President and visits of Lt. General Miller and Major General Gray, were well appreciated and provided a needed boost at a rough time. 24th MAU will hang tough.

Sporadic small arms, artillery, rockets, mortar, and RPG fire continued throughout our sector, wounding five Marines. All line companies and checkpoints received increased fire, causing the 24th MAU to maintain our state of alert at Condition One.

The 31st MAU, under the command of Col. Jim Curd, arrived on September 12 after transiting the Suez Canal. Colonel Curd and some key staff came ashore from their flagship, USS *Tarawa* (LHA-1), while PHIBRON 8 hosted PHIBRON 1. The

31st MAU and PHIBRON 1 were prepared to join the planning for contingency operations and any mission assigned.

The Christian LF at the mountain village Bhamdoun continued to be under heavy assault and had to abandon their positions. The LAF positions at Khaldeh and the MOD all came under fire. As the situation in the mountains worsened, the LAF 8th Brigade commenced a movement east to Suq-el-Garb and eventually linked up with LF units in this strategic town overlooking Beirut. Suq-el-Garb was another key position in the Shouf Mountains that the Israelis had abandoned.

On September 10, the 8th Brigade, under the command of Colonel Michel Aoun, came under a direct attack from the Druze, Syrian-backed Palestinians, and assorted Muslim militias. Artillery and mortar fire bombarded the ridgeline. Rounds landed near the ambassador's residence where Special Envoy McFarlane and his team worked. LAF casualty reports provided the next day revealed seven KIAs, forty-three WIAs, and several missing. The company commander had been hacked to death with axes, which was obviously intended to intimidate the LAF.

On September 11, McFarlane sent a flash cable to Washington stating:

> There is a serious threat of a decisive military defeat which could involve the fall of the GOL [Government of Lebanon] within twenty-four hours. Last night's battle was waged within five kilometers of the Presidential Palace. For those at the State Department, this would correlate to an enemy attacking from Capitol Hill. This is an action message. A second attack against the same LAF Unit is expected this evening. Ammunition and morale are very low, and raise serious possibilities that an enemy brigade . . . will break through and penetrate the Beirut perimeter. In short, tonight we could be in enemy lines.[2]

McFarlane also urged a modification of the rules of engagement to allow the USMNF to fire in direct support of the Lebanese Armed Forces.

The next day, coinciding with the 31st MAU's arrival to reinforce us, I received authorization from the Joint Chiefs of Staff to make the decisions regarding the use of U.S. firepower to support the LAF. As the on-scene commander, I had this authorization from the president, over the strong objections of Secretary of Defense Weinberger, if three conditions were met: "(1) if the Commander on-scene in Beirut concluded that Suq-el-Garb was in imminent danger of falling; (2) the attacking force was non-Lebanese; and (3) the Government of Lebanon requested assistance." The order emphasized "that nothing in this message shall be construed as changing the mission for the U.S. Multinational Force." (See appendix E.)

This order was a contradiction of terms in that it would mark that the Marines, for the first time, were going on the offensive in direct support of the LAF. I understood, all too well, the consequences of this decision. For all practical purposes, it would eliminate whatever appearance of neutrality and impartiality we had left.

A factor that was hard to ascertain was the operational status of the 8th Brigade. My multiple intelligence sources revealed they were holding up well to several attacks and their defenses were strong and responsive. I had observed firsthand the LAF's training and its integration of the religious groups into the army. Although the majority of the officers were Christian, they also had Druze, Sunni, and Shia field grade and company grade officers in their ranks. More than 60 percent of the enlisted ranks were Muslims. Overall, the LAF had made remarkable progress in a relatively short period. Its main deficiency was that it needed more time and training to develop the men's combat skills and mature into cohesive combat units. However, they appeared to be fighting together with determination in repulsing several fierce attacks.

The authorization to use U.S. firepower in direct support of the LAF caused several reactions. What followed was a rancorous week of requests by McFarlane and members of his staff to allow the use of naval gunfire and air strikes. To their great consternation, I blocked these requests. I thought that they were over-reacting and not considering the implications of their demands. Fortunately, I was supported in my decisions by Commodore Rick France and Col. Tom Fintel, the U.S. Army officer in charge of the U.S. mission to train the LAF. Tom had some contacts within the LAF, which added to our intelligence.

During one of my heated exchanges with Brig. Gen. Carl Stiner, McFarlane's JCS liaison officer in Beirut, I yelled, "General, don't you realize we'll pay the price down here? We'll get slaughtered! We're totally vulnerable!" In another exchange with Ambassador McFarlane, I told him directly, "Sir, I can't do that. This will cost us our neutrality. Don't you realize that we'll get slaughtered down here? We're sitting ducks!" After continuous calls to me to unleash our massive firepower against the Muslim factions, I wondered if anyone else realized where this fucking train was headed.

The crux of my disagreements with McFarlane and his staff lay in the skepticism of the doom-and-gloom reports coming out of Suq-el-Garb. The LAF 8th Brigade had a company that had been battered, but the main force was holding up and hanging tough. Colonel Aoun had a reputation of being indecisive and prone to panic, not ideal leadership traits one would want in a commander. General Tannous himself had some reservations about him.[3] Every report from the front included pessimistic news that Suq-el-Garb would fall in a matter of hours.

I had an uneasy feeling about the rush to expand our role and cut loose with this enormous firepower at our disposal. My view was to use it only if it was absolutely required to protect American and allied lives and property. Rick France and I were in complete agreement that all three of the JCS prerequisites had to be met prior to giving the order. In the meantime, we had our respective staffs pre-plot targets, update intelligence, and prepare to respond quickly when and if the order was given.

This reluctance evolved out of weighing the consequences of taking sides in an eight-sided battle while being located, for longer than year, in a static position that grew increasingly vulnerable by the hour. The MAU compound at BIA was tactically unsound (as were the locations of the French, Italian, and British MNF) and had been selected for political and diplomatic reasons. The rationale for this location had long past. The astonishing devastation wrought by the extensive use of heavy artillery, rockets, and mortars had everyone's attention. Our intelligence estimated that upwards of six hundred tubes in Druze- and Syrian-controlled territory in the Shouf Mountains could be brought to bear on our positions at BIA.

I remember well having recurring thoughts about the brutal manner in which Syrian president Hafez al-Assad had put down a revolt against his regime in Hama, Syria, in February 1982. A beautiful city, which today has an estimated population of 300,000 inhabitants and is located about 120 miles northwest of Damascus, Hama was the scene of a fundamentalist Sunni Muslim Brotherhood uprising. The precise details of the genocide that occurred would not be revealed until years later, but what was known was some of the tactics employed. Led by Assad's younger brother, Rifaat, the Syrian Army cut off and surrounded the city with tanks and artillery, then proceeded to bombard it for weeks, turning city blocks into parking lots. Assad's approach to problems was direct and ruthless. A later Amnesty International report estimated ten thousand to twenty-five thousand people died, mostly civilians.[4] The implications for anyone targeted by the Syrians and their allies were clear.

My MNF counterparts all felt this same growing vulnerability while observing violence that showed no bounds. It seemed that President Reagan's national security advisers were not thinking through the implications of their decisions, particularly the repercussions against the multinational force. As the battle to hold Suq-el-Garb heated up, the United States increased its naval forces offshore to more than a dozen warships and twelve thousand men. The French, Italian, and British were also moving forces into the area. Commodore France and I were having other problems within the chain of command during this period, which caused considerable confusion. Rick drafted the following message on September 12 to Admiral Martin requesting assistance:

Subject: Chain of Command

Originator and CTF-62 are being caught in the middle of chain of command problem. Specifically the Gen. Stiner to CJCS chain. CTF-62 is being called direct from JCS office. Stiner is requesting targeting info for tonight furnished a target grid coordinate recommended for air strike. Such requests are going through CTF-62. Tim received a call from JCS. Tonight the White House was trying to call me but never made contact. The bottom line is that apparently JCS and possibly White House is encouraging use of CAS [close air support]. These hints etc. could be handled much quicker if they went through the chain of command. Since call to Tim was direct from JCS and believe White House was attempting to contact me on this same subject. I have no way of knowing if President is making an announcement and I am sitting here not lighting the fuse to make it happen. I therefore released message requesting CAS against target recommended by Stiner through Tim and encouraged by JCS. Due to time sensitivity and source of requests I had no other choice. I don't like it and I am sure Tim feels the same way. Request your assistance in getting the situation back on track. Very Resp Rick.

I refused the air strike mission.

On September 10, I sent my commander's SITREP to Admiral Martin, COMSIXTHFLT, stating my growing concerns and observations of what was happening.

From: Col. Geraghty

Subject: Weekly Situation Report

The worsening military and political situation in Lebanon this week has pulled the MAU deeper and deeper into more frequent and direct military action. Our increasing number of casualties has removed any semblance of neutrality and has put us into direct retaliation against those who have fired on us. Within the last seven weeks we have taken 4 killed and 29 wounded in attacks on the airport. It is relatively immaterial who has pulled the trigger. The end result of this involvement is that since 22 July, the MAU has been on an increasingly greater level of alert, culminating in a near constant state of general quarters for the past two weeks. This has not been without its impact on our operations. As you know, the MAU is not designed for sustained combat ashore and this level of action has tasked my men and equipment to their maximum. I personally feel they have exhibited the requisite degree of steadfastness, skill, and resolve and have accomplished all that has been asked of them. I am concerned, however, that the end does not appear to be in sight and I perceive that the involvement in the Lebanese internal struggle has exceeded our original mandate. We have, in fact, changed the rules and are now an active participant. De facto request for support come from all members of the MNF for targeting/intelligence data, fire support, logistic assistance, liaison assistance, training, and coordination. By far the greatest impact has come from the Lebanese Armed Forces and the associated U.S. Office of Military Cooperation. We are actively their allies.

Ammunition, training, intelligence, security, and logistical assistance have been provided on an immediate and priority basis. My intelligence and operations section act as sub-operations centers for the LAF and are required to respond in order to support operations over which they have no control and of which they are not even apprised. The MAU is receiving support from assets and equipment not normally found at this level and must receive, process, and disseminate information from these assets in a timely and effective manner with our normal allotment of personnel. In many cases the originator, objective, and user of this information are not known and the support provided has not been requested from this level. Our credibility as an effective deterrent is becoming suspect with the opposition, and I have a perception that our assistance to the LAF is not only unappreciated and taken for granted, but that there are those who believe that the MAU could be doing more and are, in fact, refraining from assisting in the effort. With each bombardment of the airport and increase in the number of casualties sustained, my ability to influence those factions who desire to involve us militarily has declined. I have now reached the point where a combined artillery/NGF [naval gunfire] mission has failed to prevent attacks on the airport. In effect, I have reached my limit of response given the capabilities of the weapons within my force and the constraints of the current rules of engagement. While the above is somewhat negative, I wish to assure you that we are maintaining the course previously set and it is only an observation, that the indications of shoal water are increasing. 24 MAU will continue to do what must be done.

Very respectfully, Col. Geraghty.

On September 14, Rick France and I were directed again to go into our Landing Force Operational Reserve Matériel (LFORM) stocks to provide emergency resupply of ammunition to the LAF. During September, the helicopters of HMM-162 transported 2,424,081 pounds of cargo (including 1,345,050 rounds of ammunition). Lt. Col. Larry Medlin, the squadron's commanding officer, demanded excellence, and his Marines and sailors performed accordingly.

These large resupplies reflected only one factor concerning the fierce battles being waged to control the ridgelines in the Shouf Mountains overlooking Beirut. It became clear that the LAF had to retain its positions, but the LAF faced rigorous challenges from the Druze PSP with direct support from Syria and Iran. The stakes continued to be raised.

During the night of September 16, heavy artillery fire fell on the Ministry of Defense and the U.S. ambassador's residence. The USS *Bowen* and the USS *John Rodgers* (DD-983) conducted six naval gunfire missions, expending a total of seventy-two rounds on six separate targets. The firing from these Muslim battery sites ceased. It was becoming clear that the Druze, the Syrian-based Palestinians, and assorted Muslim militias were making a major effort to bring down the Gemayel government. The following night, the Druze PSP conducted heavy artillery, rocket, and mortar fire directed at BIA, the MOD, the Presidential Palace, and the U.S. ambassador's residence in Yarze, where we had just expanded our Marine security guards.

Accurate sniper fire was also being directed at our joint checkpoints 35, 69, and 76 near the airport. Marines responded with accurate fire directed at the sources, and this exchange of gunfire continued sporadically for the next eight days. I do not believe it coincidental that similar reports of active, accurate sniper fire was being directed at the 8th Brigade at Suq-el-Garb. It was also not coincidental that during this period we had confirmed sightings of professional, seasoned soldiers outfitted in Soviet battle dress uniforms, which were not unlike U.S. Marine camouflaged utilities, except they were brown and rust colored. It appeared that the Damascus leadership had made the decision to deploy Syrian troops closer to the battles.

During the second week of September, the LAF conducted a covert operation to repair the westernmost runway at BIA. At 5:00 a.m. on September 15, it launched five Hawker Hunter aircraft and transferred them to an emergency airstrip on a road north of Juniyah. The 24th MAU assisted in this endeavor by turning on and racing our tank and amphibious assault vehicle engines to mask the aircrafts' noise. The following morning, these 1950s' vintage jets attacked the ridgeline around Suq-el-Garb. They ran into intense antiaircraft fire, which damaged several of them. One crashed into the Mediterranean, and a search and rescue aircraft from the *Ike* picked up the pilot. One damaged jet made an emergency landing at BIA while another diverted to Cyprus, where it landed safely at the Royal Air Force Base at Akrotiri. The air strike reportedly destroyed several Druze emplacements and several Soviet-built T-55 tanks.

At first light on Monday, September 19, the Druze, radical Palestinians, and assorted Muslim militias unleashed another horrendous artillery, rocket, and mortar barrage on the LAF at Suq-el-Garb that lasted several hours. Its sheer magnitude again brought to mind the Syrians' attack on Hama. Military observers nearby, like those of us farther away, had never viewed such an expenditure of ammunition at so great a blistering rate. Marine positions at BIA were receiving sporadic shelling, and we anticipated and alerted checkpoints 76 and 69 to expect attacks on their positions. Our highest alert status, Condition One, had become the norm rather than the exception.

I had received updated intelligence reports that indicated a major assault was building. When the winds of change started blowing hard in the late summer, I had authorized my 2nd Radio Battalion Detachment, led by 1st Lt. Gary Graff, to establish some intercept sites in the foothills to enhance our intelligence-gathering capabilities. Their intelligence proved to be timely and professional. As the battle for Suq-el-Garb was intensifying, the unit intercepted sensitive and revealing battlefield communications. One of the most intriguing intercepts involved Farsi tactical communications that indicated some of Iran's IRGC contingent based in the Bekaa Valley and their leadership were involved in the attack against the LAF.

Syrian support and involvement in the attack were undeniable. The Druze PSP's forces under Walid Jumblatt were chiefly supplied and controlled by Syria. Syrian tactical radio intercepts were overt and informative, along with the artillery and mortar firing, which were originating from confirmed Syrian positions in the mountains. Syrians, Syrian-supplied T-55 tanks, and radical Palestinians based in Syria were supported by an effective supply pipeline of ammunition and military equipment. The IRGC contingent had come through Damascus earlier and established its base in the Syrian-controlled Bekaa Valley a year earlier. That base still remains active and operational.

Following an intense artillery prep fire, two battalions of infantry supported by tanks launched the coordinated ground assault on Suq-el-Garb. As the battle intensified, General Tannous received somber reports from the 8th Brigade at the Ministry of Defense's Operations Center. Soon he received a frantic radio message from Colonel Aoun, who was screaming to make himself heard above the explosions: he was running dangerously low on ammunition and would likely be overrun within the next thirty minutes. Other sources reported hearing the roar of tank engines as the tanks moved from their staging area to assault positions.

Tannous contacted me and formally requested assistance. Rick France and I had been studying events at Suq-el-Garb and were well prepared in the event that the LAF would request naval gunfire. We both agreed that the three conditions had been met since: (1) Suq-el-Garb appeared to be "in imminent danger of falling," (2) the intercepts and other sources confirmed a non-Lebanese attacking force, and (3) the Lebanese government had requested our assistance.

I gave the orders. Four U.S. ships moved into position in waters off the Port of Beirut and opened fire. Between 10:04 a.m. and 3:00 p.m., the USS *Virginia* (CGN-38), USS *John Rogers*, USS *Bowen*, and the USS *Radford* (DD-968) fired a total of 360 5-inch rounds. Overhead, F-14 Tomcats (TARPS) and A-6 Intruder fighter-bombers from the *Ike* were identifying targets and assessing the results of the naval gunfire barrage. French Super Étendard fighter-bombers from the French carrier *Foch* were also visible to discourage further exchanges. The MOD reported that the attacking forces broke and ran under the barrage, and the tide of battle turned because of the NGF support. There was no reason to order any air strikes.

In my combat operations center (COC), I communicated with Rick France on the *Iwo Jima*, the Ministry of Defense, and our liaison officers with the other MNFs. Our using NGF to thwart the assault on Suq-el-Garb allowed the LAF to remain credible, but the implications of our direct support to the LAF were still to come. It was a dilemma wherein we were obliged to provide support to prevent the LAF's defeat, but in doing so we terminated our peacekeeping mission while opening ourselves to unknown retribution. As the sun set at the end of a tumultuous day, I remarked to members of my staff that "my gut instinct tells me the Corps is going to pay in blood for this decision."

The postattack assessment from multiple sources provided mixed views regarding whether the direct support by the USMNF and Sixth Fleet had been necessary to save the 8th Brigade at Suq-el-Garb. Several observers thought the LAF had exaggerated its plight and would have held its position without our direct support. It was another occasion when I wondered if we had been had. Still, others were convinced the support had been absolutely necessary and saved the day for the LAF. After I had time to evaluate the mixed opinions and contrasting views, I came away with several opinions of my own. The most significant cause for some optimism was the fact that the LAF, with its integrated religious composition, fought and held together as a true Lebanese Army, repelled a fierce assault, and won the engagement. Druze, Christian, Sunni, and Shia officers and men, some of whom were killed and wounded, performed above our expectations. But I was surprised, given the intensity of the combat assault, that the casualties were so light. The LAF suffered eight KIAs and twelve WIAs. I was not alone in this assessment. However, with the intelligence available at the time, I am convinced that there was no other choice but to provide the LAF with the needed support.

I was also convinced that the rules of the game had changed forever with that decision, with its consequences unknown.

The next two days there was no letup in sporadic small arms fire, mortar, and artillery rounds striking our positions. Marine artillery and NGF returned fire at targets that could be identified. A rocket-propelled grenade hit the Durrafourd Building, where some of the U.S. embassy staff worked. A Druze rocket hit the main Italian MNF ammunition dump, and six French soldiers were wounded in two separate attacks. The French launched its Super Étendard fighter-bombers from the *Foch* in retaliation and for the first time hit targets behind Syrian lines. The Italians moved some fighter aircraft to the Royal Naval Air Base in Cyprus for added security. The conflict was definitely taking on an international flavor, but the implications were not so clear.

Any expectations of a reduction in the attacks' intensity dissipated on September 23 when the airport, the French and Italian compounds, and Bravo Company at the Lebanese Science University came under heavy attack. Our checkpoints 35 and 69 were particularly hit hard with small arms fire, RPGs, 20mm antiaircraft cannon fire, and mortars. Along with checkpoint 76, they were originally established as a buffer between the Israelis and the Shia-dominated town of Hay-al-Sellum. These jointly manned positions served a useful purpose of stemming the flow of arms and resupplies to the Shia militias in the southern suburbs.

The 24th MAU responded initially with counter-battery fire from the 81mm mortars and 155mm artillery against the hostile firing in the hills. The intensity and duration soon escalated our response to utilizing all of our organic weapons and naval gunfire. The fighting continued throughout the day and night when intelligence indicated that a large force of Druze PSP and PLO fighters, reinforced with six T-55 tanks and commanded by four Syrian Army officers, were staging for an assault on checkpoint 69.

At midday on September 25, we were hit with RPGs, small arms, 12.7mm machine guns, 23mm guns, and 106mm recoilless rifles. We suffered some casualties, which further exposed our vulnerability while evacuating the wounded and resupplying the isolated checkpoints. We were fortunate to get a helicopter evacuation of the wounded, and a resupply was completed owing mainly to the crew's skills and professionalism. I also concluded that under the current circumstances, the checkpoints had become too vulnerable. Their risk was no longer acceptable.

After notifying the appropriate U.S. embassy officials and Lebanese government authorities, I ordered Lt. Col. Larry Gerlach to redeploy the Marines and sailors from checkpoints 35 and 69. I immediately was deluged with calls from several people in the U.S. embassy and the Lebanese government to cancel the order. General Tannous called and made a personal plea, but I explained in great detail that my decision was final. My personal view was that if we continued the status quo, the future safety of our MNF would be increasingly jeopardized.

As the Mountain War intensified, so did the worldwide media's interest. All networks, the wire services, newspaper syndicates, major U.S. newspapers, and photo agencies sent additional correspondents, photographers, and TV crews to Beirut. International press was aboard from Great Britain, Norway, Denmark, Sweden, Finland, Switzerland, France, West Germany, Italy, Spain, Belgium, and Turkey. Independent and affiliate U.S. television stations sent crews to do stories on hometown Marines. The Joint Public Affairs Branch, ably headed by Maj. Bob Jordan, escorted a daily average of thirty to forty media people, and more than forty stayed overnight with units in the field. Because of the "fishbowl" effect and media access to all factions, many operations—such as air strikes, naval gunfire support, the placement of observers at Suq-el-Garb, and the closing down of checkpoints— had to be considered from a public affairs aspect. Since tactical considerations had to be weighed in light of the diplomatic situation, our Public Affairs Office's (PAO) coordination with the U.S. embassy and its ability to respond to press queries were particularly important.

On September 6, I had held a press conference after two Marines were killed, which intensified the media coverage. I was interviewed by the *Baltimore Sun*, *Miami Herald*, and CBS on September 10. Tom Brokaw of NBC interviewed me on September 14, and John Bennett of Scripps-Howard interviewed me a day later. On the fifteenth, in a satellite-feed interview with ABC's Ted Koppel for *Nightline*, the program also included Walid Jumblatt, the Druze PSP leader, who was shelling Marine positions at BIA. My interview with ABC provided a moment of reflection on the intensity of the international media coverage, the freedom of the press, and the responsibilities that go with it. Many of the queries dealt with my views on whether the Marines were in "imminent danger of hostilities" that would trigger the War Powers Resolution then being debated in Congress. When I was reminded in an interview with the *Washington Post* on September 16 that twelve navy warships and about ninety fighter aircraft were at my disposal for the MNF's protection, I reiterated that I had no new instructions from Washington on the expanded use of this massive power. I also confirmed my belief that our minimum use of force responses would continue to be solely defensive, as our mission stated, and proportioned to the provocations on a case-by-case basis.

I was reminded by the media that my views were in sharp contrast to the aggressive statements issued by the White House that suggested the United States was about to escalate the use of force to protect the Marines and possibly even to assist the Lebanese Armed Forces. I repeated there was no change in the peacekeeping mission despite the widespread impression that new orders had broadened the Marines' role, committing us to directly support the LAF. My superiors' response to my comments was a deafening silence.

I emphasized that my biggest worry, in addition to the shelling from the mountains, was the movement of radical Shiite Muslim armed militiamen into two neighborhoods near our headquarters at the airport. I refused to offer any judgment on whether the USMNF faced the danger of our "imminent involvement in hostilities," justifying the entry into force of the War Powers Resolution. It was interesting that many of the European print journalists looked especially for political angles, seeing the United States as supporting one faction over others.

On September 25, the battleship USS *New Jersey* arrived off Beirut. The following day, a cease-fire worked out by U.S. and Saudi diplomats and agreed to by Presidents Gemayel of Lebanon and Assad of Syria took effect. It halted the rage of the September Mountain War.

The cease-fire drew further media interest, which included my interviews with the Turkish newspaper *Hürriyet*, with *USA Today*, and with Jim Webb for a MacNeil/Lehrer Report documentary, *Marines in Beirut*, which later earned an Emmy. A former Marine, highly decorated Vietnam veteran, and noted author, Webb would later become the secretary of the navy and then the senior U.S. senator from Virginia.

On September 27, we lost an AH-1T Cobra gunship from HMM-165 (31st MAU). It crashed and sank at sea, but both pilots were rescued with minor injuries. Two days later, another event further highlighted one more vulnerability. Since late August, the USMNF had virtually lived in its highest state of alert, Condition One. As the security environment continued to deteriorate, one of the several orders published stated that only vehicles involved in official duties were permitted to leave the compound, and all would have to be accompanied by at least one security vehicle. Two soldiers attached to the 24th MAU from the Field Artillery School's Target Acquisition Battery left without permission or a security vehicle. While traveling north on the main highway into Beirut, they made a wrong turn and were picked up by a Shia militia. I was livid. Having only sketchy details about their abduction, I talked with Lieutenant Colonel Gerlach to assemble a reaction force while notifying the U.S. embassy of the kidnapping. Shortly before the reaction force was ready to launch, I was notified that the two soldiers had been brought to the Amal leader, Nabih Berri, who subsequently released them to a French liaison officer. Berri apologized for the incident, but interestingly, although the jeep was returned, one of the soldiers' pistols was not. I reported after the incident that it was particularly serious as it pointed out the USMNF's inability to react appropriately to such episodes and that it demonstrated the variety of threats to the MNF and their possible consequences.

As September was winding down, I hosted a large congressional delegation led by Congressman Samuel Stratton (D-NY). Brig. Gen. Jim Mead, commanding officer of the 22nd MAU, escorted the House Armed Services Committee (HASC) delegation, which included ten members. I provided a detailed orientation and situation briefing on the status of the MNPF mission and explained the increasing difficulties of providing security for our forces while trying to maintain the neutrality our mission required. The delegation had many questions and was very interested in the operational details involved in performing our mission.

When the delegation returned to Washington, Congressman Stratton wrote to General Kelley:

Dear General Kelley,
I wanted to take the opportunity to write you concerning the truly outstanding service of one of your officers, Colonel Timothy Geraghty, Commander,
24th Marine Amphibious Unit.

As you know, I had the honor recently to lead a delegation of 10 members of the Committee on Armed Services to Lebanon to review the difficult
military and political problem firsthand. During our visit, we were able to
spend several hours with Colonel Geraghty and his men at Beirut International Airport.

I know I speak for all the members of the delegation in expressing nothing but the highest praise for Colonel Geraghty and, of course, the personnel of the 24th Marine Amphibious Unit. The circumstances presented by U.S. participation in the Multinational Force (MNF) involve extremely difficult exercise of judgment by Colonel Geraghty as the on-site commander balancing the safety of his men with a political requirement to minimize the level of U.S. involvement in the area. It was apparent during our visit that the U.S. participation in the MNF was contributing to stability in Lebanon. This success can be attributed in no small part to the performance of Colonel Geraghty.

The Marine Corps and the United States of America can be justly proud of the service being performed by Colonel Geraghty.

Sincerely,

s/s/ Sam

Samuel S. Stratton

Head of Delegation

Congressman Samuel S. Stratton ltr to CMC, dtd 6Oct83.

Handwritten at the bottom of the letter was a note: "We also are deeply grateful for the outstanding assistance General Mead gave our delegation."

The month of September closed on a cautious, optimistic note. On the thirtieth, the airport reopened, the sectarian cohesiveness of the LAF had withstood stern testing on the battlefield, and the agreement by all parties to hold reconciliation talks in Geneva in the near future offered a glimmer of hope for Lebanon. The tenuous cease-fire provided us with a break to send some of the peacekeepers on R & R, to get hot showers and hot food, and to rest.

Unbeknownst to us at this time, the leadership in Damascus and Tehran was already working on other plans to attack us within a month. On the same date the cease-fire took effect, September 26, the National Security Agency (NSA) intercepted a diplomatic communications message from the Iranian intelligence agency, the Ministry of Information and Security (MOIS). Tehran ordered its ambassador (a known terrorist) in Damascus "to take spectacular action against the American Marines." After the failure of the conventional attacks at Suq-el-Garb, this decision reflected a shift in strategy by Tehran (and Damascus) to employ terrorism while using surrogates for plausible deniability. The Director of Naval Intelligence (DNI) didn't pass the intercept on to my chain of command until October 26—three days after the suicide bombing.

—7—

Cease-fire and Rising Danger

MOST DIPLOMATS AND THE MULTINATIONAL forces greeted the September 26 cease-fire with hope and caution. The most positive development was the agreement by the conflicting religious factions to meet with the government of Lebanon in Geneva on October 30. These national reconciliation talks had long been the Lebanese government's major goal, and the battlefield successes of the religiously integrated Lebanese Army during September provided it with a measure of strength going into the talks. It was the unanimous view of nearly all diplomats and the MNF commanders that diplomacy was the only path that could lead to some resolution of the civil war. This optimism, however, would have been tempered if we had known that Syria and Iran were already planning further attacks against the MNF before the reconciliation talks were to begin.

The U.S. and Saudi negotiators had exerted considerable energy to achieve the cease-fire along with an agreement for the national reconciliation talks. The U.S. chief negotiator was Special Envoy Bud McFarlane, who would soon be named the new national security adviser to the president. The chief Saudi mediator was Prince Bandar bin Sultan, who shortly would become the Saudi ambassador to the United States, a post he would hold for the next twenty-two years. He was ably assisted by a Lebanese-born Saudi businessman named Rafiq Hariri, who had earned a fortune in the construction business and later became prime minister of Lebanon. He was assassinated on February 14, 2005, in a massive car bomb attack allegedly carried out by Syria (see chapter 13).

Even with the wary hope for a better future for Lebanon, the hard reality on the ground was that tensions remained high in Beirut and that it was still very dangerous to travel through most of the city. The MNF, which had boots on the ground, had long come to the realization that "cease-fire" is a relative term in Lebanon. The cease-fire continued to hold, more or less, going into October, but sporadic fighting in the suburbs continued. In the early morning hours of October 3, an unidentified assailant fired AK-47 rounds at Bravo Company's sentry post 3. This fire was not returned as the target quickly disappeared. At mid-morning, Charlie Company reported that several artillery rounds landed south of its positions, and checkpoint 76 reported several rounds of sniper fire.

Fighting at the southern end of the runway outside Khaldeh continued through the night and developed into a sustained, heavy firefight. Mortars, RPGs, and heavy machine gun fire were exchanged, and the Marines cautiously observed the situation from the bunkers because of the danger of stray rounds.

From October 3 to October 5, BLT 1/8 rotated the infantry line companies for the final deployment before our relief. We maintained our ANGLICO teams at the Italian Folgore Battalion and the British headquarters. The Lebanese Army, meanwhile, received additional shipments of American tanks, armored personnel carriers (APCs), howitzers, and assorted ammunition. On October 5, a Marine helicopter transporting the U.S. defense attaché to Lebanon, who also was an aide to Special Envoy McFarlane, was hit by ground fire while en route to the Ministry of Defense. A round passed through the cockpit, causing the pilot to take evasive action. After landing at the MOD, it lost one engine but finally recovered to continue to the airport at Landing Site Red. We reevaluated the practice of using standard air transit patterns over Beirut and took actions to protect the aircraft, including staggering flight times and routes, flying at lower altitudes, and limiting nonessential helo orientation flights over the city.

At the same time, the Palestinian fighters' objective was to complete an infiltration route into the Palestinian refugee camps of Sabra and Shatila. This confrontation had led to the erection of barricades in Burj al Barajinah, Hay-al-Sellum, and Ash Shuwayfat. The LAF and the inter-militia fighting over the barricades continued to flare up, with stray rounds impacting around Alpha Company. The PLO leadership was persistent and strove very hard to break through LAF checkpoints and link with the refugee camps.

I still wonder today about the PLO's complicity in the attacks against the peacekeepers on October 23, 1983. The United States had guaranteed the security of the Palestinian fighters' families left behind in Sabra and Shatila after the fighters were deported. A Christian militia's subsequent massacre of the Palestinian noncombatants four days after the Marines' departure, along with the Sharon-directed acquiescence by the Israelis, left Arafat and his PLO leadership with a huge ax to grind against the United States. It would be well to remember that a chief operative in the suicide bombings was Imad Fayez Mugniyah, who began his notorious career with Fatah and was close to its leader, Arafat, at the time.

On the evening of October 6, another Marine helicopter (a CH-46) was hit under fire. The pilot noticed a shudder and airspeed loss during the flight and aborted the mission. A postflight analysis revealed a small arms round had hit an aft rotor blade. The same day, we received a report that the Israeli chief of the National Guard was killed by a car bomb north of Tyre. Less than two weeks later, I nearly suffered the same fate returning from the U.S. embassy to my headquarters.

Fighting between the LAF and Muslim militias broke out again on the morning of the eighth. It was scattered throughout the adjacent villages and lasted most of the day. Alpha Company received spillover fire in its area. The fighting continued to escalate and spread south to the Khaldeh triangle and north into Burj al Barajinah and Chiyah. Mid-afternoon, a French patrol operating in Al Bashurah had a hand grenade thrown at it but suffered no casualties. The same evening, Bravo Company reported that stray rounds from the fighting near Khaldeh had wounded a Marine from the Target Acquisition Battery (TAB) Detachment, but he did not require medevac. The fighting would escalate at times to heavy machine guns and RPGs, adding to the firefights' intensity.

Sniper fire intensified against the MAU positions throughout our area October 9–14. Alpha Company received well-aimed sniper fire on the ninth, wounding one Marine. Bravo Company observed three men entering a building, and moments later, sniper fire from the building began to strike the Marines' positions, although firing ceased after several rounds. Throughout the area armed militiamen were observed building barricades and manning checkpoints.

Mid-morning on October 9, Alpha Company came under sniper fire from two locations. One Marine was hit in the right shoulder. An hour later, a CH-46 helicopter at LZ Condor drew fire, with two rounds causing minor skin damage to the aircraft. It was becoming more obvious by the hour that the USMNF aircraft and men were targets of hostile snipers.

Factional clashes and sniper activity continued on October 10 with Lebanese Forces and Amal militias fighting along the old Green Line, which historically separated Muslim West Beirut from Christian East Beirut. After the Lebanese Army intervened during the evening, fighting diminished and finally ceased around midnight. During these exchanges, at 11:00 p.m. three men in a bunker fired on Alpha Company positions. Small arms and RPG rounds were directed at the company's command post. No fire was returned during this initial attack owing to the close proximity of civilians to the hostile bunker.

At dusk on October 11, sporadic sniper fire from the bunker was again directed at Alpha Company's CP. Alpha Company fired an M203 illumination round over the bunker, and the firing ceased. At 10:00 p.m., a Charlie Company sentry post was fired on from Hay-al-Sellum. The sentries fired a pop-up illumination and saw three men armed with rifles and RPGs thirty-five meters outside the perimeter fence. The sentries fired twelve rounds of M-16 ammunition at the men, causing them to flee down an alley and into the slum.

The full realization of the dangers and perilous security situation in Beirut were brought home to me on a trip to visit General Tannous at the MOD. I was being driven in the command jeep with two Marines in the rear seats riding shotgun and followed by another jeep with the security detail. After my meeting, I visited with some Marines and other MNF members at the MOD before we headed back to my headquarters at BIA. Our return route was one we had traveled many times. The escalating destruction from the artillery, rocket, and mortar barrages were readily apparent, and few civilians were on the street. I always made a point to look for children and their mothers, since if there was any trouble about, mothers will remove their children from danger. This maternal instinct crosses all cultures. I saw none.

As we proceeded through the devastated area, we came upon some make-shift barricades and an illegal checkpoint set up by a radical Amal militia. This was their territory. As soon as we realized what we faced, the order was given to lock and load weapons, or chamber a round in the weapons and put the safety catches on. When we halted, four or five angry-looking militiamen armed with AK-47 automatic rifles appeared, wearing a mixture of civilian clothes and military uniforms. They were informed that we were passing through. They started to spread out, locked and loaded, and pointed their weapons toward us. Our noncommissioned officer in charge (NCOIC) shouted the orders, and the Marine security detail quickly disembarked the vehicles while clicking off the safeties of their M-16s and spread out.

I noticed the leader of this ragtag group would look across the street to a similar armed group of militiamen. The apparent leader of this second group was also armed with an AK-47 and wore a dark blue running suit with white stripes (probably Adidas since that was the popular brand in Lebanon). After a pause that seemed longer than it probably was, the showdown ended when the Adidas-clad man gave the signal to allow us to proceed. When I returned to headquarters, this route joined a growing list of those that were put off-limits due to the ever-escalating security threats.

A major cease-fire violation occurred on October 12 when, at dusk, hostile Muslim militias in Alayh initiated heavy mortar fire against LAF positions in Suq-el-Garb. The LAF responded with heavy automatic weapons fire and artillery. This fighting quickly escalated and was the heaviest since the cease-fire agreement of September 26. No casualty report was ever received.

The trend of terrorist hit-and-run activity directed against the USMNF continued to cautiously but definitely escalate. The areas of Ash Shuwayfat and particularly Hay-al-Sellum were being used as a base of operations against the MNF. I believe professional Syrian troops and the Islamic Revolutionary Guard Corps were main instigators of these attacks because of the sightings of these troops in camouflaged battle dress, the increased accuracy of hostile sniper fire, and tactical communications intercepts, including some in Farsi, by our Radio Battalion Detachment.

On October 13 at 7:15 p.m., a hand grenade was thrown from a speeding vehicle heading west on the Corniche, the seaside road in front of the devastated U.S. embassy, the British embassy, and the Durrafourd Building. The grenade exploded near a Marine sentry post at the Durrafourd Building and wounded him in the left thigh and ankle. He was treated by American University of Beirut (AUB) medical personnel and stabilized for medevac to the USS *Iwo Jima*. Three hours later, Landing Site Red was under attack. RPGs and heavy small arms fire struck the landing site and was probably directed at a helicopter parked for repairs. Minutes later, a man threw a grenade into the Lebanese Army camp and escaped on foot to the north. Firefights continued in Hay-al-Sellum, with stray rounds striking on the Marines' northern perimeter.

The accurate sniper fire that we faced daily turned deadly on October 14. At 10:30 a.m., two jeeps traveling on the airport perimeter road came under attack. The first jeep was hit, and the driver was shot through both legs. The driver of the second jeep, Staff Sgt. Allen H. Soifert, was shot in the chest, and his jeep overturned. Both Landing Site Red and Charlie Company responded, firing at the snipers. The two wounded Marines were medevaced to the USS *Iwo Jima*; however, Staff Sergeant Soifert died shortly thereafter. Both the perimeter road and LS Red were closed to all travel.

Muslim militia activities in Hay-al-Sellum continued to increase as they sandbagged their positions and buildings and stocked them with ammunition. Militiamen, some wearing red headbands, were visible carrying weapons while manning checkpoints and bunkers daily. The night of October 14 was punctuated by bursts of sniper fire directed at sentry posts on Alpha and Charlie companies' perimeters. It continued into the morning of the fifteenth, when a Marine sniper team was dispatched to Charlie Company to deal with the threat. The team surveyed the area with sniper scopes, pinpointing the snipers actively firing at Marine positions. The team coordinated their action, then opened fire with eighteen rounds of 7.62mm ammunition at fourteen targets. Their success was evident by the sudden silence from each hostile position. The firing into our positions, however, remained unpredictable.

While this sniper exchange was taking place across our lines, a Shia religious celebration was being held in the Shiite-dominated southern suburbs. This event brought large crowds and processions with men performing bloody self-flagellation as part of a religious ritual. To an outsider, it appeared that the activities were whipping the crowd into a mindless frenzy. These demonstrations definitely increased tensions but were kept under control. However, it was reported that about a hundred civilians, some of whom were armed, were seen wearing red headbands in the same fashion that the militiamen wore when firing on Marine positions the previous two days.

During the late afternoon of October 16, small arms and machine gun fire raked the lines of Alpha Company's position. Marine snipers returned scattered fire over the next few hours, but at 7:15 p.m., the volume of fire became intense. Rocket-propelled grenades impacted around the library building at the Lebanese Science University. One hit the breezeway and wounded three Marines. Alpha Company returned fire at numerous targets, but the volume of hostile fire was too great to allow a medevac helicopter to land near its position. The British contingent offered the assistance of their armored Ferret Scout cars, which escorted a convoy with the two seriously wounded Marines to the MOD. From there a helicopter medevac took the wounded to the *Iwo Jima*. The medevac chopper was fired on en route but was not hit.

The Marines fired two Dragon antitank rounds at a machine gun bunker at 9:40 p.m. after the firing increased directly at Marine positions. At 10:03 p.m., Capt. Michael Ohler, a forward air controller with Alpha Company, was struck in the head and killed by small arms. The firefight had spread to numerous buildings to the south and west resulting in the company being virtually besieged in the university buildings. At 11:00 p.m., they suffered two more wounded with shrapnel wounds from RPG fire. The fighting tapered off after midnight; however, sporadic fire and explosions continued throughout the night.

The Italian MNF reported moderate fighting throughout greater Beirut. None was directed specifically at its positions.

On October 17, I was sent a copy of a State Department message from the American embassy in Beirut to the secretary of state in Washington, D.C.:

Subject: Condolence Letter from French Minister of Defense to USMNF Commander

1. The commanding General of the French Multinational Force contingent passed his own translation of a Letter of Condolence he received for transmittal to the Commander of the U.S. Multinational continent. Text follows:

2. Begin Text: Dear Colonel Geraghty, Today at 1:02 p.m., I received a message from the Minister of Defense. This message may be translated as follows:

    Message to be transmitted to the Colonel commanding the Marines in Beirut.

    At the side of their French, Italian, and British Comrades, the Marines of the American Detachment of the Multinational Security Force in Beirut watch over the peace. Once more, one of your men has become a victim of Duty. The United States Marine Corps continues to pay a heavy tribute to the cause we all defend. I ask you to communicate to your soldiers my profound sympathy.

    Signed, Charles Hernu, Minister of Defense.

    End text.

3.   Comment: Neither the Embassy nor the Marine contingent can recall a pre-
cedent to this message. We regard it as a heartening example of the continued
cooperation and mutual support between the MNF contingents in Beirut.
Pugh (Deputy Chief of Mission).

Scattered fighting continued in Beirut and the southern suburbs on October
18, with Marine positions being recipients of stray rounds and sniper fire. The
LAF in Suq-el-Garb came under increased pressure from artillery, tank, and heavy
machine gun duels with Muslim militias. Fighting escalated that mid-afternoon
when the LAF was hit again with heavy barrages of 122mm Katyusha rockets
while the violence within greater Beirut expanded.

Early on October 19, the fighting in the vicinity of St. Michael's Church further
intensified when the LAF and Muslim militias traded small arms and machine
gun fire, and eventually the LAF resorted to main tank 105mm rounds to destroy
hardened positions. Armed militias attempted to barricade the Shatila traffic
circle, but the LAF broke up the barricade and reopened the road. Lebanese Army
units in Khaldeh to our south also came under rocket attacks from the east, further
adding to the extremely tense situation and chaos.

During the late afternoon, a Marine resupply convoy returning from the Durrafourd Building and British embassy was attacked with a car bomb. The convoy
was hit near the Kuwaiti embassy as it was traveling east along the main road. Four
Marines were wounded and a truck damaged when the remotely detonated bomb
in the parked car exploded. BLT 1/8 executed the reaction plan and dispatched a
covering squad to the scene. Soldiers of the Italian MNF were on the scene at the
time of the blast, and one Marine WIA was medevaced to the Italians' nearby field
hospital. Intelligence sources indicated that pro-Iranian Islamic fundamentalists
conducted the attack and deliberately targeted the USMNF.

I had traveled past the same site of the explosion moments before the convoy
did. I had been making my rounds, visiting the British embassy and Durrafourd
Building, and had met with Bill Buckley to exchange information about the
deteriorating security situation throughout Lebanon. He was well aware of the
trend. After the convoy attack, Bill called me via secure communications to
inform me that I had been the target of this attack. He stated that it followed a
known pattern of Iran's and Syria's to target the opposition's military leaders and

mentioned the assassination of the Israeli general in Tyre earlier in the month. The next day, Bill sent me a three-page memo that he had written on a legal pad, laying out the steps that I should take for my protection and to reduce the Marines' vulnerabilities. I appreciated his genuine gesture even though most of the measures he recommended had already been effected. His providing assistance and personal concern well beyond his considerable responsibilities as the chief of station also reflected Bill's many fine qualities.

The French MNF was targeted again on October 20 when a jeep was bombed in the mid-afternoon by a command-detonated mine hidden in a garbage can. The mine was planted along a route frequented by French vehicles at an overpass. It resulted, however, in only one minor French injury.

With the national reconciliation talks scheduled to begin in Geneva in ten days, late October was a sensitive time diplomatically. The talks were viewed as a major step in the right direction to begin the process to end the civil war. The goading attacks on the MNF required firm, proportional responses. We needed to be careful not to do something stupid that would derail the positive diplomatic developments. To keep Admiral Martin abreast of the current situation, I sent the following SITREP on October 20:

O 201418Z Oct 83
FM CTF SIX TWO
TO COMSIXTHFLT
INFO CTF SIX ONE
PERSONAL FOR VADM MARTIN, INFO CAPT FRANCE FROM COL. GERAGHTY
SUBJ: RECENT ATTACKS ON USMNF

1. The recent series of direct attacks upon USMNF Personnel, as well as the French and Italians, signal yet another change in tactics by the extremists in this very unpredictable milieu. The MNF was unanimous in forecasting a change, but none was, of course, able to predict just what events would unfold. Although much has changed, many things are still the same; therefore, I feel I should provide you with an update of our current situation.

2. The tactics the extremists have resorted to (i.e. sniping, car bombs, etc.) are the tactics of losers who are looking for great political gains at very little personal risk. These tactics are difficult to counter, and unless we remain ever

mindful of our role, could easily provoke an inappropriate response which could seriously jeopardize our position and the cease-fire as well.

3. I believe that I have the situation firmly in hand and I can assure you I will not place my men unnecessarily at risk. Neither will I retreat behind an earthern berm and "show the flag" only from the top of my flagpole. I have instituted measures which will, I believe, eliminate unnecessary exposure, but will still make our presence known.

4. I have placed certain roads and portions of the city strictly off limits to the USMNF. We are varying our routes and times for those convoys we must send out and, additionally, I am exploring the use of boats to resupply the Embassy and to use helos in other cases. In other words, I am making our movements about the city as unpredictable as possible in order to thwart their plans while not presenting any targets of opportunity.

5. Snipers and other armed attackers around our positions at BIA and the Lebanese University will continue to be countered by the minimum amount of force necessary to eliminate the threat, but not to escalate the hostilities on a grander scale.

6. In regards to my anticipated response to future attacks, I think you should know that I am beginning to see in the tea leaves a groundswell building for us to adopt a "more aggressive defense." I get the uneasy feeling that emotions outside this theater might drive some to expect us to answer a sniper with some 105mm tank rounds. That is the last thing we should do. An inappropriate response to any provocative act will destroy our credibility and place us in even greater danger. I shall continue to respond as we have in the past.

7. The ultimate solution to these isolated terrorist attacks must, as always, come from the GOL and the LAF. In this regard, Bob Pugh has applied pressure to both the GOL and the leader of the AMAL, Nabih Berri. I, in turn, have seen Gen. Tannous and provided him with a list of positions from which we have recently received fire. I am positive that the GOL has taken, and will continue to take, steps to eliminate the threat. Albeit, small measured steps, they have already begun to move.

8. Until such time as the GOL has complete political control of the situation, we will continue to maintain our vigilance. Very respectfully, Col. Geraghty. BT

On October 20, 114 Marines, sailors, and soldiers returned from liberty in Antalya, Turkey, aboard the USS *El Paso*. On October 21, seventy-nine Marines and sailors departed for ten days' liberty in Alexandria, Egypt, aboard the USS *Austin*. On the same day, a memorial service was held for Staff Sergeant Soifert, who had been killed a week earlier by sniper fire. Conducting the service was the Sixth Fleet Jewish chaplain, Lt. Cdr. Arnold Resnicoff, who had flown into Beirut from the Sixth Fleet flagship.

While these activities were occurring at the airport, some LAF units at Khaldeh (to our south) and Suq-el-Garb were exchanging artillery fire with the Druze and Muslim militias. The shelling grew intense on the evening of October 21, the result of a Muslim militia's probe of Lebanese Army positions. It escalated into heavy artillery exchanges that lasted for several hours.

On October 22, Bravo Company received hostile fire from RPGs, heavy machine guns, 120mm mortars, and 23mm antiaircraft guns. Checkpoint 76 was also the target of sporadic small arms fire. The fighting died down after a couple of hours. That night, the United Service Organizations (USO) sponsored a performance of the group MEGA Band at MSSG-24 and BLT 1/8's headquarters and drew appreciation by all hands. It turned out to be the only USO performance during the 24th MAU's six-month tour in Beirut.

After the USO performers' departure that Saturday night, reports from all the security posts indicated sporadic firing in the mountains, but it was generally quiet by Beirut standards. What we know now was that the Iranian-supported terrorists, with Syrian complicity, were positioning the two massive suicide truck bombs for use against American and French peacekeepers in the early morning hours the next day.

—8—

Suicide Bombings and Aftermath

ON OCTOBER 23, I AWOKE as usual at dawn. As part of my routine, I slipped into my utilities and combat boots, threw some cold water on my face, and proceeded downstairs to the combat operations center (COC). After checking with the watch officer, I browsed through overnight communications traffic. Saturday night had been, by Lebanese standards, relatively quiet.

I roamed outside to view the rising dawn of this troubled country and was struck by the quiet of the morning. I saw some Marines going about their duties, others who had relinquished their overnight duties, and some who were preparing for a workout in their physical training (PT) gear. Since it was a Sunday, we were on a modified routine. Reveille was pushed back an hour to 6:30, and brunch was served between 8:00 and 10:00. The change in the routine, along with the delicious meal, was well appreciated by all hands and a welcome respite from the intense fighting of the preceding weeks.

But this morning would be anything but quiet and routine. At 6:22—soon after I returned to my quarters/office, which I shared with Lt. Col. Harry Slacum, to review the daily schedule and reports—a massive explosion rocked our headquarters, followed by enormous shock waves. Shards of glass from blown-out windows, equipment, manuals, and papers flew across my office. Fortunately, we had put duct tape on all the windows for such an eventuality, but a large section of the sandbag wall, built on the outside ledge, was blasted away. The entry door to my office, which was on the far side away from the explosion, had been blown off its hinges, and the door frame was bent. The force of the blast had cracked the reinforced concrete foundation of my headquarters. Other than superficial cuts, neither Harry nor I was injured.

With my ears ringing from the explosion, I grabbed my helmet, .45 pistol, and flak vest as I yelled to Harry, "What the hell was that?" I ran down a wobbly staircase to the operations center, where debris and papers were still floating in the air, and noticed some of the communications equipment and radios had been blown across the room. I quickly checked the Marines on duty and found them shaken, but luckily no one had received serious injuries.

I ran outside only to find myself engulfed in a dense, gray fog of ash. Debris still rained down. My view was obstructed in all directions as a sickening knot grew in my gut. I knew that whatever had happened spelled big trouble for us. My initial thought, as I stumbled through the fog, was that we had taken a direct hit from a rocket, Scud missile, or heavy artillery. As I made my way around the rear of my headquarters, I smelled the pungent odors of the explosive and concrete dust.

My logistics officer (S-4), Maj. Bob Melton, joined me in the search to find out what had happened when suddenly the acrid fog began to lift. I looked north toward the buildings behind my headquarters. Then, as I turned to the south, Melton gasped, "My God, the BLT building is gone!" As I absorbed the magnitude of the scene before me, I experienced a moment of disbelief like no other. The sickening knot in my stomach grew more intense. The BLT Headquarters building billeted more than three hundred Marines, sailors, and soldiers. I was crying hard on the inside but had no time for personal feelings. There was work to be done.

Quickly, reality set in. It was obvious that we had suffered heavy casualties, but I still did not know exactly what caused the attack. Shortly thereafter, someone reported to me that a large truck had penetrated our perimeter south of the BLT's headquarters from the direction of the airport's main terminal. The driver had rammed through the sergeant of the guard's post in front of the BLT building's entrance and detonated the truck's payload in the lobby. The explosive force of the blast caused the concrete, steel-reinforced four-story structure, which was considered one of the strongest buildings in Lebanon, to completely collapse. Its total devastation was astounding. I took in this carnage as cries for help pierced the air.

Another Marine came up and informed me that the French Paratrooper Headquarters at Ramlet el-Baida about two miles north of the airport had also

MAP 5. Battalion Landing Team Headquarters, Beirut. *USMC Archives*

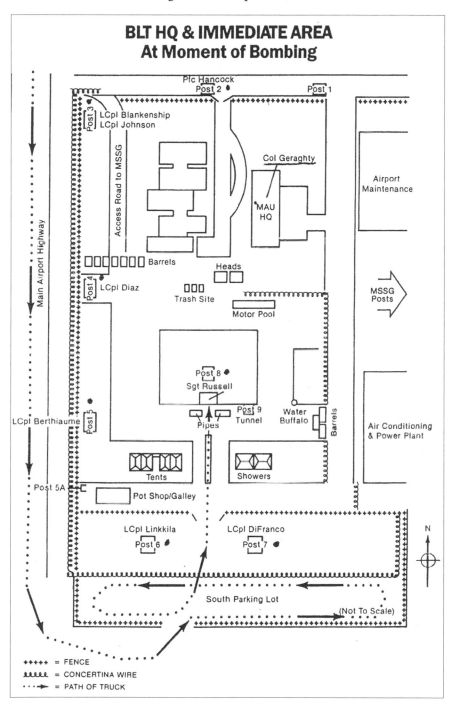

BLT HQ & IMMEDIATE AREA
At Moment of Bombing

Pfc Hancock
Post 2

Post 1

Post 3

LCpl Blankenship
LCpl Johnson

Access Road to MSSG

Col Geraghty

Airport
Maintenance

MAU
HQ

Main Airport Highway

Barrels

Heads

MSSG
Posts

LCpl Diaz

Post 4

Trash Site

Motor Pool

Post 8

Sgt Russell

LCpl Berthiaume

Post 5

Pipes

Post 9
Tunnel

Water
Buffalo

Barrels

Air Conditioning
& Power Plant

Post 5A

Tents

Showers

Pot Shop/Galley

LCpl Linkkila

Post 6

LCpl DiFranco

Post 7

N

South Parking Lot

(Not To Scale)

+++++ = FENCE
ⵣⵣⵣⵣⵣ = CONCERTINA WIRE
• • •➔ = PATH OF TRUCK

just been hit by a similar massive truck bomb. My mind raced to absorb all the details about exactly what was coming down. What about the Italians and British? Were these coordinated attacks a prelude to a ground assault? I instinctively expected follow-on attacks and began organizing revised defenses to thwart them. I grabbed the nearest officer available and ordered him to immediately reorganize and reinforce the security force from the BLT site to the 24th MAU compound's main entry point. I told him to instruct the Marines to repel and shoot any vehicles or drivers who failed to heed the command to halt. These new rules of engagement would take effect immediately. I also ordered those nearby to expedite recovery operations to rescue the injured survivors from the smoldering ruins. I knew we were going to need reinforcements and need them fast.

I hurriedly made my way back to my operations center and communications section to report via secure-voice radio to Commodore Rick France and Adm. Ed Martin. It generated a flash message to the National Military Command Center (NMCC) in Washington:

Explosion at BLT 1/8 HQS . . . a large explosion at BLT 1/8 HQS Building collapsed the roof and leveled the building. Large numbers of dead and wounded. Are using MSSG-24 and Italian MNF medical and will medevac out of LS Brown. French report a building in their sector also bombed . . . unknown injured; BLT HQS destroyed.

Then Lieutenant Colonel Slacum and I composed an OPREP-3 (operational report) Pinnacle Front Burner flash message to the NMCC requesting that the entire BLT Headquarters be replaced by the Second Marine Division's Air Alert Force (AAF) on standby 24/7 at Camp Lejeune. To buttress support, I requested an additional rifle company to augment security for the rescue operation and the anticipated follow-on attacks. As I learned more about the sophistication of the dual suicide attacks, it confirmed for me that an extra rifle company was necessary. This rationale also had led to my decision to keep my staff intact and assume responsibility for the fire support coordination center (FSCC). The battalion staff normally fulfilled this function, so my staff had to step in and restore that lost capability. Capt. Tim Tanner, the acting S-3 of the 24th MAU, established direct radio contact with all the line infantry companies (Companies A, B, and C) and the attachments. He was ably assisted by 1st Lt. Steve Mikolaski, the assistant S-3, in setting up and operating the FSCC.

We shared intelligence and coordinating information with the Lebanese Army and the other MNF peacekeepers. The Italians and the British actually occupied more vulnerable positions than the U.S. and French forces did. Given the immensity of the attacks, both the Italians and the British were taking frantic precautions to improve their defenses and reduce their vulnerability. This action was particularly important since a later study revealed that comparable destruction and casualties would have resulted at any MNF headquarters or embassy without a truck bomb having to penetrate their defensive perimeters, as ours was. In the days following the bombing, there was a major transformation around all units' positions to prevent a possible recurrence of suicide attacks. Earthen and cement barricades were dragged across all open areas to prevent high-speed entry. After evaluating the possibility of human suicide commandos, as well as the use of captured LAF or MNF vehicles and uniforms, a heavily manned and reinforced perimeter sealed off the Marine compound from these threats.

My staff reestablished the FSCC quickly and efficiently. This effort assured me that, in the event that supporting arms were required, we could provide them with our artillery, naval gunfire, and air support from the Carrier Task Force 60 located over the horizon. A proven leader, Lieutenant Colonel Slacum took over the overall coordination with the ships, the other MNFs, the Lebanese civilian rescuers, and others to ensure security, provide medical evacuations, and synchronize the multiple activities. Harry's exceptional performance of this duty, and that of my staff, was nothing short of stellar. After the FSCC was up and operating, I instructed the communications officer to set up and activate an alternative operations center in the event we got hit. He accomplished it rapidly and professionally.

To further beef up security, I requested that the Marine detachment from the USS *New Jersey* be sent ashore to assist in digging out the survivors. I assigned Maj. Doug Redlich, the MSSG-24 commander, to take charge of the rescue operation. His superb leadership, organization, and compassion accelerated the operation and saved countless lives. Doug; Dr. Gilbert Bigelow, the senior dentist; and Staff Sgt. Dennis Allston, an explosive ordnance disposal technician, were among the first on the scene following the attack. Dr. Bigelow viewed the heinous scene of dust-covered body parts, moaning wounded, and dazed survivors and immediately went back to his headquarters to find assistance and medical supplies. Doug dispatched Sergeant Allston back to his headquarters to summon the truck and engineer platoons, heavy earth-moving equipment, and people to assist with the mass casualties and medical evacuations. Major Redlich then moved through the pile of rubble that was once the battalion's headquarters and searched for victims. He discovered Sgt. Steven Russell, the duty sergeant of the guard, lying face down on the ground, severely wounded. Surprisingly, Russell was conscious. When Doug knelt down to assist him, Russell related what he had witnessed prior to the truck bomb's detonation.

Russell told Doug how he saw a large yellow Mercedes truck accelerating through the barbed-wire obstacles directly toward the BLT Headquarters. He yelled at a Marine next to him, "Get the fuck outta here!" and ran through the headquarters screaming, "Hit the deck! Hit the deck!" Right behind him, he saw the nineteen-ton vehicle crash through his sandbag guard shack at the entrance and stop in the middle of the lobby. A few seconds later, he saw "a bright orange-yellow flash at the grill of the truck." The last thing he remembered was feeling "a wave of intense heat and a powerful shock wave." His survival was, in itself, a miracle.

Russell asked for assistance to get up on his elbows so he could view what was left of the BLT building. After Doug complied with this request, he grabbed a couple of corpsmen to treat Russell. They splintered his shattered left leg, bandaged his head and left hand, and helped move him to an impromptu casualty collection point.

Commodore Rick France was leading the effort to organize the critical medical support and handling medical evacuations. He immediately sent a medical team to the airport along with several working parties from the USS *Harlan County* and USS *Portland*. He activated additional medical teams on the battleship USS *New Jersey* and the USS *Virginia*, which were soon heli-lifted ashore.

HMM-162, the MAU's air combat element, launched its two ready aircraft around 6:45 a.m. One was a medevac-configured CH-46 equipped to carry fifteen litter cases while the other CH-46 was configured to haul up to twenty-five seated personnel or several deck-mounted stretchers. Each carried ground support reinforcements along with their equipment. The helicopters were especially useful in rapidly transporting ashore working parties from all the ships to expedite the recovery operation. Upon landing at LS Brown, they were serviced and supported by the twelve-man helicopter support team (HST) assigned to the shore party platoon. They began transporting the wounded survivors from the triage stations at the bombing site and those at the aid stations near LS Brown to be heli-lifted to the multiple ships' medical facilities offshore.

Shortly after the attack, Rick France alerted the British Royal Air Force hospital at Akrotiri, Cyprus, for possible medical evacuation assistance. It was fortuitous that Maj. Gen. Desmond Langley, the commanding general of the British Forces, Cyprus, had paid us a visit a month earlier. This visit paved the way for many wounded peacekeepers to be treated at the RAF hospital there. In addition, Rick requested medevac aircraft from Stuttgart, West Germany, and recalled the USS *Austin* from a port visit to Alexandria, Egypt. Rick France and his PHIBRON 8 staff coordinated their actions with my staff ashore in implementing the mass casualty evacuation plan that we had rehearsed earlier. Thank God for that training, which undoubtedly saved innumerable lives during the recovery operation.

As the recovery operation was getting under way, rescue workers, military forces, and Lebanese civilians, along with Lebanese Red Cross workers, poured into BIA. The Italians and Lebanese construction workers were some of the first to arrive after the bombing. I had passed word to expect follow-on attacks, and the flow of vehicles and people was increasing at the airport, which was rapidly becoming a target-rich environment. Only personnel directly involved with the rescue operation were allowed into the recovery site. More large vehicles, equipment, and fifty-five-gallon drums filled with dirt were set up to control and slow the increasing flow of people and vehicles. Reporters, photographers, international press, and TV news personnel arrived in droves but were kept at a distance until we could get things under control. A platoon of British soldiers soon joined the rescue effort, and later a contingent of French soldiers arrived to help, even though the French were dealing with their own dead and wounded. The French contingent's presence sent an honorable statement that we were together in times of adversity.

The recovery operation made progress. The engineer and truck platoons brought some heavy equipment to the scene. Wreckers and chains and a ten thousand–pound forklift arrived, but it soon became apparent that we needed larger and heavier equipment (i.e., fifteen-ton cranes) to lift the large blocks and slabs of steel-reinforced concrete and get to any survivors buried beneath the rubble.

MAP 6. Rescue Operation at Beirut International Airport. *USMC Archives*

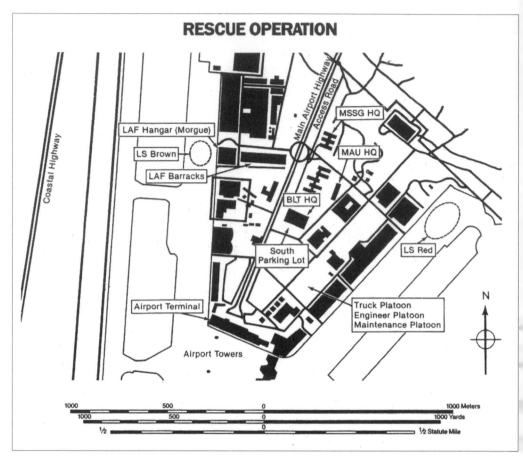

During my earlier rounds, I noticed the arrival of General Tannous, accompanied by Brigadier General Stiner. The pained, remorseful look of sorrow on the old Lebanese warrior's face reflected how all of us felt. I learned later that he was working in his office at the Ministry of Defense with General Stiner, planning future LAF operations, when the blast's loud report shattered the early morning stillness. As they both watched the huge column of black smoke rise and create a swirling white smoke ring similar to a nuclear blast, Tannous exclaimed, "God willing, I hope it's not the Marines!" As he and Stiner raced to his vehicle to head to BIA, the morning air was again pierced by a massive explosion, and a similar black cloud rose above the French compound.

General Tannous told me, "Whatever you need, you've got. We'll bring every emergency crew in Lebanon to bear on this, and I'll get you heavy construction equipment in here immediately to lift some of these layers off these people." True to his word, the need was quickly filled by Oger Liban, the largest Lebanese construction company, owned by the Lebanese-born Saudi negotiator Rafiq Hariri. This same firm had provided important assistance following the April suicide bombing of the U.S. embassy in Beirut. Its large cranes and other heavy equipment were crucial in assisting the rescuers, who were digging with shovels, picks, sledgehammers, axes, and anything they could get their hands on. The cries for help and the blood-chilling groans and moans from their buddies added to the Marines' sense of urgency, frustration, and commitment to save as many as possible. Not far beneath the surface of their steely demeanor was a fierce rage directed at the perpetrators.

Dr. Gil Bigelow had linked up with his assistant, Dr. Jim Ware, and some corpsmen and set up two separate aid stations. Just as for my alternate COC, their rationale was that if they took a direct hit from artillery or rockets, which was a definite possibility, one station would survive. Jim was placed in charge while Dr. Bigelow took four corpsmen, rushed back to the BLT site, and set up the triage station. Scores of wounded would eventually cycle through these stations, and many owe their lives to these dedicated professionals.

As soon as I was satisfied that the operations center had control of the revised security plan at the airport, the fire support coordination center, and our other locations, my command post went mobile. With Corporal Cavallero, a PRC-77 radio, and my command jeep, I moved to a visible location near the bombing site. From there, I could observe firsthand the rescue operation's progress and the new entry point's security, which revealed more heavy vehicles, more obstacles, and increasing numbers of fifty-five-gallon drums filled with dirt to impede the traffic flow into the MAU compound. I felt strongly that it was important that I be visible to my men and the rescue teams to offer encouragement and support while they carried out the heart-wrenching, gruesome task.

The incredible devastation of the bombing site resembled a scene from one of those black-and-white newsreels of Europe during World War II. It was surreal. Mangled, dismembered bodies were strewn throughout the area in a grotesque fashion. One Marine's body, still within his sleeping bag, was impaled on a tree limb. Teams of rescuers used steel cutters and blowtorches to cut through the steel reinforcement rods connecting the massive slabs of concrete. Others performed the arduous task of hammering the concrete into manageable chunks, which were then loop-tied and lifted away by the heavy cranes.

Everything was covered with gray dust. Those trees left standing were stripped of any foliage, and vehicles and other equipment were overturned masses of twisted steel. As rescue teams frantically searched the area, what appeared to be large chunks of dirt and debris would move, and we could hear mournful moans beneath the ruins. The gray dust that covered bodies and body parts added to the black-and-white newsreel effect. Many bodies and portions of bodies were totally burned. I had a tough time keeping my psychological balance. As I surveyed the carnage, I grew livid. I couldn't help thinking, Here lie the fucking unintended consequences of getting sucked into an eight-sided civil war while trying to carry out a peacekeeping mission.

As I made my way through the obliteration, I came upon Lt. Col. Larry Gerlach, the battalion's commanding officer. A Vietnam veteran who had earned a Purple Heart, he was lying on the ground near the southwestern corner of his demolished headquarters. I knew his quarters were on the second deck of that sector of the building, so he apparently was blown clear of the collapsing structure by the force of the explosion. To put it bluntly, he looked a mess. He was covered with the ubiquitous gray dust, one of his arms and a leg were in unnatural positions, and it was obvious he was suffering from multiple facial fractures and head wounds. What was so bizarre was that the blood from the multiple wounds, particularly the severe facial wounds, had coagulated into a gray crust, which added to this incredible scene. My first impression was that he was dead. Several rescuers had gathered, and as I knelt down for a closer look, I came very close to getting sick. I was surprised that he was still living but frankly didn't give him much of a chance for survival.

Fortunately, I was proved wrong. He was placed into the back of a Lebanese ambulance and rushed to the Italian MNF medical facility. Later, we learned that the Italians had transferred him to a local hospital. It took us almost three days to track him down along with about twenty other seriously wounded men who had been whisked away to local Lebanese medical facilities shortly after the attack. Larry's successful recovery can be attributed to Robin Wright, a foreign correspondent covering the war for the *Sunday Times* of London. Through her contacts and persistence, she was instrumental in locating Larry, who was immediately transferred to a U.S. hospital in Germany for further treatment. The other injured Marines and sailors were located through the relentless efforts of a team led by Capt. Barry Ford, who, with his interpreter, ran down every lead until everyone was recovered.

Our lone physician ashore, Lt. John Hudson, USN, perished in the bombing, leaving a large void to fill. Doc Hudson was genuinely loved and respected by all hands, who saw him for what he was—a courageous caregiver committed to making the world a better place. Fortunately for us, Lt. Larry Wood, the HMM-162 flight surgeon on the USS *Iwo Jima*, flew ashore with a team of corpsmen shortly after the bombing. Dr. Wood had the corpsmen set up a triage station and immediately started treating the most severely injured. His leadership, stamina, and special skills saved many untold lives. He was another quiet hero who did whatever had to be done to save the shattered lives of the injured.

By late morning, the casualty count continued to mount as bodies of dead Marines, sailors, and soldiers were positioned in rows and covered with ponchos and poncho liners. We ran out of body bags quickly and requested an emergency resupply. The bloody bodies, along with the rising temperatures, caused a repugnant odor of death and drew flies, which added to the mayhem. The treatment of the wounded, most of whom suffered severe burns along with multiple fractures and shock, nearly overwhelmed us but for the heroic efforts of the U.S. Navy medical teams from the ships offshore. They accelerated the emergency treatments and expedited the medical evacuations to the ships, the Italian medical facility, the local hospitals, and those in Cyprus, Italy, or Germany. We recovered the body of one Marine who was inside the BLT building when the bomb detonated and was hurled more than 110 yards onto the airport access road.

■

Thanks to the relentless professional performance of Rick France, the PHIBRON staff, and my staff, the first medevac aircraft landed at Beirut International Airport about 10:30 on Sunday morning. It was a U.S. Air Force C-9 "Nightingale" from Rhein-Main Air Base (AB), Germany, specially equipped and staffed for medical evacuations. Fortunately, the crew had spent Saturday night in Incirlik AB, Turkey, to pick up patients who needed routine treatment in Germany. The flight time from Incirlik AB to Beirut was forty-five minutes.

Early Sunday morning, the C-9's crew had received emergency orders to proceed immediately to Beirut and evacuate casualties after an explosion. The members had no idea how bad the situation was until they were ordered to remove all but fourteen seats and prepare the plane to carry twenty-four litters. Three flight surgeons from Incirlik AB joined the evacuation mission.

On the visual final approach into BIA, the air controller cautioned them that there was sniper fire just east of the airport. Sniper fire was also being directed at the recovery teams working at the bombing site. The Nightingale pilots noted the Marine Cobra gunships patrolling areas just parallel to the runway.

As the plane taxied next to a hangar, the pilots avoided numerous artillery and mortar shelling holes in the concrete taxiways. The crew viewed body bags containing dead servicemen piled up on the tarmac. Within seconds, Marine and U.S. Navy helicopters landed next to them with severely wounded peacekeepers on board, bringing them from PHIBRON 8 ships.

I was on the tarmac when they loaded both the walking wounded and the litter patients. Dr. Alfred Studwell, the lead flight surgeon, came up and informed me that one of the severely wounded Marines on a litter had little chance for survival. I recall looking at that young Marine clinging to life and telling Dr. Studwell to take him and do the best he could. That flight was his only chance for survival, since our medevacs were encountering accurate sniper fire.

Second Lt. Joe Bunker, one of the pilots, had to determine how much fuel to carry for the four-and-a-half-hour direct flight to Rhein-Main. After trying for forty-five minutes to get a fuel truck, they suddenly spotted one on the ramp heading for a Navy C-9 that had brought in transfer cases from Italy. Lieutenant Bunker ran out and commandeered the fuel truck and put on the needed fuel to safely reach Germany.

On the return trip to Germany, Lieutenant Bunker was in the jump seat and could hear the sound of the heart monitor directly behind him. Dr. Studwell was the only doctor aboard since the Navy had commandeered the other two flight surgeons in Beirut right before takeoff and helicoptered them directly to ships offshore. Along with two nurses, Dr. Studwell was treating the most severely wounded Marine in the special care area. Lieutenant Bunker suddenly heard the heart monitor stop and turned around to see the straight green line on the monitor and Dr. Studwell giving the Marine CPR. They eventually lost him despite an incredible effort.

Lieutenant Bunker went back to assist with the other wounded. Also on board was Senator Gordon Humphrey (R-NH) who was visiting Beirut but never got ashore because of the attack. Along with an aide, he helped out like everyone else did, which amazed the crew. How well Americans pull together in times of crisis.

Upon arrival, they were directed to park in the VIP slot where six UH-60 U.S. Army Black Hawk helicopters awaited the most serious wounded and four litter buses for the rest. The plane's pilots noted they had only forty-one hundred pounds of fuel on board, or just a hundred pounds above their legal minimum. After clearing out all the wounded from the airplane, the Nightingale taxied over to its normal parking area to remove the dead Marine away from the cameras and media.

The other wounded Marines on the flight had survived, and the next day all were in stable condition. The entire crew, led by Dr. Studwell, provided professional care and compassion that saved the peacekeepers' lives. They join the ranks of those quiet heroes who do whatever has to be done to save lives. In doing so, they bring honor to their patients and themselves.

■

The rescue workers continued their gruesome labor unabated amid the lingering danger of smoldering fires in the armory where TOW antitank missiles and heavy ordnance were stored along with burning batteries containing lithium. It was feared that the poisonous gases discharging from the burning lithium would asphyxiate those survivors trapped beneath the rubble. As the rescue teams from several nations continued their tasks, we started taking sniper fire from Hay-al-Sellum. The bastards would never be satisfied. This sporadic sniper fire continued for many days throughout the rescue operation, even though I ordered countersniper fire to precisely neutralize its source. It worked temporarily, but the snipers resumed at their will.

Shortly after noon on Sunday, a Royal Air Force C-130 from Akrotiri, Cyprus, landed and was loaded with twenty more severely wounded survivors. The crew immediately returned to its base for the men's emergency treatment. Later, a stream of U.S. Air Force C-9s and C-141s flew into BIA, at considerable risk, to load the wounded and immediately take off for destinations in Germany and Italy. The airport had been closed for several days before the attack, and afterward, we were still taking small arms fire from the surrounding villages. To look upon the rescue scene, one couldn't help but be struck by how so many undertook the enormous, dangerous exertion of providing assistance. As dust-covered bodies were pulled out of the rubble heap, many were thought to be dead but later found to have a pulse and surviving. Lebanese Red Cross workers performed CPR on rescued individuals and moved them to aid stations. Marines, sailors, soldiers, and the airmen from the medevac planes joined the Italians, British, French, and Lebanese military along with civilian workers and labored feverishly to save those trapped and pleading for help. As one Marine rescuer put it, "The ground itself was crying."

Rescue teams hammered at the concrete slabs and chunks of steel-reinforced concrete to get to the shouts beneath the rubble. Bodies of the dead and wounded were carried out by stretchers, cots, ponchos, poncho liners, and later, the plywood partition walls used in our administrative areas. Jackhammers, blowtorches, and hacksaws continued to be employed to break through the concrete and the reinforcement rods. The heavy cranes lifted gigantic concrete slabs to facilitate the rescue teams' access to the groaning men beneath the rubble. All of the rescuers looked like ants on an anthill, but no one slowed down or vacillated. It crossed my mind again that such a large gathering of rescue workers presented a very lucrative target in a location where the gates of hell had already opened. The more I surveyed this heinous scene of absolute madness, a seething rage again rose within me toward those who committed this despicable act of war against peacekeepers. The rows of dead bodies and body parts and the shattered, burned bodies of the severely wounded all added to my disgust to this act of pure terrorism. The more I thought about it, the angrier I became and resolved that this attack had to be answered with swift and precise retribution—not for revenge but for simple justice. It took some time for me to get this fury under control. There were too many decisions to be made and lives to be saved to divert my attention to personal feelings.

One of the busiest on this gruesome scene was the MAU's Catholic chaplain, who provided assistance and ministered to the dead and wounded. Lt. Cdr. George Pucciarelli, who earned parachutist wings while serving with a force reconnaissance company, was highly respected as a man of the cloth, a leader, and a counselor for all Marines and sailors. He was working with the Sixth Fleet's Jewish chaplain, Lt. Cdr. Arnold Resnicoff, who had flown into Beirut to conduct memorial services for Staff Sergeant Soifert.

Both chaplains became heavily involved in digging and searching for survivors. When finding a seriously wounded individual, they would guide rescue teams and assist in the recovery. When bodies were pulled out from beneath the smoldering piles of twisted steel and chunks of concrete, each chaplain would minister to the wounded and help stabilize them. The work for all was both physically and emotionally exhausting.

By chance, Father Pucciarelli found Chaplain Danny Wheeler's purple stole and guided a rescue team to the location where he thought his Lutheran colleague was buried. It was a stretch that Chaplain Wheeler could be there, and more than three hours had passed since the bombing. Using questions to establish voice contact with the still-conscious injured, Father Pucciarelli asked, "Who's there?" An answer finally came back, "Chaplain Wheeler." Father Pucciarelli answered, "Just hang on, buddy, we'll be right there."

The rescuers had discovered that it was often easier and safer to burrow down past entombed victims, then tunnel back up. It was very risky and dangerous since large chunks of concrete were falling into the tunnels and striking the rescuers. With parallel rescue efforts ongoing throughout the piles of rubble, one of the ever-present real dangers was that any movement of the multiton slabs of steel and concrete could shift and crush the rescuers along with the trapped.

Chaplain Wheeler came very close to dying during this incredible rescue effort. When a large piece of debris was pulled from the tunnel, the entire weight of the rubble settled on the minister's back, pinning his head with a vise of pressure too great to sustain. Chaplain Wheeler felt himself blacking out, and he panicked. He was within millimeters of being rescued or crushed to death. Father Pucciarelli again reassured him that he would be fine. After what seemed like an eternity, Charlie Company commander Capt. Chris Cowdrey's face appeared in Chaplain Wheeler's line of sight. "Hey, Chaplain! Can you move your legs?" Both his legs were pinned by rubble. Further efforts using a sledgehammer caused more chunks of concrete to slam into the crypt, but the persistent rescuers eventually pulled him free. It was one of those special moments of thanksgiving in an otherwise miserable day of never-ending sorrow.[1]

As I worked my way from my remote CP through the rescue operation, other problems arose besides the intermittent sniper fire. Looters were caught taking personal belongings, which were scattered throughout the airport complex. The security guards and rescue personnel did not take lightly to this intrusion. Several nasty incidents nearly occurred involving angry, frustrated guards—buddies of victims—and the looters. Many looters were perplexed by the guards' anger and surprised when we expelled them from the site. There was definitely a culture gap here.

Meanwhile, rounds of ammunition stored in our armory, which were located in the basement, were cooking off and mingling with the moans of the buried victims. The instability of the piled ruins continued to create safety hazards that caused all to pray while they toiled. Vehicles destroyed near the site caused gasoline from ruptured tanks to seep into the basement. Besides small arms ammunition, the TOW missiles stored there also posed a danger, which only added to my anxiety.

And the challenges never ended. Also stored in the basement were sensitive communications equipment and cryptographic materials, some of which were scattered throughout the area. The job to retrieve this classified material fell on 1st Lt. Glenn Dolphin, a talented communications officer. Through his team's persistent efforts, they found a splintered wooden storage box in the basement that still contained crypto key cards and tapes used to encode. It was a lucky find for us but reaffirmed the fact that we would never retrieve all the cryptographic materials. As is routine in such a crisis, we had immediately notified headquarters of this worst-case scenario, and a worldwide emergency code change had already been put into effect.

The destruction of many records, particularly the service record books (SRBs), led to a painfully delayed casualty reporting system to notify the victims' next of kin (NOK). First Lieutenant Claude Davis, the personnel officer (S-1) of the 24th MAU, worked tirelessly to provide sensitive and professional leadership to ensure the information was precise and correct. The casualty reporting system must guarantee accurate information and proper notification of the NOK. The requirement for absolute accuracy overrode all other considerations since no one wanted to hurt anyone needlessly with wrong information. This necessarily delayed NOK notification became so problematic that different resources had to be activated to relieve the mental anguish of waiting families and friends. AT&T came forward and donated the use of international telephone lines, which allowed survivors to notify their families that they were not killed or seriously wounded in the attack. It took time to make needed repairs and install the lines, but soon they became operational. My staff set up procedures for all hands to call home and speak with their loved ones. An integral part of the procedure, as well as a long-standing Marine tradition, was that enlisted Marines were allowed to be first in line. Continuity and respect for Marine traditions were evident and necessary, particularly in times of adversity. While this communication brought joy and appreciation to many families, one can only imagine the gnawing fear among those families who waited so long for a call that would never come.

In the early afternoon on Monday the twenty-fourth, I received notice that President François Mitterrand of France was en route to the MAU compound. Accompanying him were the French defense minister Charles Hernu and Gen. Jeannou Lacaze, the chief of staff of the French armed forces. The security detail surrounding the presidential party was the largest and most intense that I had ever witnessed. They arrived after visiting the devastated French paratroopers' headquarters. Gen. François Cann, the French MNPF commander, later provided details about that bombing. A truck driven by a suicide driver and loaded with high explosives had crashed through barricades and a hail of gunfire into the nine-story building and detonated. The eventual casualty toll was fifty-eight killed and scores wounded.

After visiting the MAU bombing site, President Mitterrand and his party went to our central morgue, which we had established in a Lebanese Air Force maintenance hangar adjacent to our primary Landing Site Brown. By nightfall, we had gathered close to two hundred bodies in green body bags and stored each in an aluminum casket container called a transfer case. Many of the body bags contained assorted body parts to aid in the identification of each corpse, which was accomplished later in Germany. The transfer cases were stacked four wide and four high on aluminum pallets, sixteen per pallet, and secured with nylon straps. There must have been almost a dozen pallets lined in a row and spread deep into the darkened hangar.

As the party entered the hangar, I greeted and saluted the men. President Mitterrand graciously greeted me and, through an interpreter, offered his condolences to the fallen American peacekeepers. When we moved deeper into the hangar, I noticed the look of astonishment on President Mitterrand's face as he stopped and looked past me to view the stacks of caskets on the pallets. His eyes opened wide, and his face became pallid. It was an expression that I will take to my grave. He muttered something softly under his breath that I could not hear. He opened his hands, palms up, and appeared to gesture at the mayhem that had descended on the peacekeepers of both of our nations. He then requested that he and his party be allowed to pay their personal respects to the deceased. President Mitterrand led the group in front of *each* pallet of caskets, making the sign of the cross and saying what appeared to be a silent prayer. Each member of the presidential party displayed a sincere, quiet reverence and remorse for the fallen Americans that was beyond description. That they were alone, without press coverage, showing their genuine respect was extraordinarily moving.

What was even more remarkable was when they completed their private condolences at the last pallet of caskets, President Mitterrand asked me what was occurring in the back corner at the hangar's far side. This area was lighted with large floodlights and was purposely isolated and shielded with large curtains so that the dedicated working party of Marines and sailors could perform the grim task of collecting body parts while respecting the privacy and dignity of the deceased. When I explained this through the interpreter to the president, I was surprised when he and the party requested to go there. I then escorted them all the way across the cavernous hangar, and President Mitterrand and his party again paid their solemn respects to the fallen peacekeepers. When the presidential party departed, it was apparent to me that these men expressed the same heartfelt condolences for the American dead that they must have shown earlier to their fallen French peacekeepers not far away.

The solemn decorum President Mitterrand and his party displayed in their private tribute to the Americans, along with the assistance of the French MNF contingent that aided our rescue operation even though they had their own rescue operation in progress, showed me a special quality of the French. Added to the personal message of condolence from Minister of Defense Hernu the previous week, it convinced me that the French will stand with us in times of bad fortune.

I was notified later that evening that the U.S. Air Force C-141s carrying the requested battalion replacement headquarters and rifle company were inbound to Beirut. Given the time and distances involved, their arrival within thirty-six hours confirmed the capabilities and readiness of the Second Marine Division's Air Alert Force. I had been confident that Major General Gray would ensure my emergency request was promptly filled.

Lt. Colonel Ed Kelley, the commanding officer of Battalion Landing Team 2/6 Replacement Headquarters, stepped off the lead aircraft and was met by the recently arrived U.S. ambassador to Lebanon, Reginald Bartholomew, and me. I was surprised to learn that the additional rifle company I had requested for security reasons had been scratched. Kelley also expressed surprise since Echo Company was scheduled and ready to deploy. With all of the activities at our site and our obvious vulnerabilities, I quickly added that denied request to my growing list of concerns. I then took Lieutenant Colonel Kelley and his operations officer, Major Cunningham, past the bombed ruins where recovery activities continued under floodlights through the night. After giving them a quick orientation of the area, including Lieutenant Colonel Kelley's temporary headquarters, I provided an update on the current situation at BIA and the Beirut environs. Ed then left to meet with the infantry company commanders, my staff, and attachment leaders. To his credit, he returned mid-morning the following day stating his readiness to assume responsibilities as the new commanding officer, Battalion Landing Team 1/8. His leadership provided a seamless transition of command that was prompt, ready, and professional.

The previous day back in Washington, President Reagan requested that CMC Gen. P. X. Kelley attend a National Security Council (NSC) meeting at the White House. The president appointed General Kelley his personal representative to go to Beirut and determine what additional security measures could be taken to improve the Marines' protection. The general departed Andrews Air Force Base at 9:00 a.m. on Monday, the twenty-fourth, aboard Air Force Two. His party included Presidential Assistant Edward V. Hickey and Congressman John P. Murtha (D-PA), a former Marine. When General Kelley arrived at Rhein-Main Air Force Base in Germany later that day, the weather was wet and dreary, adding to the melancholy mood. He was met by the base commander, who informed him that a C-141 from Beirut had arrived shortly before with 140 caskets aboard. In General Kelley's own words:

> I asked if I could go to this aircraft to pay my respects to our fallen comrades. As I emerged from my sedan, I was not prepared for the flood of emotion which overcame me . . . for I had never seen before, and Lord willing I will never see again, an aircraft as large as a C-141 . . . filled to capacity

with caskets . . . caskets of those Marines, Sailors, and Soldiers who had been so very much alive and full of youth and vitality during my visit to Beirut several weeks earlier. On this cold and windswept night . . . in a distant land . . . I watched as young Airmen from our Air Force respectfully and tenderly removed each casket . . . one by one . . . and I silently asked the question: "Lord, where do we get such men?"[2]

The following morning, General Kelley was heli-lifted from Rhein-Main AFB to the U.S. Air Force Regional Medical Center in Weisbaden to visit with the severely wounded medical evacuees recently arrived from Beirut. At the same time, Marines were landing and the U.S. Army Rangers were parachuting onto the small Caribbean island of Grenada.

General Kelley recalled an incident that occurred while he moved through the intensive care ward and talked with the wounded, one that touched on the valor and commitment of the peacekeepers. He mentioned seeing "a young Marine with more tubes going in and out of his body than I have ever seen in one body. He couldn't see very well. He reached up and grabbed my four stars, just to make sure I was who I said I was. He held my hand with a firm grip. He was making signals, and we realized he wanted to tell me something. We put a pad of paper in his hand—and he wrote, 'Semper Fi.'" As his aide-de-camp, Lt. Col. Frank Libutti, later related, "General Kelley's face reflected a combination of joy and tremendous pride all wrapped around this very heavy emotional environment. This guy in a single act, in a moment, captured . . . the courage of that man and his love for the Corps and his country. And more than anything, the faithfulness, the loyalty . . . the opposite of despair, you know, 'Semper Fi.'" Always faithful.[3]

In a tribute to the wounded Marine, Lance Cpl. Jeffery L. Nashton, General Kelley later presented him with the four-star insignia in a shadow box. Semper Fidelis flows both ways—up and down the chain of command.

General Kelley landed in Beirut on Tuesday afternoon amid intelligence warnings of another terrorist attack. Sniper fire was still sporadic at the airport. He went immediately to the bombing site to get a firsthand look at the destruction and ongoing rescue operation. He seemed to make a point of studying the devastated building from several different angles to gain a true understanding of the bombing's magnitude. From my standpoint, his presence and encouragement to the exhausted rescue force provided a much-needed boost in morale. The commandant's show of support reinforced his personal concern.

Later aboard the flagship *Iwo Jima*, Rick France and I provided an updated briefing on the current status of our casualties and our tenuous security situation. I explained that the BLT Replacement Headquarters under Lt. Col. Ed Kelley had arrived, had been integrated, and was operational. I also mentioned that my requested additional rifle company did not deploy and was withdrawn at the last moment. Later, in a closed-door meeting with Rick France, myself, General Kelley, and General Richard Larson, deputy commander in chief of the European Command, the conversation quickly became heated. After discussing the casualties' status and other issues, our attention turned to security. Besides the unremitting sniper fire, we were receiving continuous intelligence to expect further terrorist attacks. Hearing EUCOM had scratched the extra rifle company, General Kelley pointedly asked General Larson what the rationale was for refusing a field commander's request for additional resources in a time of national crisis. He reiterated that it was my judgment that the extra rifle company was required immediately in a deteriorating security environment. General Larson told Kelley to calm down and that EUCOM was evaluating the requirement for this request. General Kelley was having none of that explanation and heatedly told General Larson that the current security situation demanded action—not analysis from a staff far removed from the reality on the ground in Beirut. I remember Rick France and I exchanged glances, wondering if we were going to have to step between two four-star generals before the end of the meeting. After further intense discussions, the issue was finally resolved, and Echo Company deployed from Camp Lejeune a couple of days later. We all felt much better after its arrival in Beirut.

On Wednesday, October 26, Vice President George H. W. Bush arrived in Beirut, and simultaneously we returned to our highest alert, Condition One. At dawn, we were attacked with small arms, mortars, and RPGs along our eastern perimeter near the town of Ash Shuwayfat, a Druze stronghold. We responded with 81mm HE mortars and small arms; the attack ceased around 7:00 a.m.

Vice President Bush and his party flew aboard the *Iwo Jima*, where Rick France and I briefed them on the current situation ashore. Besides a sizable U.S. Secret Service protective detail, his group included Ambassador Bartholomew. Vice President Bush visited the wounded in the sick bay, speaking quietly to each of the men and honoring their service by presenting them with the Purple Heart medal. He was obviously moved by their sacrifice. The vice president then departed by helicopter to the airport, where he inspected the havoc at the site of the attack. We were still receiving sniper fire despite security being very tight. It was another time when my stomach rumbled just thinking of the possibility that Vice President Bush could be hit.

He was determined to see firsthand the devastation at the site, so we suited him with a helmet and flak vest over his white shirt, which unfortunately highlighted his VIP status. He is also a tall man, which translated in the Beirut lexicon as presenting a bigger target. As I escorted him around the site, he commented on the magnitude of the attack and the cowardliness that caused it. He asked several pertinent questions, and I noticed the Secret Service detail's growing uneasiness, which I shared, at his prolonged exposure and vulnerability in a country running amok. The vice president did not reflect any such discomfort.

He departed via a Super Sea Stallion helicopter, escorted by two of our Cobra gunships, for a visit with President Gemayel at the Presidential Palace. President Gemayel and Vice President Bush's visit lasted about an hour, after which Vice President Bush made no comment to the waiting international press.

Later, we made arrangements for him to meet with my MNF counterparts: French Gen. François Cann, Italian Gen. Franco Angioni, and British commander Lt. Col. John Ferguson of the Queen's Dragoon Guards. As he had when he visited the wounded aboard the *Iwo Jima*, the vice president made it a point to personally thank each individual and express our nation's gratitude for their service to the peacekeeping mission and their assistance in the recovery operation. It was clear to any observer that Vice President Bush's personal, sincere remarks touching on the service of the Multinational Force had a profound effect on this special group of peacekeepers. Later, each of my counterparts conveyed to me their gratitude and respect for the vice president's visit and his comments.

The vice president asserted to the press after the meeting that the bombing "damn sure hasn't shaken the courage of the Marines in Beirut." He later sent me a personal note stating how impressed he was with the Marines' and sailors' discipline and high morale. His sincerity and personal concern were deeply appreciated by all hands amid all the turmoil. His safe departure also caused a big sigh of relief from all security personnel.

On October 27, President Reagan addressed the nation. His speech drew in part from a memo by a member of General Kelley's party, Ed Hickey, the White House director of Special Support Services and the father of four Marine sons (see appendix B). It provided a poignant personal assessment of the situation in Beirut.

The relentless pace of the rescue efforts at the site continued around the clock while the physical and emotional toll on the rescuers became more apparent. Any abatement of their determination to save their buddies was not an option. Groups of seriously wounded survivors would be located, but they were trapped between the pancaked ceilings and floors. It became obvious to the rescue force that one trapped group of about six Marines, mostly staff noncommissioned officers (SNCOs), could not hold on until the heavy concrete slabs could be removed. Rescuers working with the heavy-lift cranes labored frantically to reduce the pressure, and corpsmen relieved each other during the agonizing vigils. Each of the trapped Marines had been given morphine, and despite everyone's best efforts, eventually they all died, one by one. As the rescue teams reached others buried beneath the piles, they found that many had been crushed to death and most had suffered severe burns. It soon became clear that all of the remaining wounded had to be rescued immediately or they would die very soon from shock and blood loss. It was literally a race against time, and we were losing. The recovery operation was beginning to sound like a broken record: by the time we finally reached those trapped, they had succumbed. This only added to the rescue team's frustration and personal pain.

Amid the havoc, the rescue operation continued 24/7 for a week. When we could finally get down to some of the bodies later in the week, they were still warm. Those victims who remained trapped under the tons of concrete were comforted as much as possible. Many of the rescuers held hands with them, softly speaking and praying with them until they quietly passed on. Digging out the broken bodies of many who could possibly have survived if only we had been able to get to them sooner caused fatigue and a sense of hopelessness. This unrelenting reality only added to the men's anguish, frustration, and swelling fury.

The security concerns for VIPs, meanwhile, did not end with Vice President Bush's departure. In order to fulfill a major purpose for his trip, General Kelley wanted to meet with General Tannous and all the other multinational force commanders. During two earlier visits to Beirut, the commandant and General

Tannous had developed a special rapport, and General Tannous had mentioned to me then how impressed he was after meeting General Kelley. During their current meeting at the MOD, it was evident that General Tannous held the Marines in high esteem and that both leaders had a high respect for each other. At the conclusion of this meeting, I escorted General Kelley to visits with the Italian, French, and British commanders. Traveling through the streets of Beirut at this time was very hazardous and getting worse. The visits were conducted without any major disruptions, except for his trip to General Cann.

General Kelley was riding in the front seat of my jeep and his aide-de-camp, Lieutenant Colonel Libutti, was in the rear seat with me. As we were weaving our way through the traffic-jammed streets to the French paratroopers' headquarters at Ramlet el-Baida, our vehicle and security convoy came to an abrupt halt. An unruly mob was milling about the crowded urban area. Easily identified as American jeeps, the security vehicles to our front and rear blew their horns in an attempt to keep the convoy moving. The procedure in such situations, particularly when carrying VIPs, is to keep moving at all costs. Don't stop, even if it means pushing vehicles out of the way. As the mobs came right up to us, the security detail was ordered to lock and load its weapons. I exchanged anxious looks with Libutti. Both of us knew we did not want to linger in this situation. Similar thoughts that I had had previously during the vice president's visit came to mind: we do not want an assassination of the commandant of the Marine Corps.

I yelled at my driver, Corporal Cavallaro, to lay on his horn and move, even if we had to drive on the median. The security vehicles were also starting to move forward with horns blaring. After some anxious moments, we finally got moving again while drawing some hard looks from the angry mob. We were lucky, and it took quite a while for my overworked stomach to calm down. But General Kelley seemed unfazed by the whole ordeal. When we arrived at the French site, he commiserated with General Cann over the loss of his fifty-eight paratroopers in the nearly simultaneous suicide truck bomb attacks.

That evening, General Kelley conducted a meeting at my headquarters to discuss and review the substance of his report to the president. All key principals were in attendance and contributed to the report's content. Ambassador Bartholomew and General Larson were among the attendees. Among the topics was a list of initiatives under way or contemplated for increasing security and decreasing vulnerabilities associated with the large concentrations of Marines:

- Lebanese Army Armored Personnel Carriers have been positioned at the main terminal and at the traffic circle in front of the entrance to Beirut International Airport (BIA).
- Vehicle access to command posts is now restricted to emergency and military vehicles.
- Civilian pedestrian access to the command post has been restricted to one location.
- 24th Marine Amphibious Units (MAU) was placed in an indefinite "Condition 1" (highest level) alert status.
- All entrances to the command posts have been blocked and reinforced.
- All rifle companies have reinforced the perimeter fence lines adjacent to their positions.
- An additional .50-caliber machine gun has been positioned to cover avenues of approach into the command post.
- Additional guard posts have been established throughout the MAU area, and an additional rifle company was sent from Camp Lejeune to provide security during the period of the recovery operations.
- Mobile reconnaissance patrols with antitank weapons have been established within the BIA perimeter.
- BLT 2/6 command element arrived at Beirut on 24 October to replace BLT 1/8 command elements.
- Definitive action is underway to strengthen the 24th MAU positions and to reduce vulnerability to terrorist attacks by isolating and barricading command and control and support areas.

Source: Gen. Kelley's testimony before Senate Armed Services Committee on October 31, 1983, 15–16.

Upon agreement and completion of his report, General Kelley left for Washington. En route, he stopped in Naples to visit with the wounded at the U.S. Naval Hospital there and presented each of them with the Purple Heart medal.

The 24th MAU had already set in motion a series of actions to preclude future terrorist suicide attacks. Besides the concrete-filled and earthen barricades positioned throughout all open areas to prevent high-speed penetration of our perimeter, the MAU compound was ringed with an anti-vehicle ditch and an anti-vehicle berm. We had also instituted the following:

1. The airport road was reduced from four lanes to two.
2. Access into the perimeter was restricted to MNF and U.S. embassy vehicles only.
3. The number of entrances to the MAU command post was reduced to three, all of which were covered by .50-caliber machine guns and blocked either with a five-ton truck or heavy steel gates made of railroad tracks.
4. M-60 machines guns, loaded with 7.62mm armor-piercing ammunition, covered all roads and open areas leading into or in the proximity of the airport area.
5. With the exception of those Lebanese who worked at the airport's power plant, all civilian personnel were excluded from the compound, and all LAF troops were relocated outside the fence line.
6. The number of interior guard posts was increased, and all posts were armed with light antitank assault weapons (LAAWs).
7. All but ten security guards were removed from Green Beach.
8. The Corniche in front of the Durrafourd Building and the British embassy was blocked off completely, and the position reinforced with an armored assault vehicle.

Fighting in the Beirut suburbs continued throughout this period. In my weekly report, I stated that "the myriad of intelligence reports involving planned bombings of the MNF and diplomatic locations, coupled with rumored U.S. retaliation in the southern suburbs, only increased the already high tensions in Beirut." On October 29, a large congressional delegation toured the MAU compound, and I provided an updated briefing regarding the current security situation and the steps I was taking to reduce our vulnerabilities. Its members were Representatives G. V. "Sonny" Montgomery (D-MS), John P. Hammerschmidt (R-AR), Sam B. Hall (D-TX), Bob Stump (R-AZ), Earl Hutto (D-FL), Larry J. Hopkins (R-KY), Ike Skelton (D-MO), Solomon Ortiz (D-TX), Roy P. Dyson (D-MD), Bill Richardson (D-NM), and Guy V. Molinari (R-NY).

Interestingly, an incident occurred upon their arrival that provided a harbinger of where the investigations were headed. When I met the delegation to escort the members to the devastated bombing site and then to my headquarters, Representative Hopkins raced up to me, put his face right in mine, and screamed,

"You are going to eat a shit sandwich!" I didn't blink, move a muscle, or say a word. But I did glare at him. After a period, he apparently sensed my mood and finally backed off. So much for impartiality. I believe the emotional visit was exacerbated by the delegation having visited some of our wounded survivors in Germany before coming to Beirut. This visit was only the beginning of the many investigations into the bombings.

On Sunday, October 30, exactly one week after the attack, the final transfer cases carrying the remaining peacekeepers' bodies and body parts departed BIA for Germany via two C-141s. At the same time, the USS *Harlan County* opened fire with its .50-caliber machine guns and sent warning shots in front of several rapidly approaching Zodiac boats. They turned away but confirmed that the asymmetrical warfare aspect of terrorism was present and evolving. The terrorists would be coming at us in every conceivable way, and we were on their home turf.

The frantic weeklong rescue operation finally ended for the utterly exhausted rescue force. With dignity, solemn determination, and love for their fallen brothers, they had done what had to be done. In spite of heroic efforts by many teams, the hard truth was that no survivors were extracted from the deadly pile of rubble after the day of the attack. Only the dead were pulled out after that. They died as they had lived, with honor and courage. However, I added the lingering memories of them to a list that grinds on my conscience frequently but also helps me remember this special group of warriors.

In my commander's comments in my SITREP to headquarters on October 31, I stated:

> While the cutting edge of the MAU took some heavy nicks this week, it proved to be made of well tempered steel. Those that have tried to dull the blade have found that it can't be done from a distance and they have had to move close aboard to achieve their aims to win in Lebanon. They must place their ship along side ours and they will find that BLT 1/8 has been rehoned and that 24 MAU has fixed bayonets. The support from the MARG during the bombing was without equal. They placed their ships in harm's way and were first to respond. Many Marines owe their lives to the Sailors of TF61.

On November 4, the 24th MAU conducted a memorial service to recognize the service and sacrifice of those peacekeepers who perished in the dual suicide truck bombings. Ambassador Bartholomew, Deputy Chief of Mission Robert Pugh, and their wives attended along with General Tannous. Each commander of the French, Italian, and British MNF and their representatives were also present for the respectful and emotional ceremony.

Earlier that same morning, the Israeli military headquarters in Tyre, Lebanon, south of Beirut, was struck by a suicide truck bombing that mirrored the modus operandi used against the Marines and French paratroopers ten days earlier. The truck bomb eluded many of the same defenses that we were later castigated for not having and detonated its load in the vicinity of the headquarters. There were sixty killed and thirty wounded.

Ironically, as I delivered the eulogy to honor our peacekeepers for their sacrifice, the Israeli Air Force was bombing Shiite strongholds near Alayh, northeast of the airport. While the resounding noise of the jet aircraft and bombs did not disrupt the service, it definitely had everyone's attention. The Israelis' response, taken before the dust had settled on the terrorist attack in Tyre hours before, sent a clear message that there are consequences for terrorism. I wondered when the United States was going to seek a comparable retribution for these acts of war.

■

On November 5, as the advance party of the 22nd MAU arrived for the turnover, Companies A and E came under fire. On the seventh, all units on the perimeter again came under heavy fire, which continued for more than six hours. It ended only after a deluge of rain and hail descended upon us.

The deteriorating security environment, particularly around the isolated Lebanese Science University where Alpha Company was positioned, was growing more precarious by the hour. Under the excellent leadership of Capt. Paul Roy, the company had withstood some of the most fierce firefights and mortar attacks thrown at us. After discussing their predicament with Lt. Col. Ed Kelley, I decided to withdraw them during the early morning hours of November 8. We were forced to use a truck convoy, because the accelerating threats of antiaircraft fire throughout the entire Beirut area had long halted the preferred option of using helicopter transports. Sensing a vulnerability, however, the Muslim militias launched a fierce attack on the evening of November 7 against Alpha Company. The Marines vented their frustrations and rage and responded with a ferocity that the militias had not seen previously. The attack was quickly terminated, but our response carried an implicit message to the perpetrators that the rules of engagement had indeed changed.

Under cover of darkness at 3:00 a.m. on November 8, a truck convoy arrived at the scientific facility and loaded Alpha Company for the dangerous four-mile circuitous trek back to the airport. In accordance with the ever-present Murphy's Law, the convoy had a mechanical breakdown and flat tires on the return journey, delaying its arrival by more than three hours. With another sigh of relief and a silent prayer of thanksgiving, Alpha Company was taken directly to Green Beach and safely embarked aboard the USS *Harlan County* to assume responsibilities as the MAU's reserve company. Since the truck convoy did not encounter any militia opposition during its long return trip, I suspect the intense encounter with the Marines the previous night had sent a message that was received loud and clear.

On November 10, the MAU celebrated the 208th birthday of the Marine Corps. After the traditional cake cutting, I reported, "Our birthday celebration was low-key, but traditional, and from our watch, 24 MAU added another page to the history of Marines in Lebanon." I also received the following Marine Corps birthday message:

> Before long, you will turn over your responsibilities to 22nd MAU. All Americans are deeply in your debt. Even as we grieve your sacrifice, we take pride in your excellence as Marines on this, the 208th Birthday of the Corps. Please know we are thinking of you and look forward to welcoming you home — Our Marines.
> "Semper Fidelis,"
> Ronald Reagan

On the same day, a delegation of the Investigations Subcommittee of the House Armed Services Committee arrived in Beirut to examine the bombing site and take testimony from numerous witnesses. Hearings were conducted for two days aboard the *Iwo Jima*. As a result of an urgent request by General Kelley upon his return, Secretary of Defense Weinberger convened on November 7 the Department of Defense Commission on Beirut International Airport Terrorist Act, October 23, 1983. Charged with conducting an independent inquiry into the circumstances surrounding the terrorist act, this commission eventually took the name of its chairman, Adm. Robert L. J. Long, USN (Ret.). During the commission's visit to Beirut, I escorted Admiral Long and members of his staff to meet with Ambassador Bartholomew, General Tannous, and all of the MNF commanders. They conducted interviews and took testimony in Beirut and later in Rota, Spain, during our return voyage home.

On November 19, with the completion of the backload of all our equipment and personnel, I officially passed command and control of the U.S. contingent of the Multinational Force, Beirut, to an old friend, Brig. Gen. Jim Joy, commanding general of the 22nd MAU. At noon, the *Iwo Jima* and the *Portland* left Lebanon to join the already departed *El Paso*, *Austin*, and *Harlan County* heading toward home. In my final situation report, I stated, "24 MAU stands relieved as Landing Force, Sixth Fleet 2-83 and U.S. Contingent to the MNF, Beirut, Lebanon. Proceeding on duties as assigned. Able to respond to any combat mission. Able to respond as Marines."

On November 29, while crossing the Atlantic and prior to our arrival at Morehead City, North Carolina, the 24th MAU received the following message from Commandant Kelley:

1. Courage, sacrifice, and heroism characterized the Lebanon tour of 24 MAU. Under the most trying and difficult conditions, each unit's performance shines as a witness to the world that Americans stood firm in the defense of peace and freedom.
2. The exemplary bravery of the MAU Marines, Sailors, and Soldiers has been indelibly written on the pages of American history. No one—standing or fallen—served in vain. Every man's devotion to duty will continue to be an inspiration to all who desire to live as free men.
3. On behalf of a grateful nation, I thank God for men like you in the service of this country.

On December 7, the 24th MAU arrived at Morehead City to an enthusiastic welcome from families, friends, bands, and the national media. Two days later on the parade field at Camp Lejeune, the 24th MAU passed in review before the commandant of the Marine Corps, who welcomed us home with the following remarks:

When I met the first flight of your fallen comrades as they arrived at Dover, Delaware, after the mass murder of 23 October, I asked the question—Lord, where do we get such men? As you stand here today, I ask the same question. Where do we get such men of courage—such men of dedication—such men of patriotism—such men of pride? The simple answer is that we get them from every clime and place—from every race—from every creed—and from every color. But each of you has one thing in common—you are a Marine or that special brand of Navy man who serves alongside Marines.

Two days ago, an entire nation opened its heart in grateful recognition of your safe return.

You gallant Marines and Sailors of the 24th have earned your rightful place in the glorious history of our Corps. You can stand tall and proud in the knowledge that you have selflessly given of yourselves in the service of your country, your Corps, and of free men everywhere.

In the joy and emotion of your safe return, let none of us forget those brave Marines and sailors who made the supreme sacrifice—or forget the wife who will never again see her husband—the child who will never see its father—or the parents who will never see their son. They, too, have made the supreme sacrifice!

By the authority given to me this day by the Secretary of the Navy, I hereby recognize your significant contributions, under conditions of great adversity, by authorizing each of you to wear the Combat Action Ribbon.

You and your precious families—those loved ones who have participated in a lonely and anxious vigil these past months—have my deepest and sincerest respect and admiration. God bless you!

Two hours later, in a private meeting with Generals Miller and Gray, I was relieved of my command.

The U.S. embassy in Beirut following the suicide bombing of April 18, 1983, that killed sixty-three people, including seventeen Americans. Six CIA officers died, including the station chief, his deputy, and the CIA's national intelligence officer. It seriously affected American intelligence-gathering capabilities in the region. *USMC*

CIA Station Chief William F. Buckley, the author, and Lt. Col. Bill Beebe (his back is to the camera), executive officer of the 24th Marine Amphibious Unit. In early 1984, Hezbollah kidnapped, tortured, and murdered Buckley. *USMC*

Maj. Gen. Al Gray, commanding general of the Second Marine Division, confers with the author during his visit to Beirut in September 1983. *USMC*

Referred to in the press as the Marine barracks, the Battalion Landing Team Headquarters building at the Beirut International Airport provided protection against frequent artillery fire from Lebanon's many warring factions. *Long Commission Report*

On Sunday morning, October 23, 1983, a mushroom cloud rises from the BLT HQ. *USMC*

When the huge bomb destroyed the BLT HQ, the Marines suffered their greatest loss of life in a single day since Iwo Jima. *FBI*

Marines survey the ruins of the BLT HQ. Rescue operations lasted for seven days. *FBI*

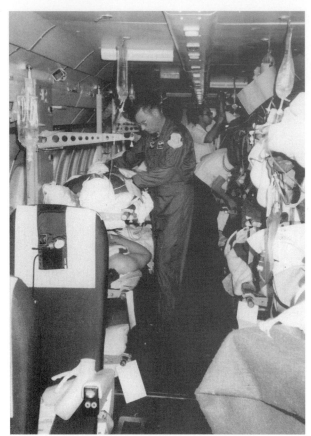

Col. Alfred Studwell, MD, USAF, attends to the wounded aboard a C-9 Nightingale en route to a U.S. military hospital in West Germany. Prompt medical care was credited for saving many lives. *Joe Bunker*

Left to right: The author, Vice President George H. W. Bush, and Marine commandant Gen. P. X. Kelley at the bombing site. *USMC*

Gen. Ibrahim Tannous, commander of the Lebanese Armed Forces; the author; Vice President Bush; and Commandant Kelley. When he saw the smoke rising from the airport, Tannous had exclaimed, "God willing, I hope it's not the Marines!" *USMC*

The author speaks at a memorial service in Beirut twelve days after the bombing. *USMC*

Hezbollah terrorist Imad Fayez Mugniyah, whose bloody résumé included not only the Marine barracks bombing but those of the U.S. embassy, the French paratroopers' headquarters, and many other atrocities. He met his fate in a car bombing in 2008. *AP*

Mastafa Mohammad Najjar was the senior commander of the Islamic Revolutionary Guard Corps in Lebanon's Bekaa Valley in 1983. This unit provided security, planning, training, and operational support for Hezbollah's suicide bombings against the French paratroopers and the U.S. Marines. Najjar was named Iran's defense minister in 2005. *AP*

─9─

Warriors' Compassion

BEFORE DISCUSSING THE BOMBING investigations, I should describe one of the most striking performances during the aftermath of the attack, one that occurred thousands of miles from the Beirut scene. The difficult weeks that followed showed Maj. Gen. Al Gray's ability to assume an extraordinary leadership role when unexpected challenges were thrust upon his shoulders. Ironically, after a lifetime of preparation for command in combat, one of his most memorable accomplishments was not on the battlefield but in a garrison setting, helping some of his Marines far from home.

It was 6:22 a.m. in Beirut and just past midnight at Camp Lejeune, North Carolina, when the commanding general of the Second Marine Division received a frantic phone call, his first notification that a serious incident had happened in Beirut. It was approximately ten minutes after the explosion.

Here the special bond of trust between General Gray and his juniors came into play. The call—an urgent, unofficial early alert—came from Marine Forces Atlantic in Norfolk, Virginia. The staff duty officer, one of Gray's admirers and a former reconnaissance platoon commander, was Maj. Joe Crockett. A holder of the Navy Cross, Crockett knew Gray needed to be notified of the bombing as quickly as possible, so without any authority to do so, he had called. With a heavy heart, he reported, "It doesn't look good. Looks like maybe thirty or forty have been killed." Little did General Gray understand that, at the moment of that phone call, he was soon to be completely consumed in an epic national tragedy. Gray told his wife, Jan, "We have a bad problem in Lebanon. I'm going in to division headquarters." Next, Gray began to think through the initial preparations for assembling numerous casualty notification teams. Gray later reflected that his arrival at headquarters at 2:00 a.m. and his work during the following four hours were critical to his overall plan to react to the tragedy.

When the chain of command was stressed by the difficulties of first reporting and then having to describe this major tragedy, the structure's complexity caused innumerable communications problems. In its simplest terms, command authority flows from the president to the secretary of defense, through the Joint Chiefs of Staff to the commander in chief of U.S. Forces Europe (USCINCEUR). However, exacerbating the reporting process was the fact that the bombing incident occurred on a Sunday morning and far from the headquarters of the commander in chief, Europe (CINCEUR), which at that time was focused primarily on NATO's Soviet Bloc threat from the East. Low on CINCEUR's surveillance and attention level would have been the deployment of a small force at the outer limits of the CINC's territorial responsibilities. The volume of communications traffic through this extensive chain of command—which dealt with the security status, casualties, location of wounded, identification of the dead, and the requirement for absolute accuracy—made the reporting process complicated and cumbersome. These and other diverse considerations led to the near-total confusion of command and control procedures to effectively manage the massive movement of casualties back to the States. In discussing this multilayered command, the Long Commission's report cited that all commanders within the entire operational chain of command were partially at fault for not identifying the increasing terrorist threats to the MNF positioned in Beirut (see fig. 1).

Gray waited until official word came down the chain of command before alerting his division staff officers to return to the headquarters building. It would take about four more hours before it reached his division. In the meantime, he spoke to Lt. Gen. John Miller, his immediate force commander in Norfolk, and began receiving the first fragmentary details on the bombing. The reports on casualties continued to grow. With several additional calls from General Miller, Gray gained a fair idea of the gravity of the Beirut explosion. At five o'clock, a local news release went out, and at six o'clock, the duty officer exercised the "frost call," or an alert to key personnel. By this time, Gray had assessed the tragedy and directed that a casualty assistance center be activated.

FIG 1. Chain of Command. *USMC Archives*

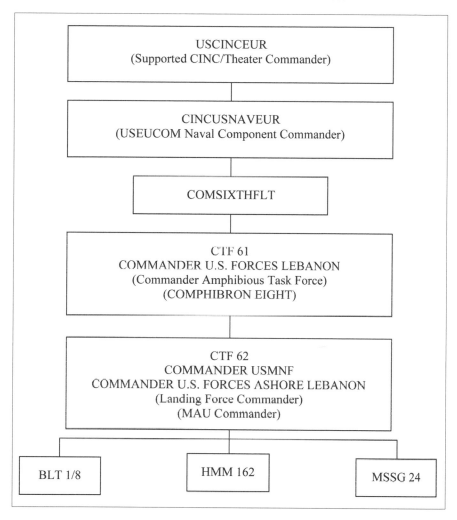

Most Americans vividly remember the bombing. However, few appreciate the extraordinary humanitarian outpouring, caring, and casualty assistance that immediately began for the families of the dead and wounded. What is so often lost at the higher levels of command in an emergency situation is who the survivors are and how they are fairing. Tragically, the preeminent issue is usually the care of the wounded and dead. Dealing with the families has to be delayed in order to focus on higher priorities. It would be a stressful, chaotic period.

When the first report of the bombing reached Headquarters Marine Corps in Arlington, Virginia, key personnel were assembled. During the immediate hours that followed, there was no definitive casualty information. The initial reports sent to the States indicated the Battalion Landing Team's headquarters element was decimated and no longer an effective command element. Information was sketchy at best; no senior leaders could be located, and their survival was thus in doubt. However, in sharp contrast, through the use of modern satellite communication technologies, the international news media became the primary source of information from the bombing scene. The first video coverage began to sweep across American television screens, depicting the worst fears. The White House issued its first Situation Report (see appendix C).

On Capitol Hill, congressional public affairs staffers and military liaison officers were besieged with inquiries, which obviously could not be answered accurately or in a timely fashion. By the end of the day, a huge collection of international media was at Camp Lejeune and actually camped on the lawn in front of the division headquarters. Rumors about the bombing rippled through Camp Lejeune, the homes of hundreds of families in and around it, and the adjacent military bases. Questions as to the status and welfare of Marines, soldiers, and sailors saturated the base's limited telephone system. The local commanders of other small detachments assigned to the BLT and dependent wives, parents, and relatives all pleaded for answers.

Meanwhile, the Marine Corps' public affairs hotline number was publicized over the radio and on national television news programs. The country woke up to news of the bombing, and its reaction was an overwhelming state of shock. The flood of telephone calls far exceeded the available lines to properly handle the inquiries, generating further confusion across the country. Many concerned callers with sons and relatives in the 24th MAU waited twelve to fifteen hours before getting through on the hotline. At the Second Marine Division, the number of calls from distraught wives and parents was equally heavy as they sought answers on the status of individuals. The division's representatives could do nothing except to say they were "trying to get more information." It was a lose-lose situation for everyone.

Back at Camp Lejeune, Gray initially ordered fifty officers and senior staff NCOs and then fifty more to serve casualty assistance duties. They were assembled and given a quick course on proper procedures. With these initial decisions made, Gray's staff began to function with its new mission. True to his character, he left his division headquarters at one point and went outside to be alone for a few moments. As he later reflected, he went for a walk, had a chew of Red Man tobacco, and figured out what else needed to be done.

He put the division staff on a twelve-hours-on and twelve-hours-off schedule, and in spite of the enormity of the bombing, he ordered that all units continue their scheduling training. Amid all this activity, Gray was alerted that the 22nd MAU, which had just deployed for the Mediterranean area, was ordered by the National Command Authority (NCA) to be diverted to the Caribbean island of Grenada, where it would oust a communist-supported group of rebels that had taken over the island's government. (Within several days, the island was secured, and the Marine units re-embarked onto their amphibious ships and began their twelve-day movement into the eastern Mediterranean area.) Additionally, there was also an immediate need to deploy more Marine units to Beirut to replace the devastated 1st Battalion, 8th Marines. The Air Alert Force's BLT Headquarters (Command Element) mounted out along with Echo Company to provide extra security around the demolished bombing site.

More than twenty-four hours would pass before the first Beirut casualty list from the 24th MAU arrived at HQMC; however, this report included the names of only eighteen dead and sixty-three wounded. Hundreds were still unaccounted for, so this partial report was disappointing to everyone. Television crews projected steady coverage of the disaster around the world. This real-time coverage was saturated with pictures of dead and wounded Marines. Unfortunately, those reports only aggravated and heightened the tension throughout the United States and particularly at General Gray's division headquarters. Questions arose across the country, particularly from dependents and families, as to why the Marine Corps was not providing more timely information. Yet nothing could be done until accurate accountability information on each individual could be established.

Brigadier General Joy recalled, "As the flow of wounded and dead began returning to the United States, it became even more complicated. Every individual in the 24th MAU had been accounted for. If he was alive, fine. If he was wounded, where was he? Was he aboard a ship? Was he in a hospital in Lebanon, or in an American hospital in Germany? Or was he already in the States? If so, where in the States?" The division was desperate for more accurate and timely information on its Marines and sailors, but little was forthcoming in a timely manner. "We needed information for the families—to keep them advised as to what was going on."[1] Hundreds of families had to be dealt with in a professional and wholly compassionate manner.

By noon on the twenty-fifth, the first direct telephone contacts were made between HQMC and the shattered 24th MAU Headquarters. We commanders on the scene believed that all the medical, dental, and service records had been destroyed in the explosion, records that were absolutely critical to identifying the dead. Without such basic documentation, HQMC and the Second Division's personnel officers sought any other available medical or dental records that might be located in the States.

Another two days passed before the BLT's medical and dental records were uncovered in the building's wreckage. Fortunately, most of these records had survived the blast; however, as mentioned earlier, almost all the service record books on individual Marines and sailors had been destroyed. Each service record book contained an emergency data page that listed the next of kin to be notified in case of injury or death. When the news of the missing service record books reached Camp Lejeune, a computer-generated personnel roster and a record of emergency data for everyone on the 24th MAU's rolls were produced by the Second Division and dispatched to Lebanon to facilitate personnel accountability. Adding to the lack of detailed information available from the Marine Corps, CNN television continued showing vivid pictures of the chaotic situation in Lebanon as the dead soldiers, sailors, and Marines were carried from the collapsed building. For the first time, satellite technology enabled live television to bring a terrorist bombing halfway around the world into America's homes.

On the scene in Lebanon, as a means to identify the injured and missing, the 24th MAU began a 100 percent identification of every American assigned to the U.S. Multinational Force. This enforcement was difficult because the Marines and sailors had to be able to move freely to and from the ships and into the BIA encampments. "Welfare reports" confirming the well-being of every survivor began to arrive at HQMC the evening of October 26. By late afternoon on the twenty-eighth, seven messages containing the names of casualties had been received from the MAU. Personnel accountability, a sacred command responsibility, was belatedly taking form.

Inaccurate and incomplete information kept the scope of the disaster vague. It had taken fifty-two hours before a list of 192 missing personnel that the 24th MAU transmitted went up the lengthy and cumbersome chains of command and before any reports finally reached HQMC. After approximately seventy-two hours had elapsed since the bombing, the external pressures for information were considerable. Later in the day, the initial list was reduced to 170 missing. This adjustment also caused problems in identifying who was still on the list and who had been removed.

At Camp Lejeune, three separate major commands had been quickly organized into a mutually supporting team to handle the massive casualty assistance program. General Gray had been the driving force to establish a common disaster control center and prepare for the difficult task of notifying local families on the status of their killed or wounded Marines.

That same week, the Second Division's biannual inspection by the HQMC inspector general (IG) was scheduled. The IG called General Gray and offered to postpone or cancel the weeklong event, but Gray elected to proceed.

Early on October 24, General and Mrs. Gray visited the newly organized casualty coordination center to see how it was prepared for the anticipated large number of casualties. Gray had envisioned (correctly) a much larger base of operations and support effort. Within hours of his inspection, all kinds of additional support began to materialize. More phones were installed, a fleet of commercial vehicles was assigned for casualty notification calls, and the first group of officers, designated for the casualty calls, appeared in full dress uniforms, ready for their difficult missions ahead.

Gray's first priority was to ensure that everything would be in place to provide the local next-of-kin rapid notification and follow-up assistance once confirmed casualty reports began to flow. This vital information was updated to pass on to the NOK who were located outside the local area. His concern was that once correct and verified information became available about a deceased or wounded serviceman, the officers should be prepared to immediately notify the NOK and provide on-scene follow-up assistance wherever the NOK may be located. His second priority (but equally as important as the first) was to get an accurate situation report on the total casualty statistics. As the casualty coordination center began to function, the division's conference room was turned into an information-gathering center. The conference room walls soon became covered with charts displaying the gruesome toll of the suicide terrorist bombing.

Gray seemed to be everywhere at the same time as he responded personally to worried families and relatives across the nation. An additional thirty officers and all available chaplains were assembled in a central barracks area. They were directed to bring their dress uniforms and be prepared to remain until all casualty notifications were completed. Once a name was received through the division's casualty coordination center, an officer was assigned that particular casualty, and he, along with a chaplain, was directed to deliver the official notification to the family at the appropriate time. The officer would then stay with the family through its personal crisis. In the case of a death, the officer would be assigned with the family until released by the casualty coordination center, which in most cases was not until all death benefits were taken care of and/or the family was relocated.

Each casualty assistance officer was directed to provide all possible assistance to his assigned family. General Gray repeatedly met with these officers to stress the need for their deepest understanding of the bereavement every family was experiencing. To ensure that every family received the attention General Gray expected, his rapidly expanding computer database produced a report that showed, on a single sheet of paper, specific information on every next of kin located throughout the country. This report contained detailed information on each casualty, the addresses and phone numbers of his primary and secondary NOK, the date and place of interment, the status of death benefits processing, other personal data, a brief summary of how the primary NOK was doing, and finally any special needs or requests the NOK may have expressed.

Next, General Gray set up a program so that either he or another senior officer representing the Second Marine Division went to every funeral throughout the nation. Gray personally attended more than 140 funerals while he and Mrs. Gray served as the commandant's special representatives. The Grays were present to express the Marine Corps' sympathy for the loss of each family's sailor or Marine. Every funeral was a sad and highly emotional experience, as the families poured out their shock and grief to the Marines attending that service.

Additionally, Gray spent hours each day on the telephone. He was completely committed to caring for his Marines, his sailors, and their families. To the best of his ability, he presented a stalwart leadership image in a time of confusion and misunderstanding. The circumstances that led up to the bombing tragedy would be deeply ingrained in General Gray's mind forever. He began to take steps to ensure such an event would never happen again to the Corps. And as fortuitous circumstances would later transpire, this determination to better prepare Marines to operate in a rapidly changing world would become his focused mission as the Marine Corps' twenty-ninth commandant.

On October 29, Americans watched on television as the first remains arrived at Dover Air Force Base. During the next eleven days, the 241 soldiers, sailors, and Marines killed in the Beirut suicide bombing were brought home. The last three arrived in the States on November 10, the Marine Corps' 208th birthday. But at Camp Lejeune, there would be no celebration to commemorate the birthday. There was too much pain. The Marines' focus remained on burying the dead and caring for the bereaved families.

On November 4, the president of the United States and Mrs. Ronald Reagan visited Camp Lejeune for a solemn and emotional memorial service. It was held in a small outdoor amphitheater overlooking New River Inlet, behind the Second Marine Division Headquarters. Honoring all who lost their lives in the terrorist attack, it was a gut-wrenching and profoundly emotional scene captured on television by the national news media. Wives, fathers, mothers, children, grandparents, and relatives from all stations of life who had journeyed to share a painful moment with other strangers were now bound together forever.

Following the memorial service, General Gray sent a letter to all the next of kin, describing the service and offering his continuing assistance. The letter contained several documents: a videotape of the service, the memorial service program, a copy of the signed presidential proclamation directing the flag be flown at half mast, and a copy of a magazine called *The Word*, which featured a tasteful pictorial on the members of the 1st Battalion, 8th Marines and the bombing. Months later, the forty-five miles of highway from Camp Lejeune to Morehead City would be designated Freedom's Way, and 241 individual trees were planted to memorialize every American serviceman lost in the Beirut bombing.

Every year since 1983, a Beirut memorial service is conducted at Camp Lejeune on October 23. More than two decades have passed, but General Gray has kept in touch with many of the families. In a long and distinguished career, his leadership and compassion during that period will remain among his finest hours.

The personal assistance and comfort he provided to the Beirut bombing victims, survivors, and families continue to this day. He has given a new dimension to our Corps' motto of Semper Fidelis.

■

The tragic terrorist bombing also generated a global response, reflecting the support and sympathies of countless friends and allies. On November 9, 1983, Gen. P. X. Kelley sent me a message that highlighted these feelings:

Subject: Outpouring of Concern for Lebanon Marines

1. Since the tragic events of 23 October there has been an outpouring of concern from people and organizations throughout the world for you. From small towns in middle America to the far corners of the world, I have received hundreds of letters and telegrams from sympathetic and appreciative individuals and organizations expressing their heartfelt concern for Marines and Sailors of 24th MAU and your families and their deep appreciation for your sacrifices and your continued dedication to duty.

2. The tremendous volume of letters and telegrams received precludes presenting extracts from even a fraction of them; however, I have chosen a few salient ones that I felt were worthy of passing on.

   A. From the Commandant General Royal Marines, "All Royal Marines grieve with you over your losses in Beirut and your families are very much in our minds."

   B. From Northside High School, Memphis TN, "Northside Cougars care for our Marines in Beirut. . . . We send our love and prayers."

   C. From a former Marine in Alabama, "Want you to know that we support you and all your endeavors. We want you to know that if we are not with you in body, we are with you in spirit."

   D. From the Swiss Military Attaché, "I'm shocked by this terrible act of violence and would like to express to you my condolences."

   E. From Lt. Gen. Park Hee Jae, Commandant of the Korean Marine Corps, "ROK Marines offer their condolences to those U.S. Marines who sacrificed their lives for peace and freedom."

   F. From the Mayor of St. Petersburg Beach, FL, "The city government and its employees wish to extend their deepest sympathies for the loss of American lives in Beirut."

G. From the Commanding Officer, 1stBn, Royal Welch Fusiliers, "Our deepest commiserations on your recent losses. . . ."

H. From a young woman in Milwaukee, WI, "May God watch over all of you."

3. Similar messages were received from the German Navy, the Brazilian Marine Corps, NATO, Retired Dutch Marines, and a host of other sources throughout the United States and around the world. It is most heartening to know that so many people outside our Corps care so much for our Marines and Sailors and understand and appreciate the difficult and demanding mission that has been given to 24th MAU.

4. As always, you and your brave men are in my thoughts and prayers. God bless you and Semper Fidelis!

■

Most of the young men who sacrificed their lives in Beirut were based out of Camp Lejeune and called the adjacent town, Jacksonville, home. They were known as fathers, neighbors, fellow church members, and Little League baseball and soccer coaches. The Jacksonville community, which reflects the indomitable American spirit and values, was particularly stunned by the loss of these men. On the afternoon of this tragic bombing, a commission met to seek permission to plant memorial trees along Lejeune Boulevard, the main traffic artery joining Jacksonville and Camp Lejeune, to honor the fallen patriots. This action saw an immediate response, and funds began arriving to support the project. It became the birth of the Beirut Memorial.

Following the tree dedication, contributions continued to come in, and the commission sought to erect a simple marker to depict the history and significance of the trees. Camp Lejeune offered the commission four and a half acres of highly visible land on Lejeune Boulevard, which expanded the commission's original vision of the memorial's final form. Through the efforts and generosity of many individuals, businesses, organizations, government bodies, churches, schools, and families, both locally and from far away places, the commission raised a total of $244,000. Featuring a statue of a lone Marine keeping vigil over his fellow comrades, the memorial was dedicated on October 23, 1986, with approximately two thousand people in attendance.

In 1992, a group of Beirut veterans wanted to establish a fraternal organization dedicated to keeping the memories alive of those comrades who had made the supreme sacrifice. Led by Maj. Bob Jordan, the Beirut Veterans of America (BVA) was founded, and they adopted as their motto "The First Duty Is to Remember." Membership is open to military members who served in Lebanon dating back to the 1958 mission. It is going strong with more than a thousand members. BVA sends out a quarterly newsletter called *Root Scoop*, which keeps the Beirut family abreast of everyone's news, and has published a directory to facilitate the members and families maintaining contact.

Each year, in the days surrounding October 23, hundreds gather at the Beirut Memorial Remembrance for camaraderie and renewing friendships. The remembrance is dedicated to the history of the peacekeepers who served our nation so valiantly in Lebanon, where the war on terrorism began. Each year's event includes a traditional candlelight vigil at 6:00 a.m. at the foot of the Beirut Memorial, where each name, etched on the marble wall, is read aloud by veterans and family members. Later, a more formal ceremony includes military music, pageantry, and commemorative comments by key military and community leaders. A wreath is laid at the foot of the statue of the lone Marine standing perpetual guard at the site.

The Marine Corps Scholarship Fund (MCSF) is a nonprofit, nonpartisan organization that assists the Marine Corps family in many areas. Since its founding in 1962, it has provided more than twenty thousand scholarships valued at more than $31 million, with particular attention given to children whose parent was killed or wounded in action. The foundation's slogan is "Honoring Marines by Educating Their Children."

The fund awarded more than $1.1 million in education bonds to the child of every American serviceman killed in the attack: three children from the U.S. Army, eighty from the Marines, and nineteen from the U.S. Navy. That these bonds were awarded regardless of the father's branch of service honors *all* members of the peacekeeping team who sacrificed their lives so their children can live in a better world. What better tribute could be provided in remembrance of their fathers than offering financial assistance for these dependents' higher education. Through the years, it has been heartening to watch and see the children of the fallen peacekeepers grow into responsible young adults.

■

The strength, courage, and quiet determination displayed by the families and friends of those peacekeepers who died in the service of our country have been inspirational to all of us who have come to know and love them. There are countless stories of how they picked up the pieces, helped one another, and carried on to raise their children and honor the memory of their lost husbands, sons, brothers, and friends. Many years later, my response to General Kelley's question—"Where do we get such men?"—remains the same: look no further than their families and friends.

The Marine Corps is a family, a close family. The devastating terrorist suicide bombing on October 23, 1983, demanded fast decisions and immediate actions for security, replacement forces to reconstitute the BLT, notification to higher headquarters, and most important, organization of the rescue operation. As previously detailed, Commandant Kelley's exceptional leadership, personal care, and dedication to the USMNF as President Reagan's personal representative in Beirut during these dark days was above and beyond what I expected. He paid respect to those who sacrificed their lives, treated the wounded with compassion, and gave unmitigated support to the rescue teams and those who continued to carry out the mission. His leadership and support never wavered throughout the investigations and the aftermath.

To be honest, I would have understood if General Kelley, along with Lieutenant General Miller and Major General Gray, had backed away from their personal support of the 24th MAU and the families. Others could perform the countless tasks in caring for them and in providing personal assistance. The opposite happened. The Corps' senior leadership, led by the commandant himself, displayed a personal commitment and involvement with the families that continue today. For this dedication, they have earned the everlasting respect and hearts of the 24th MAU and their families.

_10_

Investigations

BEING RELIEVED OF MY COMMAND so abruptly upon our return to the States on December 7 caused a disquieting stir not only within the 24th MAU but also the Second Marine Division. Those few who did call me asked what was happening. Why so fast? What was the reason given? The suddenness with which it happened, without any public information or explanation, fed the rumor mill. It inferred that it was a relief for cause, which in itself suggests dereliction of duty. The pall hanging over Camp Lejeune at this time only added to my sense of remorse. My emotions were on autopilot.

I had figured my relief was coming. The partisan tone of the investigations and the sheer immensity of the suicide attack and massive casualties signaled to me that I would not retain my command for a second float. The reality was that the 24th MAU had a rapid turnaround, so the lock-on phase and workup for returning to the Mediterranean were short. As a principal witness in the ongoing investigations, which would require me to testify at congressional hearings, my time and attention to my duties would naturally be divided. Politics dominated the environment, and I was radioactive in some circles. The House Armed Services Committee investigation and Long Commission investigation would be released before the end of the year. The 24th MAU had hard training milestones to be met, and they conflicted with my commitments.

Lieutenant General Miller and Major General Gray heard the rumbles shortly after the announcement of my relief and, I believe, were caught off guard by the misunderstandings and the intention of their decision. To explain its rationale, they called together all officers of the 24th MAU and the Second Division. General Miller noted that I had been through a stressful ordeal and needed a break. He explained the short turnaround for the 24th MAU along with my extensive commitments, including congressional testimony, did not allow my participation in the critical workup phase for the next deployment. General Miller apologized for the misunderstanding and pointedly reinforced that my relief of command was not for cause. I appreciated his gesture.

THE LONG COMMISSION'S REPORT

Under the auspices of the Department of Defense, the Long Commission focused on key areas: the mission, the rules of engagement, the chain of command's responsiveness, the intelligence support, the command responsibility for pre-attack security and postattack security, the adequacy of procedures for handling casualties, and the military response to terrorism. The commission presented its findings, conclusions, and recommendations to Secretary Weinberger on December 20, 1983.

THE MILITARY MISSION

The commission concluded that the presence mission was not interpreted the same way by all levels of the chain of command. Also, the chain of command should have recognized the perceptual differences regarding that mission, including the supposed responsibility of the U.S. Multinational Force for the security of Beirut International Airport, and should have corrected them.

The commission discussed in detail that the security of the USMNF was dependent on four basic conditions: it would operate in a relatively benign environment, the Lebanese Army would provide security in areas where the MNF operated, the mission would be of limited duration, and the MNF would be evacuated in the event of attack.

The commission noted that as the political and military situation evolved, three factors adversely impacted those conditions. First, the mission required that the USMNF be perceived as neutral by the Lebanese confessional factions, but the tasks assigned to the MNF included direct fire support to the LAF. Next, Iran and Syria had a deep-seated hostility toward the United States plus the capability to advance their own political interests through terrorism. Then, the diplomatic efforts to secure the withdrawal of all foreign forces from Lebanon faltered. The commission noted that these factors resulted in the continued erosion of the U.S. Multinational Force's security.

From my viewpoint, the security of BIA as a responsibility of the U.S. Marine commander was never in any mission tasking. This point was clear to everyone I spoke with or briefed. The Marine presence enhanced the Lebanese Army's responsibility of providing security at the airport, but providing security for the BIA was never a mission of the USMNF. There was certainly no confusion on this issue from Admiral Martin (COMSIXTHFLT) down through the chain of command.

The commission also noted that the security environment had changed significantly by late summer 1983. Furthermore, "appropriate guidance and modifications of tasking should have been provided to the USMNF to enable it to cope effectively with the increasingly hostile environment. The Commission could find no evidence that such guidance was, in fact, provided."

Although there was unanimous consent throughout the chain of command that the environment had changed, all of us had taken positive and proactive steps to improve the security posture. Commodore Rick France, the fellow MNF commanders, Admiral Martin, and others worked tirelessly to cope with the dynamic changes. Dialogue was brisk, intense, and continuous.

The mission, however, remained unchanged, since it was considered still valid and so stated by higher authority. Further, the rules of engagement remained in consonance with the mission; specifically, it centered on self-defense only. During this period, adjusted guidance and modifications were made within these parameters to enhance our security posture. As an example of personal involvement, Admiral Martin visited Beirut on at least ten different occasions to supervise firsthand the changes being made to advance our overall security.

THE RULES OF ENGAGEMENT IMPLEMENTATION

The commission "viewed with concern the fact that there were two different sets of ROE's being used by the USMNF . . . after the U.S. Embassy bombing on April 18, 1983." It concluded that this contributed to a mind-set that detracted from the USMNF's readiness to respond to the terrorist attack on October 23, 1983.

During testimony, it was pointed out to the commission that the mission for the USMNF *elsewhere* in Beirut did not change when U.S. embassy security became a USMNF responsibility. The special situation at the embassy, however, required more stringent ROEs. The external security role at the embassy required providing security to a nonorganic establishment as opposed to our own positions. Because of this mission modification, separate ROEs were required at the U.S.-British embassy. Consequently, a modified ROE (Blue Card) was put into effect at the embassy while there was no change (White Card) at other USMNF positions. It was considered that the criteria of self-defense, always contained in the ROE specified by the White Card, remained adequate.

All sentries at BIA had self-defense ROEs and additional guidance and instructions for searching vehicles and passengers entering the Marine compound through our controlled checkpoints. Sentries on duty at the BLT Headquarters were not at a compound entrance. Therefore, physically breaching a barrier was the terrorist's only access option. All guards at these interior posts understood that breaching a barrier was sufficient to act in self-defense at their USMNF positions. This fact was substantiated when the sentries fired on the suicide truck on October 23 as it broke the barrier. External three-tiered concertina wire fencing with engineer stakes was considered to be sufficient against anticipated threats—namely, car bombs and infiltrators—to permit time for effective engagement. The White Card did not require a call for local forces to assist in all defense efforts at the expense of timely engagement. Self-defense was always authorized.

The Chain of Command and Exercise of Command Responsibility

The commission concluded "that USCINCEUR, CINCUSNAVEUR [commander in chief, U.S. Naval Forces, Europe], COMSIXTHFLT, and CTF 61 did not initiate actions to effectively ensure the security of the USMNF in light of the deteriorating political/military situation in Lebanon."

Members of the commission stated that they were fully aware that the entire chain of command was heavily involved with, and supportive of, the USMNF. The crux of their criticism centered on the fact that the overall security then in place, and all elements of supervision by the chain of command, were ineffective in preventing a nineteen-ton truck laden with high explosives from breaching the Marine compound's perimeter and from subsequently detonating a bomb that we now know was equivalent to more than twenty thousand pounds of TNT. A suicidal driver using a large truck to detonate an immense bomb was unprecedented and, therefore, not anticipated.

The conclusion that the chain of command did not initiate actions to effectively ensure the USMNF's security was unsubstantiated. Representatives from all levels toured USMNF positions at the airport and other locations, received detailed briefings on the mission and threats, and were updated on defensive measures. Security measures for a broad range of threats were taken in a timely manner.

Contrary to the commission's report, the evidence was clear that Commodore Rick France and I responded properly and promptly to the worsening threats during the summer and fall of 1983. We kept our senior officers informed and did not hesitate to voice our concerns, to take action where called for, or to act according to the full extent of their instructions.

On October 20, one day after I barely missed being the victim of a car bomb and three days before the suicide bombing, I sent a personal message to Admiral Martin that reflected my concerns. In this update, I pointed out that while an attack could not be predicted, I had taken precautions to maximize our alert posture. This assessment reflected the continuous review of security and our posture, and characterized the command's oversight function.

From my perspective, security measures had been discussed at length within the chain of command and actions were taken to mitigate the known threats. The European Command maintained a EUCOM Liaison Team within the U.S. embassy that served as the U.S. military representative on the Multinational Force Coordinating Committee. My executive officer usually attended these meetings, and the EUCOM team reported the proceedings directly to EUCOM via their own radio net. One could say the team members were EUCOM's eyes on the scene and were intimately familiar with mission operations in Beirut. The deployment of the Field Artillery School's Target Acquisition Battery and the tactical aerial reconnaissance pod system, and the cancellation of patrols as hostilities increased are all examples of EUCOM's direct guidance and concern for the USMNF's security.

Vice Admiral Martin personally visited Rick France and me in Beirut numerous times during our tenure. He often stayed several days to be updated and to oversee defensive initiatives taken against known threats. Admiral Martin was straightforward and aggressive in stating his guidance to Rick and me. His staff's personnel were also frequent visitors, particularly the Sixth Fleet Marine Officer Colonel Pat Cacace, who spent more than a month in Beirut closely observing and providing on-scene guidance to area commanders. Additionally, Admiral Martin gave frequent direction to Commodore France and me via our secure voice communications net.

Vice Adm. M. Staser Holcomb, deputy CINCUSNAVEUR, visited Beirut on July 6, 1983, and implemented a requirement for a weekly commander's summary message to improve information available to all staffs within the chain of command. This requirement was generated by his criticism of the presence of higher command liaison representatives in the Beirut area. I suspect he had Brig. Gen. Carl Stiner in mind since Stiner had been Gen. John Vessey's representative on Ambassador Robert MacFarlane's staff and had sent daily SITREPS directly to Vessey, circumventing the chain of command.

Both Rick France and I, many times jointly, extensively briefed all visitors concerning the mission, its changing environment, anticipated threats, security, the concept of the operation, and intelligence matters. We had candid discussions with official visitors on all occasions. Advice and direction were given verbally on these occasions, and improvements were incorporated. The commission's report equated the lack of significant documented criticism to indifference. This assumption was incorrect.

Rick France and I worked closely in evaluations of all security matters. Many of the reports to higher authorities were joint messages involving implemented security improvements or modifications. Rick came ashore almost every other day during periods of increased hostilities to keep updated on the ever-changing conditions. We did not document all the myriad matters discussed and acted on, and that fact should not have been considered unusual to any observer familiar with the close relationship of CTF 61 and CTF 62. Judgments were made as conditions changed; security actions were evaluated and modified constantly through the chain of command. That extensive criticism was not leveled at the U.S. Multinational Force was not indicative of tacit approval. Instead, it showed that all inspectors were closely involved in daily assessments of security measures taken to counter the known threats.

INTELLIGENCE SUPPORT

The commission concluded that although I received a large volume of intelligence warnings concerning potential terrorist threats, I was not provided with the "actionable intelligence" necessary to defend against the broad spectrum of threats we faced. The commission further stated the human intelligence was ineffective, being neither precise nor tailored to our needs.

One could hardly argue with these conclusions. I was inundated with intelligence from numerous sources but none with any specificity. There was a paucity of U.S.-controlled HUMINT, which was not a surprise after policy decisions made in previous years when I worked at the CIA. I also was well aware that Bill Buckley was working very hard to improve the intelligence collection capabilities. It should not be forgotten that many key CIA officers working in Beirut to advance our intelligence proficiency had been killed in the U.S. embassy suicide attack six months before the BLT bombing. Most intelligence officers recognized that there was a dearth of actionable intelligence and HUMINT to gain any significant insight to the multiple threats we faced, particularly after the Israel Defense Forces' withdrawal in early September 1983.

The commission recommended that the secretary of defense establish an all-source fusion center that would tailor and focus all-source intelligence support to the U.S. military commander involved in military operations in high-threat, dynamic environments. This recommendation was implemented. It also advised the secretary of defense to take steps to establish a joint CIA-DOD examination of policy and resource alternatives and immediately improve HUMINT support to the USMNF contingent in Lebanon and other areas of potential conflict. Although some initiatives were implemented to improve our HUMINT capabilities, it remains one of our most deficient areas in collecting actionable intelligence.

COMMAND RESPONSIBILITY FOR 24TH MAU SECURITY

The commission concluded that the security measures in effect at the airport were neither commensurate with the increasing level of threat nor sufficient to preclude catastrophic losses suffered by the suicide attack. It also found that while it appeared to be an appropriate response to the indirect fire being received prior to the bombing, the decision to billet more than 350 Marines and sailors in a single structure contributed to the catastrophic loss of life.

The commission also stated that I must take full responsibility for concentrating such a large number of personnel under my command, thereby providing a lucrative target. Additionally, it said that the BLT commander should take responsibility for billeting so many members in a single structure and that both of us had modified prescribed alert procedures and emphasized safety over security, thereby degrading the MAU compound's security. Specific mention was made that sentries on the internal posts did not have loaded weapons.

The commission went on to say that although it found the MAU and BLT commanders to be at fault, it also recognized that a series of circumstances beyond our control influenced our judgment and actions relating to the USMNF's security. The commission recommended that the secretary of defense take whatever administrative or disciplinary action he deemed appropriate, citing our failure to take necessary security measures to prevent the bombing.

As a baseline for examining these issues, it has already been acknowledged that the overall security then in place and all elements of supervision by the chain of command were not effective in preventing the nineteen-ton truck laden with explosives from penetrating the BLT Headquarters building perimeter and detonating its explosive load. Further, the use of a large truck with a suicide driver was unprecedented and therefore not anticipated.

It is self-evident that fewer men would have been lost had dispersed billeting been effected. Moreover, had no lucrative target such as the BLT existed, possibly the attack would not have occurred. However, the chain of command was well aware of the rationale for using the BLT Headquarters building for secure billeting and had ample opportunity to register any disapproval. The truth is that once the heavy artillery and rocket attacks targeted the USMNF, we had no other option available. I had to move personnel into any accessible hardened sites. If I hadn't, the casualty rate would have been unacceptable and avoidable. I would have (and should have) been relieved of my command if I had *not* taken this action. We were not operating in a vacuum, and the decisions I made were a matter of record. Countless visitors were hosted in (and on top) of the BLT building, such as General Vessey, Admiral Holcomb, General Kelley, Secretary John Lehman, and Chief of Naval Operations (CNO) Adm. James D. Watkins. None voiced the opinion that the building was a poor choice.

In reviewing the rationale for selecting the BLT Headquarters building, the Long Commission's investigators determined the decision was based on several factors. BIA was an important symbol of the new Lebanese government's control and influence. Also, Israel would not agree to withdraw from BIA unless the IDF was replaced by U.S. forces. The location of the airport, away from the inner city of Beirut and the refugee camps, was favorable. It facilitated both ingress and egress for the USMNF contingent ashore and enabled the Marines to visibly assist the Lebanese government in an area of practical and symbolic importance.

The BLT Headquarters building was occupied from the outset for other reasons. The steel and reinforced-concrete construction of the BLT Headquarters building was thought to offer ideal protection from a variety of weapons. The building also afforded several military advantages that could be gained nowhere else within the BLT's assigned area of responsibility. First, it provided a good location to effectively support a BLT on a day-to-day basis. Logistic support was centrally located, thus enabling water, rations, and ammunition to be easily allocated from a single, central point to the rifle companies and attached units. The battalion aid station could be safeguarded in a clean, habitable location that could be quickly and easily reached. Motor transport assets could be parked and maintained in a common motor pool area. A reaction force could be mustered in a protected area and held in readiness for emergencies. The building also provided a safe and convenient location to brief the large delegations of U.S. congressmen, administration officials, and flag and general officers that flew in to visit Beirut. In sum, the building was an ideal location for the command post of a battalion actively engaged in fulfilling a peacekeeping and presence mission.

Second, the building was an excellent observation post. From its rooftop, a full 360-degree field of vision was available. From this elevated position, forward air controllers, naval gunfire spotters, and artillery forward observers could see into the critical Shouf Mountains area. Also from this position, observers could see and assist USMNF units in their positions at the Lebanese Science and Technical University. Further, this observation position facilitated control of helicopter landing zones that were critical to the MAU's resupply and any medical evacuation. In sum, many of the key command and control functions essential to the well-being of the USMNF as a whole could be carried out from the building. No other site within the bounds of the airport area afforded these advantages.

Last, the building provided an excellent platform upon which communications antennae could be mounted. In that the supporting ships were initially as far as three thousand to six thousand yards offshore, antenna height was a major factor in maintaining reliable communications with the supporting elements of the Sixth Fleet. Reliable communication with the ships of the carrier strike force (CTF 60) and Amphibious Squadron 8 (CTF 61) was critical to the defense and safety of not only the USMNF but also to the U.S. embassy, the U.S. ambassador's residence, the Durrafourd Building, and our allies in the MNF as well. Reliable communications meant that NGF missions could be directed at hostile artillery and rocket positions in the Shouf Mountains when they fired into the airport. Line-of-sight communications are also essential in calling for and adjusting air strikes. Moreover, such communications were key to the rapid evacuation of casualties via helicopter to secure medical facilities offshore.

In summary, the commission decided that a variety of valid political and military considerations supported the selection of this building to house the BLT Headquarters. The fact that no casualties were sustained in that building until October 23, 1983, attested to its protective capability against the incoming fire the BLT Headquarters received while it simultaneously provided the best available facility to allow the USMNF to conduct its mission.[1]

During the six months prior to the bombing, we suffered only one casualty in the vicinity of the BLT Headquarters. It is germane that during the same period, the French MNF, which utilized dispersed billeting in some thirty-six locations, had suffered more than fifty casualties and, in fact, had consolidated its billeting just prior to the suicide terrorist bombing that caused the loss of fifty-eight French paratroopers. So, precisely at the time the commission suggested we ought to have been dispersed, the French were also consolidating to improve their security. My decision to utilize the BLT Headquarters for billeting was based on all known and perceived threats prior to October 23, 1983.

As for the details of the BLT's defenses, we placed engineer stakes and concertina wire to form a physical barrier between the Marine positions and half of the airport parking lot. This obstruction kept out civilian foot traffic. The wire barrier was also deemed by our engineers to impede the progress of a car or pickup truck sufficiently to allow it to be taken under fire.

The gates within the wire barricade and between the BLT building and the adjacent parking lot were open on the morning of October 23. The standing policy was for them to be closed. The necessity for having the gates open had increased, however, with greater use of the parking lot. The specific rationale was that the parking lot was the lone emergency medevac LZ left after I closed other areas for security reasons, and it was the only physical fitness/training area (and basketball court) where the Marines could exercise. Working out was important for morale since most of the men had been under prolonged stress with no liberty and needed an outlet.

Heavy pipes had been emplaced in front of the BLT Headquarters in June and remained thereafter as part of a continuous reevaluation of the security posture around the building. Their primary purpose was to prevent vehicles from parking in front of the building and detonating car bombs. These pipes were approximately sixteen inches in diameter and forty-two feet long. Between the two pipes was a six-foot opening to allow a jeep access but not a 6 x 6 truck. This opening was blocked by a tubular steel base. Only VIP tours or the commanding officer's (i.e., Lt. Col. Larry Gerlach's) jeep had access to this area. Perpendicular to the pipe barrier was another similar section of pipe that served two purposes: to provide orderly traffic flow and to prevent a straight shot from the parking lot to the opening between the two pipes. Exceptions were made occasionally when supplies were received and required off-loading through the front entrance; however, the pipe barrier was always replaced immediately afterward. Only on one specific occasion, when the engineer's forklift was unavailable to move the pipe, was this action delayed. This situation was corrected immediately.

There were nine security posts located around the MAU/BLT command post area:

- Posts 1–3 guarded the main access road to my CP and were always manned by two Marines with magazines in their weapons.
- Posts 4 and 5 were located along the main airport road to the west. Their primary function was to prevent vehicles and persons from parking or loitering along this thoroughfare. Their main concerns were car bombs and shooting directed at the BLT area. Magazines were not in the weapons, but at the ready, because of the high volume of civilian traffic in the area.
- Posts 6 and 7 were located in the parking lot south of the BLT building and faced the main airport terminal. Their main duties were to surveil the airport parking lot and again prevent loitering of personnel and vehicles near the wire obstacles that divided the parking lot area. Magazines were not in the weapons but were at the ready.

  The rationale was that this parking lot was heavily used by civilians for parking and as a storage area for high-value items, such as trucks full of lumber.

On the weekend, this parking lot became a picnic ground and recreation area for many of the civilians from Beirut because of its secure nature. For the same reason, the preliminary reconciliation talks were also planned to be held at BIA.

Posts 6 and 7 were rebuilt during the June and July time frame and moved to provide both better surveillance and fields of fire to cover the wire barrier and a larger area for a helicopter LZ. It later became the primary medical evacuation and resupply landing zone.

- Posts 4–7 were manned with two men in accordance with the MAU Alert Condition Order. This number was modified at times depending on the operational situation. Reduced manning (one man per post) occurred only during daylight hours and never during Alert Condition One.

- Post 8 was located on the BLT's roof and was used for surveillance of the airport road and parking lot during Condition One only.

- Post 9 was located in the basement of the BLT Headquarters and guarded the tunnel entrance into the BLT building. Two men guarded this post during the hours of darkness and Condition One. One man guarded this post during daylight and normal routine (other than Condition One).

All posts were manned by Marines with their M-16 rifles. The antiarmor LAAW weapons were not issued since there was no armor threat. Two other factors were also relevant: LAAWs cannot be fired from inside a bunker owing to the back blast, and the main terminal at BIA was directly in the line of fire.

It should also be noted that during Alert Condition One, four additional posts were manned on the third floor of the BLT Headquarters. These posts were located in the floor's corners and were manned by M-60 machine gun teams from the Headquarters and Service Company. The number of machine guns employed was a function of weapons availability. However, at a minimum, the parking lot area and the airport road were covered by M-16s, if enough machine guns were not available.

POSTATTACK SECURITY

The commission found that security measures enacted since October 23, 1983, had reduced the USMNF's vulnerability to catastrophic losses. It also included in its report that the security measures implemented or planned for implementation at this time were not adequate to prevent continued attrition of the force.

The commission recognized that the current disposition of the USMNF forces may have been the best option available but stipulated that a comprehensive set of alternatives should be immediately prepared. The commission recommended that Secretary of Defense Weinberger direct the operational chain of command to develop alternative military options for accomplishing the mission while reducing the risk to the MNF.

CASUALTY HANDLING

The commission concluded that the speed with which the on-scene U.S. military personnel reacted to rescue their comrades trapped in the devastated building and render medical care "was nothing short of heroic." The rapid response by Italian and Lebanese medical personnel was also recognized as invaluable.

The commission found no evidence that any of the wounded died or received improper medical care as a result of the evacuation or casualty distribution procedures. However, it did question the evacuation of the seriously wounded to Germany rather than to the British hospital at Akrotiri, Cyprus (a transit time difference of four hours versus one hour), which the commission felt increased the risk to some patients. It also questioned the decision to land the aeromedical evacuees in Germany at Rhein-Main rather than at Ramstein, which may have increased the risk to the most seriously wounded. However, in both instances, the commission found no evidence that patients suffered any adverse medical impact.

The commission recommended that the secretary of defense direct the Joint Chiefs of Staff to review the medical plans and staffing of the operational and administrative chains of command to ensure appropriate medical support to the USMNF. It granted that the specific actions taken to treat the wounded and transport them to treatment were excellent.

Regarding identification of the dead, the commission determined that the process used was conducted very efficiently and professionally, despite complications caused by the destruction or absence of identification data. It recommended that the secretary of defense direct the creation of duplicate medical and dental records and ensure that fingerprint files for all military personnel were available. It also recommended the development of state-of-the-art identification tags.

MILITARY RESPONSE TO TERRORISM

The commission stated that the bombing was a terrorist act sponsored by sovereign states or organized political entities for the purpose of defeating U.S. objectives in Lebanon. It posited that international terrorist acts endemic to the Middle East were indicative of an alarming worldwide phenomenon that posed an increasing threat to U.S. personnel and facilities. It stated that state-sponsored terrorism was part of the spectrum of warfare and required an active national policy to deter attacks and reduce effectiveness. The commission recommended that the secretary of defense direct the JCS to develop a broad range of military responses to terrorism, along with political and diplomatic actions by the National Security Council.

The commission also concluded that the USMNF was not trained, organized, or supported to deal effectively with the terrorist threat in Lebanon and stated much needed to be done to prepare U.S. military forces to defend against and to counter terrorism. It advised the secretary of defense to direct the development of the necessary counterterrorism doctrine, planning, organization, force structure, education, and training.

In response to the Long Commission's report, Secretary of Defense Weinberger signed several memorandums addressed individually to the secretaries of the army and the navy, the assistant secretary of defense for international security affairs, the deputy undersecretary of defense for policy, and the chairman of the JCS. Each addressee was referred to the portion of the report that came under his purview and was requested to report to Secretary Weinberger on actions being taken to correct deficiencies or to implement the recommendations made by Admiral Long and his staff. The service secretaries addressed the commission's recommendations that administrative or disciplinary action be taken with regard to Lt. Col. Larry Gerlach, Commodore Rick France, and me. In the memorandum, Secretary Weinberger mentioned only "administrative action." The chairman of the JCS outlined actions he had taken with respect to the commission's recommendations on all major military topics, which laid the groundwork for significant changes and modifications.[2]

■

CONGRESSIONAL INVESTIGATION

The House Armed Services Committee conducted its own investigation and released a report titled *Adequacy of U.S. Marine Corps Security in Beirut*. The Investigations Subcommittee was tasked with examining U.S. policy objectives in Lebanon, how the Marine mission contributed to those objectives, whether the risks to the Marines were adequately assessed, and whether sufficient precautions were taken to counter them. On November 1, the full committee held two days of hearings, which included testimony from Gen. P. X. Kelley; Brig. Gen. James Mead, USMC; former ambassador to Lebanon Robert Dillon; and officials from the Department of State and Department of Defense. A subcommittee delegation arrived in Beirut on November 12 to conduct extensive interviews with Commodore France, Al Bigler (the U.S. embassy's security officer), and me, among many others. On December 14 and 15, the subcommittee heard sworn testimony from Commodore France, General Vessey, Gen. Bernard Rogers, and me. Its final report was made available on December 19, a day ahead of the Long Commission Report.

The HASC members were particularly critical that the chain of command did not reevaluate the USMNF's security posture and that the numerous high-level visitors were not sensitive to the increased security needs. As I mentioned previously, the chain of command and visitors were well aware of our security situation, and we took positive and effective action to improve our defenses against the known threats. We were responsive to their guidance and made modifications accordingly.

The subcommittee highlighted several factors that had put the USMNF in the crosshairs of the opposition:

(a) The United States showed its backing for the Lebanese central government by training and supporting the Lebanese Army.

(b) The USMNF provided direct naval gunfire support to the LAF at Suq-el-Garb in September, and it did not sit well with the Druze and other Muslim militias.

(c) We were welcomed by many Lebanese who saw us as the catalyst to remove the foreign occupying forces from Lebanon, but that did not happen.

(d) The Israelis' withdrawal south of the Awali River made the Marines an easier target for the opposition elements. When the Marines were initially deployed at Beirut International Airport, it was tolerable because the IDF occupied the high ground east of BIA. When the IDF withdrew on September 4 without coordinating with the LAF to assume the vacated positions, security for the MNF, particularly for the Marines at BIA, was irrevocably diminished.

(e)   Witnesses testified that the success of the Marines' mission was the key factor in why the Marines became the militias' target. Ambassador Philip Habib said, "I would argue the reason they object to the Multinational Force is they don't like the positive element that derives from the presence of the Multinational Force and maybe they want to weaken the position of the Lebanese authorities." I stated as much in my testimony: "The current terrorist threat that we are under over there is, I feel, a direct result of that earlier success. . . . I feel they are dedicated to our failure in the peacekeeping role."

(f)   Another possible reason is provocation. I testified, "I think a lot of the shelling and the casualties that we took there over the months were really bait to force us to take a large response into a village. And we didn't do that."

(g)   General Vessey stated it most succinctly: "It is important for us to recognize most clearly that it is not where we are that makes us the targets, it is who we are. And that is a very key point. We are going to get shot at because we are the United States of America."[3]

The witnesses went into some detail on the rationale as to why the Marines were located at the Beirut International Airport when they returned the second time. General Mead testified the presence mission required him to strike some balances. Initially, he intended to occupy the high ground four to eight kilometers east of the airport, but several diplomatic and political considerations overruled that selection. The Israelis wanted to maintain control of the airport and Sidon Road east of the airport. Diplomatic negotiations denied the airport location to them but granted them access to and control of Sidon Road. If the Marines were located on the high ground, the Israelis would have had to pass through Marine positions, "which to the Moslems [*sic*] shows the perception of cooperation between the MNF and the Israelis which was unacceptable from a political standpoint."[4] Even though the Marines did not want to accept the airport position, they did because of both the low order of threat and diplomatic requirements.

The subcommittee also dealt with the changing circumstances and their effect on the mission. The mission had remained basically the same since September 1982, but the circumstances in Beirut had changed drastically. By the summer of 1983, the differences were obvious and significantly affected the manner in which the mission could be conducted.

The subcommittee concentrated on the substantial changes that contributed to the deterioration of security. One was that the May 17, 1983, agreement between the Lebanese government and Israel had raised hopes beyond reasonable expectations. The Lebanese people looked forward to a withdrawal of all foreign forces, and when this didn't occur, there was a backlash from Muslim militias. The uncoordinated withdrawal of Israeli forces to the south initiated the September Mountain War, which irrevocably changed the atmosphere to unbounded violence. It never was the same after this war started.

The most significant event was our direct naval gunfire support for the LAF at Suq-el-Garb, which reinforced the Muslims' belief that the United States had moved even further from impartial peacekeeper to Christian supporter. I testified, "The support that was provided at Suq-el-Garb was, in my opinion, a departure from our neutral peacekeeping role to direct support of the Lebanese Armed Forces (LAF)." Commodore Rick France testified he regarded this authority to support the LAF as a change of mission. He stated,

> We felt the naval gunfire in defense of the mission ashore was a sound, tactical move, but naval gunfire in support of the Lebanese Armed Forces was a definite change of mission and, of course, one of the things we had emphasized all the way through there was maintaining our neutral presence, and this meant especially regarding the civil war in Lebanon because the Marines were surrounded by the Shia.[5]

The subcommittee investigators also concentrated on the interpretation of the mission and visibility versus security. All of the Marine commanders interpreted the presence mission to require "visibility"—that is, high visibility—and felt our security often conflicted with the requirement for visibility. The subcommittee felt this conflict was at the center of many of the decisions made and led to inadequate security that exposed the Marine compound to the truck attack. General Mead made the point that going into mole-like behavior, or digging deep and not getting out among the population, had affected morale and been detrimental to accomplishing the mission. I emphasized the same point, stating, "It is a balance of carrying out the mission at the same time as providing the security. And that is what you are constantly weighing." One of the first things I did upon arrival was to make our patrols joint operations, manned with Lebanese soldiers and the Marines. Many of these soldiers were Sunni, Shia, and Druze, which promoted the sectarian integration of the Lebanese Armed Forces. Being Lebanese, they also helped defuse several potentially dangerous situations through their language skills and local knowledge.

The problem with the interpretation of the presence mission led to pointed queries about why we didn't just hunker down or put up dirt barricades or various tank traps. In hindsight, this suggestion seems logical, even though we never had a tank or other armor threat. In reality, a presence mission while being invisible to the populace seemed contradictory to us. Again, we were not operating in a vacuum; our interpretation of the mission was well known and approved throughout the chain of command.

An important issue that was downplayed during the investigation was that we were operating with the French, Italian, and British forces—the other members of the multinational force—without a single headquarters. This mission required close, continuous cooperation and coordination to ensure all patrols, operations, and activities were productive while contributing to the mission objectives. I had liaison officers in each of their respective headquarters as well as a liaison team at the Ministry of Defense for the Lebanese Army. If we had built a fortress at BIA, the other MNF peacekeepers would have had to assume our responsibilities. I don't think shirking our duty is what the American people expect from the Marine Corps.

The key factor that drove the changes in the environment and security was the ever-expanding threat. In a relatively short period, major changes occurred that moved us from a permissive milieu to being directly targeted. When the Muslim militias wanted to register their disagreement with the Lebanese government during the late summer of 1983, the howitzers, rockets, and mortars rained down on Marine positions daily. The intensity of the hostile fire required decisive countermeasures to protect the USMNF. They included my decision to consolidate my forces into hardened structures rather than leaving them in the open. It was a no-brainer, as they say, given the available options. We employed limited, precise counter-battery fires to silence the hostile firing positions. It proved effective while avoiding major escalations.

The introduction of professional snipers in the surrounding Shiite villages adjacent to our wire and east of Marine positions also posed a deadly threat. Their accurate fire on exposed personnel and activities caused casualties and disrupted helicopter operations among other things. The snipers, many in camouflaged utilities, were likely Syrian soldiers and others who had Iranian connections. My response was to use the same philosophy we had employed in countering the artillery fire: we did not escalate but rather responded in kind but with greater accuracy and deadlier sniper skills. By implementing our Marine countersnipers against the hostile snipers, we eliminated them quickly and efficiently. This proved effective in reducing this threat, but like the artillery threat, it continued sporadically for the remainder of our tour.

The threat of car bombs was palpable and evident since Beirut had come to be known as the car bomb capital of the world. Just as the French, Italian, and British MNFs did, we moved convoys throughout the city to show our presence, to visit the embassy, and to reinforce and resupply our multiple locations. We received more than a hundred car bomb threats during our tour in Beirut. This threat became personal on October 19, 1983, when one of our convoys was hit with a remotely detonated car bomb near the Kuwaiti embassy. As a result, we changed our times, trips, routes, and size of the convoys to make them as unpredictable as possible and not lucrative targets.

We also faced the threat of kidnapping, as evidenced when the two U.S. Army soldiers left the compound without permission and ended up captives. The incident brought home to me the very real possibility of hostage taking similar to the Iranian takeover of the U.S. embassy in Tehran in 1979. In fact, after the MNF's departure from Lebanon, intelligence revealed that the wave of kidnappings, tortures, and murders had a distinct Iranian signature that is still evident today.

In reality, all the multinational forces were overwhelmed with a multitude of threats, which we all dealt with as they developed and responded to in accordance with the mission. The intelligence volume was incredible but so general and lacking in specificity as to render it unactionable. The burden fell on us to be alert at all times and counter all threats, which was physically impossible. Iran and its client, Syria, were well aware of this vulnerability.

A subject that investigators would repeatedly question me on was command responsibility. Their core question came down to whether I accepted responsibility for not preventing the suicide attack. I repeatedly stated that "the Commander is responsible for everything, everything the command does in the final analysis, or fails to do." From my standpoint, this stance is a military absolute that Marine officers learn early in the Basic School. A maxim that exemplifies this point is that as a commander, you can delegate authority, but responsibility can never be delegated. The fact that I was repeatedly questioned on this subject gave me the impression that some expected me to try and shirk this responsibility.

During the HASC investigation, it went so far that Investigations Subcommittee chair Congressman Bill Nichols read to me the following from a Marine field manual:

> Command is the authority which a Commander in the military service lawfully exercises over his subordinates by virtue of rank or assignment. Command includes the authority and responsibility for effectively using available resources and for planning the employment of organizing, directing, coordinating, and controlling military forces for the accomplishment of assigned missions. It also includes responsibility for health, welfare, morale, and discipline of assigned personnel.
>
> The Commander is responsible for everything the regiment does or fails to do. He meets his responsibilities by sound planning, by making timely decisions, by issuing effective orders, and by personal supervision and leadership. His duties require a thorough understanding of the tactical and technical employment, the capabilities and the limitations of all organic units, and of the units which may be attached to or in support of the regiment.[6]

At the conclusion, the chairman asked me if I agreed with this definition, and I stated, "I do, sir." The subcommittee concluded that inadequate security measures had been taken to protect the MAU from the full spectrum of threats. They found me to have made "serious errors in judgment in failing to provide better protection for his troops within the command authority available to him." Commodore France was adjudged to be equally culpable.

The dissenting view of the committee's report was more discerning:

The presence of the Marine Amphibious Unit (MAU) in Lebanon as part of a Multinational Force with the French, Italian, and the British might be one of the most difficult assignments the Marine Corps, or any other military unit, has been given.

The mission was, and continues to be, presence, notwithstanding that it has been described in varying ways by many news reports and individuals including the President of the United States.

The mission of the American contingent as part of the Multinational Force was described by the President of the United States as follows in his notification to the Speaker of the House under the War Powers Act:

To provide an interposition force at agreed locations and, thereby, provide multinational force presence requested by the Lebanese government to assist it and the Lebanese Armed Forces.

We say it might well be one of the most difficult assignments because, in performing the mission, the MAU commander constantly had to weigh the method of accomplishing the mission (presence) with the threats that were perceived or became apparent since September, 1982. Those threats changed significantly over the 13 months preceding the bombing of October 23, 1983, WHILE THE MISSION REMAINED PRECISELY THE SAME.

The Investigations Subcommittee report accurately, and in chronological order, states the threats to the MAU and how each threat was neutralized, from the series of clashes with the Israelis to the artillery fire from the mountains, to the snipers, and to the car bomb attacks on the American convoys and patrols. The crux of the investigation was to find the facts surrounding the tragic terrorist attack on the compound October 23, 1983, and to affix culpability, if any, for the incident. We dissent from the majority in affixing culpability to the MAU and amphibious operation commanders.

We agree that all in the chain of command must be held responsible. By definition, commanders are responsible for all that occurs or fails to occur in their command. In fact, all of those in the chain of command who gave testimony, from Colonel Geraghty up through General Rogers, concede their responsibility and accept it. Culpability is quite another matter. To determine culpability, one must first keep in mind the mission given the American contingent and, in the interest of simple fairness, also keep in mind that the commanders on the scene, in the days leading up to October 23rd, did not have the benefit of 20-20 hindsight or the luxury of Monday morning quarterbacking.

Only with hindsight do we feel the field commanders can be faulted for failing to perceive and protect against a threat of the nature and magnitude of the successful terrorist attack of October 23rd.

Just prior to the terrorist attack, the prime threat the unit focused on was the continuous bombardment by artillery, rockets, and mortars upon the Marine positions. The field commanders had taken precautions guarding against casualties from this threat, including billeting the Marines, Soldiers, and Sailors in the BLT building, which the evidence supports was the most protective structure in the area of responsibility assigned to and available to them.

There is little doubt in our minds that, had the ground commanders dispersed their troops as much as possible and suffered the almost inevitable casualties that would have resulted from the threat perceived as primary at the time (artillery, etc.), in retrospect some would have faulted the commander for failure to use the BLT to safeguard the troops. It appears the ground commanders were in a "damned if they do, damned if they don't," Catch-22 position.

In 20-20 hindsight, some have argued the Marines ought to have anticipated the kind of attack that was carried out on October 23rd and prepared adequate defenses against it. Others point out that the Marines were on a diplomatic mission rather than a combat mission and also point out that the intelligence reports did not provide specific warnings of possible terrorist attacks of this origin or magnitude. The 20-20 hindsight condemnation of the Marines' security is not so clear when viewed in conjunction with the successful terrorist attack on the Israeli position in Tyre, Lebanon, on November 4, 1983, just 10 days after the attacks on the French and the Americans a few miles north in Beirut on October 23rd.

The Israelis are not, nor have they been, limited in their preparedness or actions by a mission described as "presence." In fact, the Israeli's [sic] very existence has been challenged and their country and forces in the Middle East attacked and continually terrorized. The concentration by the Israelis on intelligence in that part of the world is necessary for their survival on a day-to-day basis. Yet—given the experience of the Israelis in dealing with terrorist threats over the years, their extensive intelligence capabilities and many of the same defenses which the Marines, in retrospect, were criticized for not having—on November 4, 10 days after the American and French attacks, a carbon copy attack was successfully carried out against the Israelis.

We seek in no way to minimize or remove from the shoulders of all the commanders in the chain of command the responsibility they have for all that occurs or fails to occur within their respective commands. However, to assign culpability, for not defending against this specific type of attack, to those who did not have the benefit of 20-20 hindsight, while remembering that the mission had not changed although the conditions had changed drastically, is unfair. It is admittedly difficult, if not impossible, to carry out the mission of presence as assigned without exposing the force to significant danger of casualties. The record is replete with efforts by the commanders to alter methods of operation to provide safety for those in their command while still attempting to perform the mission assigned which was, and is, presence.

Much has been said both in the hearing and in the media concerning the fact that sentries on duty in the compound, while having ammunition with them, did not have magazines in their weapons. A great deal of testimony was taken in this regard concerning the efforts of the commanders to balance the need for security with the danger of accidental discharge of weapons causing injuries to Marines and innocent bystanders. Indeed, the testimony shows numerous injuries suffered by Marines from accidental discharges—injuries to friendly forces—and, subsequent to October 23rd, the accidental discharge of an antitank weapon into the Beirut airport tower, as well as an incident where innocent press members were fired upon and injured by Marine guards.

Notwithstanding the obvious danger, we feel that weapons of the sentries on duty should be loaded at all times. We make this criticism knowing that, in the future, whether in Lebanon or elsewhere, there will be injuries to friendlies as a result of this policy and that in so stating, we will have to share the responsibility for such accidental injuries. But, the security of American forces, wherever they are, must be paramount. Also, in making this criticism, we take no consolation in the fact that none of the testimony given would indicate, nor in conversation with other members of the committee has it been suggested, that had the sentries' weapons been loaded as were the Israelis', the result would probably have been the same, given the size and speed of the vehicle, the determination of the suicidal driver and the enormous power of the bomb.

We feel another point must be made. Terrorist attacks of the kind the Multinational Force suffered on October 23rd in Beirut and other attacks of the recent past—most noteworthy, those at the Embassy in Kuwait, the busy department store in London, the Navy recruiting center on Long Island, and the Capitol in Washington, D.C.—will continue throughout the world until such time as the leaders of the civilized world put aside their differences and act in a unified and effective way to curb terrorism. It is impossible to secure our persons and property against individual wanton acts, but we must insure that severe sanctions will be directed at the sources of terrorism.

David O'B. Martin

Bob Stump[7]

There was a subtle irony in testifying on Capitol Hill before the subcommittee, answering queries regarding why we did not anticipate and prevent the suicide truck bombs in Beirut, where mayhem reigned and civil war was rampant. The hearings were conducted under extraordinary security measures whose necessity had become so evident as a result of the Marine barracks' attack. While I was being castigated for not preventing this unprecedented attack when I was stationed in the middle of an international airport and countering innumerable threats as a vicious civil war raged around me, the security response across the nation's capital and New York City showed that this new terrorist tactic was perceived as deadly and authentic, even in the relatively benign environment of America.

Immediately after the October 23 attack in Beirut, the Secret Service had placed large vehicles and barricades at gate entrances to the White House, redirecting traffic patterns, and eventually closed Pennsylvania Avenue in front of the presidential residence. (This closure remains in effect today.) The Secret

Service informed me later that they were shocked by the modus operandi of the attack and the bomb's massive destructive force. Heavy vehicles, soon reinforced by concrete barricades, were also deployed at all entrances and access routes on Capitol Hill and later to other U.S. government buildings throughout the capital.

On December 12, two days before the congressional hearings, Sgt. Maj. Richard Dudley and I had attended a presidential luncheon hosted by the Congressional Medal of Honor Society in New York. President Reagan was the keynote speaker and received the society's highest honor, the Patriot's Award. Sergeant Major Dudley and I had flown into New York with the assistant commandant of the Marine Corps. As our motorcade approached the downtown hotel where the luncheon was being held, all of us were astounded by the security, heavy vehicles, and equipment surrounding the entire building and the traffic control points to prevent a similar suicide truck attack. Our nation would take a long time coming to grips with this new terrorist threat.

The subcommittee's summary reemphasized the security risk the Marines faced in Beirut. It stated:

> Both the Marine ground Commanders who testified, consistent with the view of the Marine Corps leadership, interpreted the political/diplomatic nature of the mission to place high priority on visibility and emphasized to the extent of allowing greater than necessary security risks. The Subcommittee was particularly distressed to find that the security of the MAU was less than that provided at the interim U.S. Embassy in Beirut.[8]

What was not mentioned was that the magnitude of the bomb, coupled with our static location for more than a year in the middle of an operating airport, would have caused comparable devastation if it had detonated offsite on the airport access highway that ran just a hundred yards from the western side of the BLT building (see chapter 12). A British explosives expert determined that a similar explosion, even in the outer lanes of the Corniche in front of the U.S.-British embassy perimeter that was guarded by the Marine external security force, would have devastated the embassy. As a consequence, the four-lane Corniche was totally closed to all vehicle traffic after the attacks on the Marines and the French paratroopers.

Representative Dan Daniel (D-VA) read a statement in the record to summarize his views: "Colonel, when an officer accepts command of troops, he accepts not only the responsibility of accomplishing a mission, but the guardianship of those who serve under his command." He continued, "The military hierarchy exists and can function because enlisted personnel entrust their well-being and their lives to those with command authority. When those in command either abdicate that authority or neglect that guardianship, more is lost than lives. Lost also is the trust that enables those who follow those who lead."[9]

As he was reading his statement, I made it a point to look directly into the eyes of each committee member. Few returned my gaze. After reading his statement, I was asked if I had any comment. I stated, "No, sir." But I bit my tongue hard. What I wanted to say was that I would leave the judgments of trust, neglect, guardianship, and responsibility to history and to those who served with me during this tumultuous period—and not to politicians who have a political agenda.

The subcommittee concluded by strongly urging the administration "to review its policy in Lebanon . . . from the standpoint of how the Marine mission fits into the policy to determine, if continued, deployment of the Marine unit, as part of the Multinational Force of French, Italian, and British units, is justified." But the writing was already on the wall. The multinational peacekeeping force was withdrawn from Lebanon two months later.

■

I understand the necessity and purpose of the Long Commission and the HASC investigation. It is important that, as a nation, we investigate and analyze the circumstances surrounding any tragedy and learn from our mistakes. Being the primary target of both investigations, I supported their purpose and goals while accepting responsibility as the commander.

The Long Commission recommended that "the Secretary of Defense take whatever administrative or disciplinary action he deems appropriate, citing the failure of the BLT (Battalion Landing Team) and MAU (Marine Amphibious Unit) Commanders to take the security measures necessary to preclude the catastrophic loss of life in the attack on 23 October, 1983."[10]

On December 27, 1983, after receiving the Long Commission Report, President Reagan stated at a news conference that "today's terrorists are better armed and financed; they are more sophisticated; they are possessed by a fanatical intensity that individuals of a democratic society can barely comprehend." (A more prophetic assertion could not be stated.) For this reason, the president continued, he did not believe that the Marine commanders on the ground, "men who have already suffered quite enough, should be punished for not fully comprehending the nature of today's terrorist threat. If there is to be blame, it properly rests here in this office and with this President. And I accept responsibility for the bad as well as the good."[11]

Secretary Weinberger's opinion was that the president was not to be blamed for whatever people on the ground in Beirut did or failed to do.[12] I agree with this view, and my acceptance of responsibility and command accountability was never an issue. By virtue of the president's acceptance of responsibility, he perhaps realized that circumstances causing the suicide attacks reached beyond the capabilities of the people on the ground to prevent such attacks. As previously mentioned, the French, Italian, and British commanders and General Tannous were unanimous in stating that we could not deter these type of attacks while performing the peacekeeping mission. Another likely supporter of this view would be the commander of the bombed Israeli headquarters in Tyre.

Secretary Weinberger nevertheless ordered the issuance of "nonpunitive letters of instruction" to me and Lt. Col. Larry Gerlach. On February 9, 1984, Major General Gray delivered the administrative letter to me, signed by Secretary of the Navy John Lehman.

THE SECRETARY OF THE NAVY
WASHINGTON, D.C. 20350
8 February 1984
From: Secretary of the Navy
To: Colonel Timothy J. Geraghty, United States Marine Corps,

Subj: Administrative Letter

1. I have carefully reviewed the "Report of the DOD Commission on Beirut International Airport Terrorist Act, October 23, 1983," dated December 20, 1983. I also have reviewed official reports from the chain of command and the report of the Investigations Subcommittee of the Committee on Armed Services, House of Representatives, "Adequacy of U.S. Marine Corps Security in Beirut," December 14, 1983.

2.   This incident occurred while you were Commanding Officer, 24th Marine Amphibious Unit.

3.   In my view of the circumstances surrounding the tragedy, I fully recognized that this act of unprecedented terrorism is unique in the history of our country; and that it was perpetrated by state-sponsored terrorists who were fanatical in their zeal to embarrass the United States and disrupt our national policy in Lebanon. Moreover, I took note of your vigorous and effective efforts to lead your men in a mission that grew more ambiguous during your tenure—in an environment that grew steadily more hostile. I noted, with great admiration, the heroic efforts of you and your Marines in the aftermath of the tragedy.

4.   As the Commanding Officer, 24th MAU, you were responsible for the security measures taken by your subordinates. Together with the BLT Commander, you were directly responsible for the security of the MAU/BLT compound and the BLT Headquarters on October 23, 1983. The tragedy speaks for itself. It is obvious, in retrospect, that the planning and implementation of security measures did not provide adequate security.

5.   Although this letter will not be placed in your official record, it is intended as a nonpunitive reminder that your actions, as commander, were not sufficient to prevent this tragedy.
John Lehman

Larry Gerlach, virtually a quadriplegic whose vision was still blurred and his hearing still diminished by the bombing, received his letter while lying in his bed at the Boston Veterans Administration hospital.

—11—

Lessons Learned

THE PRESENCE OF THE MULTINATIONAL peacekeeping force in Lebanon in 1982–83 undoubtedly contributed to the Lebanese government's stability while saving innumerable lives. Our successes, albeit limited, were obviously worrisome enough to the primary powerbrokers in Iran and its ally Syria that they felt compelled to launch the suicide truck bombing operations against us. Looking back, it is easier to comprehend why Iran moved the Islamic Revolutionary Guard Corps during 1982–83 into the Syrian-controlled Bekaa Valley during the height of the Iraq-Iran War. The IRGC established a base of operations to carry out Iran's strategic goals. It founded, financed, trained, and equipped Hezbollah to operate as a proxy army. Hezbollah has expanded today to challenge the Lebanese government, which cannot control it, much less disarm it. Through Hezbollah, Iran and Syria have used Lebanon as a base to conduct border raids and rocket and missile attacks on Israel. Iranian persistence and determination has paid off handsomely in terms of regional influence, political power, and military prowess without suffering any consequences. It is no wonder that their destructiveness and brashness continue to grow in ever-expanding circumstances. This trend is not going to change until they are confronted and punished.

The seeds of modern-day terrorism and suicide bombings were sown in Lebanon in 1983. The evolution of this insidious movement began with the suicide bombings of the U.S. embassy and the Marines' Battalion Landing Team Headquarters and continued with the kidnappings, murder, torture, and intimidation of Americans and fellow Westerners. As previously mentioned, all these shameless acts against humanity have been carried out without any retribution or strong countermeasures. The peacekeeping experience in Lebanon demands that we carefully review these events and learn how we can better prepare ourselves to preclude any recurrence of this tragedy. What were the lessons and did we learn them?

LESSON LEARNED 1: KNOW YOUR NEXT STEP

Among my lingering memories of the Beirut peacekeeping mission is the apparent inability of the national policy advisers to think through the implications of their decisions. I was making decisions daily in a rapidly changing, dynamic environment, especially after the Israel Defense Forces pulled back to the Awali River in early September 1983. Adding to this development was Israeli prime minister Menachem Begin's announcement on August 28 that he was resigning. By this time, whatever goodwill the Israelis had generated by expelling the PLO from Lebanon had been squandered by their Sharon-directed excesses. In the eyes of much of the world, the Israelis were perceived as dangerous and arrogant. Their withdrawal, which the IDF did not coordinate with the Lebanese government or the MNF, triggered the predictable initiation of violent attacks, which simultaneously changed our peacekeeping mission. As the MNF was drawn into the conflict in order to protect itself and the diplomats ashore and to support the Lebanese Armed Forces, we quickly intensified our response to include the full array of our firepower just for self-defense. I had no other choice. As the September Mountain War grew ever more violent, the course of events on the ground changed our peacekeeping role, but no one in the chain of command had officially modified our mission. I found myself in an increasingly untenable tactical position. At this time, the Soviet Union had resupplied the Syrian Army with $2 billion worth of new equipment and supplies, and the Syrians in turn supported the Druze and Shiite militias along with radical Palestinian factions.[1] Their battles against the LAF and Phalangists, who were backed by the Israelis, were vicious and brutal. Not only had the Soviets reequipped the Syrians with new, sophisticated weaponry and supplies, Soviet advisers manned surface-to-air missile sites inside Lebanon.[2] The Marines were caught in the middle. Our national policy opened the door to unceasing combat; the Muslim opposition selected the time and place.

At this juncture, we had three options: withdraw, reinforce and reposition our forces, or maintain the status quo. Secretary of Defense Caspar Weinberger and Gen. Bernard Rogers, the commander in chief of the European Command, preferred withdrawal, but it carried some undesirable consequences. As the leader of the free world, the United States could not unilaterally withdraw and leave its NATO allies—France, Italy, and Great Britain—to complete the job. The larger issue was that during this hot period of the Cold War, U.S.-Soviet relations were very strained. On September 1, three days before the IDF withdrawal south to the Awali River, the Soviets had shot down Korean Airlines Flight 007 en route from New York to Seoul. The subsequent diplomatic fallout added to an already tense period.

The reinforcement or repositioning of the MNF seemed to me to be the most viable option. Even if the United States did not want to increase the size of the MNF, we could (and should) have redeployed some of the force to other locations, including offshore ships. During the summer, Lt. Col. Larry Gerlach and I fully supported the idea of sending some of the Marines located at BIA to the high ground south along Sidon Road. We were taking proactive steps for that eventuality if so ordered. Nothing ever came of it, but I thought it made sound tactical sense. I had felt an ever-growing anxiety about our static position at BIA, which made no tactical sense and grew increasingly vulnerable during the September War's astonishing violence.

Secretary Weinberger finally decided to stay with the status quo and not change the mission. The situation on the ground most certainly had changed, and we were now involved with not only the incessant shelling of our positions but also endless firefights with seasoned Syrian troops and the IRGC directly across our wire in the Shiite villages to the east.

It was hoped that one result of the 1983 U.S.-brokered accord between Israel and Lebanon (known as the May 17th Agreement) would be the withdrawal of all foreign forces from Lebanon. But President Hafez al-Assad of Syria objected to the pact, stating he had no intention of withdrawing his troops. Secretary of State George Shultz said the Syrians were left out of negotiations because they considered Lebanon part of Syria. In a revealing comment, Assad told him, "We don't have an embassy in Lebanon. We never have because you don't have an embassy in Chicago."[3] So when the IDF withdrew south, the Syrians actually reinforced their forward positions and moved troops outside the Marines' perimeter at BIA. Ironically, the United States, which had condemned Israel for invading Lebanon initially, then appealed for the IDF to remain and help maintain order in the rapidly deteriorating security environment.

After the IDF withdrawal, the Marines moved into the crosshairs, to the surprise of few. As we exercised our right to self-defense, confrontations inevitably escalated in both intensity and scope, and the peacekeeping mission soon evaporated. The Muslim militias, Syrians, and Iranians knew how to play this game. They created circumstances that quickly dissolved our purpose—a peacekeeping presence—and then used our self-defensive responses to rally and fan the flames of discontent among the Muslim factions. I was perplexed about how to deal with these developments, realizing they were creating a no-win situation for us. It was becoming more evident that the rapidly changing security atmosphere conflicted with the conditions set for the presence mission. It made me wonder, how the hell have we ended up in this position? The Marines were getting sucked into the renewed civil war, and there was little we could do to avoid that reality.

One of the most profound lessons learned was revealed later when intelligence officials stated that the red flags were flying, but no one put it all together. It is my belief that after the IDF withdrawal, followed by the September Mountain War and the cease-fire, there was enough evidence to strongly convey to national security advisers that the peacekeeping mission had definitely changed and that radical Islamic militias led by Iran and Syria were targeting the MNF. The Sharon-led IDF had its own agenda, and its uncoordinated withdrawal begged the question, Who is left holding that bag when they leave town? The answer came fast and fierce within hours, culminating in the dual suicide truck bombings six weeks later.

The most acrimonious exchanges I had with anyone while in Beirut were with Ambassador Robert McFarlane during the September Mountain War when he and his staff pressured me to provide naval gunfire support for the LAF's 8th Brigade at Suq-el-Garb. This request highlighted their failure to think through their decisions' implications. In fairness to McFarlane, he admitted on the bombing's tenth anniversary that the national security advisers did not consider what the next step was. He stated that, in short, there was no American interest in Lebanon and that "we put the Marines into a feel-good mission without thinking through the vulnerabilities."[4]

The fundamental lesson to be learned was in our leaders' misjudgment of the dramatic changes in Lebanon's security environment, which essentially changed our peacekeeping mission, and their failure to then reexamine our vulnerabilities.

The Beirut experience has an overarching lesson: force-building and peace-keeping do not mix, particularly in the Middle East. The NGF at Suq-el-Garb was clearly an escalation but consistent with U.S. policy to prop up the LAF and the government of Lebanon. The force-building mission (and the Marines' training of the LAF) supported this policy but in doing so blurred the peacekeeping mission, which required neutrality. The two missions are intrinsically contradictory, especially in a region where complicity and shifting alliances are common practice. We now know that Iran and Syria, which play by a completely different set of rules, were fanning the flames of this contradiction among their Muslim supporters and further exacerbated an already combustible situation.

LESSON LEARNED 2: THINK HARD BEFORE DEPLOYING PEACEKEEPING FORCES TO THE MIDDLE EAST AGAIN

The United States represents a beacon of hope, freedom, liberty, and equality for all people. This leadership role carries many responsibilities and obligations. These inherent values cherished by freedom-loving people everywhere are anathema to the Islamic jihadists and their ilk, who seek only to expand their brutal oppression and subjugation of all. It is precisely these values and what the United States represents that make any U.S. peacekeeping force in the Middle East a prime target. Additionally, our alliance and friendship with Israel has been a cornerstone of U.S. foreign policy since the latter's founding in 1948. However, this friendship and support also makes the notions of U.S. neutrality and impartiality difficult, if not impossible, in carrying out a peacekeeping role and mission. The MNF in Beirut was careful to establish and maintain its neutrality while the diplomats were attempting to resolve the political and sectarian issues. We tried to provide the stability for them to do their work. Nevertheless, perceptions are frequently more profound than reality.

The Israelis stated they entered Beirut to prevent a bloodbath, but as Secretary Shultz noted, "it appeared they facilitated—and perhaps even induced—just that." Relying on Israeli and Lebanese promises, Ambassador Habib had assured the Palestinians that all precautions would be taken to protect the camps after the PLO fighters departed. The first MNF had not been designed to perform such a job. The resultant international outcry, demanding action to provide security to the noncombatants in Beirut, led President Reagan to consider the deployment of a new MNPF. After the massacres in the camps, Secretary Shultz stated that the United States was partially responsible and obligated to join our allies in a new MNFP.[5]

The president's decision to send a new MNPF to Beirut highlighted the growing schism between Secretary of State Shultz and Secretary of Defense Weinberger. Among the U.S. goals was to extricate Israel "from the swamp it had gotten itself into," as Secretary Weinberger put it.[6] The president sought not only the Israelis' withdrawal from Beirut but also to begin the process for all foreign forces' full withdrawal from Lebanon. The DOD proposed that no MNF be redeployed anywhere in Lebanon until foreign forces had both agreed to depart and then done so. How to induce them to leave was the State Department's problem.

It is my opinion that the overriding consideration to return the MNF to Beirut lay in the repercussions of the noncombatants' massacre in the Palestinian camps. In a revealing conversation between the French ambassador to the United States, Bernard Vernier-Palliez, and Secretary Shultz during negotiations for French support of the president's position, the ambassador agreed to support the president. However, he privately commented that the French felt particularly burned as a result of the massacre because French troops had removed the protective land mines around the refugee camps. "We do not trust the Israelis," he said sharply.[7]

Adding to this unstable environment was more and more information that pointed to Israeli complicity in the massacre, as described in chapter 1. Bowing to pressure, Prime Minister Begin requested a judicial commission be set up to investigate the massacre. The Kahan Commission issued its report on February 8, 1983, recommending the dismissal or censure of top Israeli officials, including Defense Minister Sharon. The Israeli cabinet voted to accept the report, and Sharon eventually resigned.

After the short and successful initial Marine deployment to supervise the PLO evacuation, an unanticipated series of events led to the international crisis in which the United States had the responsibility, if not the obligation, to lead a response. I believe it was the collective guilt of all the MNF nations that drove this decision in Washington, Paris, London, and Rome. All felt some sense of responsibility for the massacre. These circumstances provided the genesis of the presence mission with all of its attendant risks and dangers. These dangers would become more evident as the security environment deteriorated rapidly and irrevocably during the late summer of 1983.

When one considers peacekeeping operations in the Middle East, it is predictable that U.S. peacekeepers would be intentionally goaded into action in self-defense. The hostile opposition controlled the time, place, duration, and means of attack. By ratcheting up the provocations, at their time and choosing, they caused the focus of the peacekeeping mission to quickly shift. The lesson is to be aware that the hostile opposition drives this train and careful thought must be given on how peacekeepers can respond and maintain their credibility.

The Beirut experience exposed the extreme difficulty of sustaining neutrality in a hostile environment where the savvy street-thug mentality reigns and confrontation is inevitable. Since security is a prerequisite for political and diplomatic accommodation, the hostile opposition knows how to disrupt security and prevent stability. Our national policy officials should ponder long before ever again deploying U.S. peacekeeping forces to the Middle East.

LESSON LEARNED 3: A PRICE IS PAID FOR NOT RETALIATING

The scope and immensity of the dual bombings on October 23, 1983, demanded retribution. This savage act of war was overt, pure terrorism, which should have precipitated a unified, timely retaliation. It never happened. Was there a lack of intelligence to identify the perpetrators? How come the French, who had lost fifty-eight paratroopers in the near simultaneous suicide attacks, had little doubt about who caused the attacks and realized the necessity for retaliation? Why was President Reagan confident enough to know who the perpetrators were and ordered retaliation shortly after the attacks? Why were those presidential orders never carried out? The answers to these questions require close scrutiny.

A military unit's primary line of defense is its adversary's understanding that an attack invites retaliation. This principle is particularly true of a peacekeeping unit. If the USMNF were to be hit, the United States would retaliate swiftly and significantly. I recommended that the U.S. negotiating team deliver this message directly and emphatically to Assad in Damascus. In support, U.S. Navy aerial reconnaissance missions and other sources had identified lucrative targets to bring home the consequences for attacks. We knew Iran and Syria would be, or would control, our likely attackers and that conveying this message of retaliation to them would give them pause before launching any major terrorist attacks. This effort was especially pertinent in light of the fact that they were known to have conducted the suicide attack on the U.S. embassy in April 1983 and had escaped then without any retaliation.

On October 23, 1983, the day of the BLT attack, President Reagan chaired two National Security Policy Group (NSPG) meetings and announced his intention to retaliate with military force against the perpetrators and to coordinate this U.S. action with the French. Before the end of the day, President Reagan felt confident that he knew the identity of the perpetrators and signed National Security Decision Directive (NSDD) 109, which held Iran and Iranian-supported Hezbollah responsible and authorized countermeasures against them. The NSDD 109's military component, entitled "Responding to the Attacks on the USMNF Contingents," remains classified. It is germane that the president's action was authorized *before* he learned of the September 26, 1983, NSA intercept from Iranian intelligence to its ambassador in Damascus "to take spectacular action against the American Marines." The director of Naval Intelligence did not reveal that intercept to Adm. James Lyons, deputy CNO, until October 25, 1983, two days after the attack.

Here again the acute disagreements between the Department of State and the Department of Defense on the execution of our Lebanese policy created a perfect storm. It certainly did not contribute to a unified response at the national level. Vice President Bush, Secretary of State Shultz, National Security Adviser McFarlane, and Secretary of the Navy John Lehman all supported taking retaliatory action. Gen. John Vessey, chairman of the JCS, found the idea morally unacceptable and "beneath" the U.S. military to strike back at terrorists for a cowardly bombing. Secretary of Defense Weinberger was also strongly opposed, since he, along with others, were concerned that such action would make the Marines more vulnerable.[8]

In a television address to the American people on October 27, 1983, President Reagan affirmed that justice would be dealt to the perpetrators. The retaliation was planned for when he returned in mid-November from a five-day trip to Asia. Upon his return on November 14, President Reagan approved the air attack plan at a meeting of the NSPG. Three aircraft carrier task forces—USS *Eisenhower*, USS *Independence*, and USS *Kennedy*—were on station in the eastern Mediterranean. Discussions with the French proceeded through Deputy National Security Adviser Adm. John Poindexter and President Mitterand's military adviser, François

Saulnier. The plan included air attacks on the Sheikh Abdullah barracks in Baalbek, a known IRGC-operated Hezbollah training facility in the Bekaa Valley. President Reagan listened to all sides and then made the decision to go. The U.S. and French planners agreed that D-day would be November 17.

On November 16, French defense minister Charles Hernu called Defense Secretary Weinberger for final coordination of the combined air operation. What transpired next depended on different accounts, but the outcome was clear. Secretary Weinberger claimed he was unaware of the planned joint air strike and had not received any orders or notifications from the president. He wished Hernu and the French pilots good luck, saying, "Unfortunately, it is a bit too late for us to join you in this one."[9] In any case, and to their credit, the French went ahead with the retaliatory strike on their own. To our discredit, the United States *never* did respond, a message not missed by Syria and Iran. More than a quarter century later and after countless acts of terrorism, neither terrorist state has suffered any consequences.

What happened between November 14 and November 16 is subject to debate. Both Ambassador McFarlane and Admiral Poindexter believe that Weinberger intentionally overruled a presidential directive.[10] According to Poindexter, Rear Adm. Jerry Tuttle, the commander of the carrier task force in the Mediterranean, reported he had received the approved strike plan and was waiting to execute the orders. (It should again be pointed out that by this time the NSA intercept from Iran to its ambassador in Damascus ordering an attack on the Marines was *known* to the responsible parties.) As Admiral Lyons testified twenty years later, the targets were selected and all systems were go for the joint air strike. In his memoir, President Reagan said he cancelled it because the experts were not absolutely certain we would be hitting the right targets. He also expressed his desire not to kill innocent bystanders. He further noted that the French and Israelis were convinced they had enough intelligence and conducted air strikes at the same redoubts in the mountains that U.S. intelligence had selected for retaliation.[11] In his journal entry later, he wrote that the National Security Council was "a divided group." In an obvious response to the discord and to prevent any recurrence, the NSC later forwarded to Shultz, Weinberger, Casey, and Vessey a number of decisions that the president had made on his own to prevent any repeat of this inaction.[12]

In his memoir published seven years later, Secretary Weinberger restated the reason for calling off the joint air strike with the French on November 16: he had not received any orders or notification from the president or anyone else prior to French defense minister Hernu's phone call.[13] Considering the importance of showing some national resolve against those who had massacred the MNF peacekeepers and bombed the U.S. embassy, it would have seemed prudent for him to inquire further. After all, the planned retaliation had been completed and was ready for execution by forces under his own purview.

Perhaps more telling was Weinberger's assertion that the suicide terrorists who had attacked the Marines and French peacekeepers were "to this day unknown"—despite overwhelming intelligence to the contrary. It further exposes the complete disconnect among the president's national security advisers. Substantial intelligence, corroborated by multiple sources, revealed who was responsible. In addition to the NSA intercept, Secretary Weinberger himself charged in November 1983 that "circumstantial evidence" pointed to Iranian involvement with the "sponsorship, knowledge, and authority of the Syrian government."[14] U.S. intelligence also confirmed that the same group had been responsible for the suicide bombing that had devastated our embassy the previous April and had been trained at the IRGC's training site near Baalbek.

In my judgment, the refusal of the United States to join the French in the retaliatory air raid sent a message that the powerbrokers in Tehran and Damascus received loud and clear: terrorism works. It was only a few months later that the CIA's station chief in Lebanon, William Buckley, was kidnapped and tortured to death by Imad Mugniyeh, Hezbollah's operations chief. His murder was only the beginning of an astounding increase in terrorism worldwide.

At dawn on December 3, 1983, the Israelis conducted a major air strike against Syrian targets east of Beirut. Later in the day, F-14 Tomcats from the USS *Kennedy* flew their routine photoreconnaissance mission and were fired on by the Syrians, who used Soviet heat-seeking surface-to-air missiles (SA-7s). In response, the president ordered a retaliatory air strike and pointedly did not specify the time frame or any other specifics. With Secretary Weinberger in Paris on NATO business and Secretary Lehman visiting U.S. forces in Central America, Deputy Secretary of Defense Paul Thayer was in charge at the Pentagon. When the retaliatory strike was launched the following day, the U.S. Navy lost an A-6 Intruder and an A-7 Corsair II to SA-7s. One pilot was killed, and his bombardier-navigator was captured and released a month later by the Syrians.

The botched raid raised many questions about what went wrong. Secretary Lehman said that by issuing orders through the same heavily laid chain of command that had produced the Marine barracks tragedy, the Pentagon had predictably produced this fiasco. Later, he provided a scathing analysis, stating the specific causes for the failed air strike. Among them were:

1. the bloated bureaucracy of the Pentagon and chain of command while micromanaging the operation
2. EUCOM's rejection of the Navy's plan to strike the Baalbek terrorist training centers, which were by far safer to hit and more significant targets than destroying a few Syrians firing hand-held SAMs
3. the choice of small, inconsequential, and valueless targets, which Admiral Tuttle, who was responsible for the air strike, stated were not worth a damn and Secretary Lehman labeled as absolutely useless
4. the decision not to use the USS *New Jersey*'s sixteen-inch guns, which could have easily reached the target but President Reagan was misinformed and told that they lacked the range and accuracy and could not be used
5. its timing

Perhaps the most egregious error Lehman cited was the time selection for the raid and the subsequent changes made for no apparent reason. Admiral Tuttle received a warning order on the afternoon of December 3 that there would likely be a retaliatory strike, so he planned for a time over target of 11:00 a.m. on December 4. He ordered his two wing commanders from the *Kennedy* air wing and the *Independence* air wing to plan their strikes and load their aircraft accordingly. The changes to the target list, which EUCOM directed, required major modifications to the operation. The nature of the scattered antiaircraft sites demanded an enormous effort to de-arm and unload high-explosive bombs and replace them with cluster bombs. Admiral Tuttle and both wings labored through the night, hoping to meet the 11:00 a.m. launch time for an 11:30 a.m. time over targets. At 5:30 a.m., Admiral Tuttle was informed the execute order had changed the launch time to 6:30 a.m. He immediately demanded more time but was given only an hour's delay. Strike crews normally must begin briefing two hours before launch time, so they were forced to scramble to take whatever aircraft were available without any time to brief. Twenty-eight aircraft launched, but none had the proper load-out of weapons. Some aircraft had only two bombs.

The time crunch gave the commanders no chance at deception, surprise, countermeasures, or to fly at medium altitudes (ten thousand to fifteen thousand feet). They also had two routes over one target area, a ridgeline northeast of Beirut, which Admiral Tuttle had previously rejected owing to its high concentration of SAMs. Adding to this situation, the pilots arriving at the target areas had the sun directly in their eyes, and they had to dive to very low release altitudes to visually acquire the targets, which were in the hills' shadows.[15]

The micromanaging outside the theater caused a flawed plan to be executed prematurely for no good reason. As was the case when U.S. participation in the scheduled U.S.-French joint air strike on November 16 was canceled, here was another disconnect between President Reagan's desire to send a political message and some of his national security advisers' refusal to retaliate. The botched raid likely had the opposite effect that the president intended, emboldening the Syrians and Iranians.

■

At the Congressional Medal of Honor Society's presidential luncheon in New York in December 1983, I'd been honored to meet President Reagan. His presence as he entered the room was impressive and pervading. At the short receiving line, the president told me how proud our nation was of the courage, discipline, and sacrifice of the Marines in Beirut. He was very gracious. On behalf of the Marine Corps, I thanked him for his kind words, and simply said, "Semper Fi, Mr. President."

But as I was being escorted to the dais, I accidentally bumped into Secretary of Defense Weinberger. Standing face to face a few feet apart, we looked at one another. I believe he recognized me. As I took a step toward him to pay my respects, his face became very flushed. He suddenly looked down at some cards he was carrying and raced off in another direction.

The luncheon was a memorable occasion, and it was an honor to be on the dais with President Reagan and among our nation's most revered heroes. However, to be honest, I felt very uncomfortable there, particularly having just returned home from a tragedy and a failed mission.

LESSON LEARNED 4: AMBIGUITY IS A USEFUL WEAPON

The 1973 War Powers Resolution was passed following congressional concern over the presidential use of force. President Richard Nixon's veto was overridden by Congress. The law was born out of the distrust between the legislative and executive branches during the Vietnam conflict. One key provision of the act requires that a president terminate combat in a foreign territory within sixty to ninety days unless the president receives congressional authorization to continue. Since its passage, no administration, Democratic or Republican, has acknowledged the law's authority as it was believed to deprive the president of his constitutional authority as commander in chief during periods of hostilities. The measure's purpose was to foster an atmosphere of cooperation and partnership when making decisions to commit U.S. forces to hostile situations.

History has shown the War Powers Resolution has had the opposite effect. It pits two branches of the U.S. government against each other on essentially procedural grounds at the precise time that national unity is needed to deal with a crisis. The resolution is a political issue to be sure but less so than one calling into question the constitutional roles and responsibilities of Congress and the executive branch on the conduct of war and the authorization to deploy U.S. forces into a country.[16]

When the Marines were initially deployed to Lebanon, President Reagan refused to invoke this law and avoided giving Congress a role in reviewing the Marines' deployment. Reiterating the position of all previous administrations that the president's authority as commander in chief cannot be circumscribed, he "informed" Congress rather than "notified" it of the mission.

The second deployment involved another presidential letter informing Congress while ignoring any provision of the War Powers Resolution. The president gave no time limit for the deployment; instead, he linked the Marines' withdrawal to the prior removal of all foreign forces from Lebanon and the reassertion of the Lebanese government's control. All remained relatively quiet between the executive and legislative branches until August 29, 1983, when two Marines were killed and the IDF commenced its withdrawal. Congress debated several proposals and adopted a resolution that the imminent involvement in hostilities section of the War Powers Resolution had come into effect with the death of the two Marines. The resolution also fixed a time limit of eighteen months from its enactment for the continued Marine deployment.

The question the media asked me at this time was whether the firing at Marine positions was directed at us or was spillover fire directed at nearby LAF or allied positions. It was difficult at times to discern the difference, but I maintained the point that it becomes irrelevant as to who was firing and what their intentions were if peacekeepers, allies, or diplomats were killed or injured. If the firing had been determined to be directed at the USMNF, this finding would have triggered the imminent involvement in hostilities section of the War Powers Resolution. Further, the debate would have had to include whether Syria knew about the shelling (most of which was coming from Syrian-controlled territory) and, if the Syrians did, whether they had any control over it.

As mentioned earlier, the Marines were not alone in this dilemma. Our fellow French, Italian, and British peacekeepers were also recipients of the barrages while they were trying to sort out similar problems. French foreign minister Claude Cheysson provided a hint of an appropriate response in the situation in late August 1983 after the French contingent had been fired on for about three hours. He told Secretary of State Shultz that he called Syrian foreign minister Abdul Halim Khaddam to tell him that French aircraft and missiles were poised to strike back. "The bombardment stopped eight minutes later," he said.[17] Our allies, however, were obviously not affected by the War Powers Resolution debate.

General Kelley warned Congress on September 13, 1983, that "any Congressional use of the War Powers Resolution to set an artificial deadline for withdrawal from Lebanon could encourage more hostile fire and endanger the Marines there." He further cautioned against any movement "to start a time clock moving, which could give the wrong signal to forces that are potentially hostile to our Marines that they're going to be withdrawn." In asking Congress not to set a schedule for our withdrawal from Lebanon, he said, "If the time is too short, our enemies will wait us out; if it is too long, they will drive us out." His message was simple: never tell your enemies your plans. Ambiguity in war is essential.[18]

I may have been naive, but from afar I always believed there existed a majority of both Democratic and Republican members of Congress, along with the president, who made a sincere effort to express their concern for our welfare and safety. Two weeks before the suicide truck bombings, I received two extraordinary, thoughtful letters from separate party members of the congressional delegation that had visited us in Beirut on September 24, 1983 (see appendix D). One letter was from Congressman Samuel S. Stratton (D-NY), the leader of the delegation, and the other was from Congressman Bill Nichols (R-AL). Their letters expressed congressional concern for our welfare and a prevailing tone of optimism for our mission.

On October 12, 1983, President Reagan signed the Lebanon War Powers Authorization Resolution into law, although Secretary of State Shultz immediately made it clear that should the Marines still be in Lebanon, the administration would not feel bound to withdraw them at the end of the congressionally authorized eighteen months. Eleven days after the bill was passed, the suicide truck bombing hit the Marine BLT building. The magnitude and devastation of the bombings of the U.S. and French compounds doomed the following week's national reconciliation talks in Geneva before they began and triggered a major change in U.S. national policy to withdraw the USMNF within four months. Iran and Syria had done their homework.

The botched U.S. retaliation response against the Syrian antiaircraft attacks on December 4 only added fuel to Congress's discontent. Faced with waning congressional support, the collapse of the LAF's 4th Brigade, and the subsequent seizure of West Beirut by Muslim militias, President Reagan reluctantly announced on February 7, 1984, the redeployment of the U.S. Multinational Force. It was soon followed by the French, Italian, and British forces. As with his earlier decision to deploy the Marines the second time to Beirut following the massacre at the Sabra and Shatila camps, the president was left with few options, considering the abyss into which Lebanon was spiraling. Some of the Marines and sailors said that the laughter heard coming from the Shouf Mountains was that of the Syrians and Iranians who wrote this play.

Over the years, the War Powers Resolution has remained a contentious issue. The Supreme Court has refused to provide a definitive ruling on the law's constitutionality, further adding to the confusion. On May 19, 1988, Senate majority leader George Mitchell said that he believed the War Powers Resolution is unconstitutional. In remarks on the Senate floor, he observed that the resolution expanded congressional authority "beyond the power to declare war to the power to limit troop deployments in situations short of war." He concluded, "Into the very situation that requires national steadiness and resolve, the War Powers Resolution introduces doubt and uncertainty. This does not serve our Nation. The War Powers Resolution therefore threatens not only the delicate balance of power established by the Constitution, it potentially undermines America's ability to effectively defend our national security."[19]

On July 8, 2008, an independent, bipartisan commission stated that the 1973 War Powers Resolution is ineffective, possibly unconstitutional, and should be repealed. Cochaired by former secretaries of state James A. Baker, III, and Warren Christopher, the commission recommended that Congress repeal it and substitute a new statute that would provide for meaningful consultation between the president and Congress on matters of war. Secretary Baker commented, "The rule of law is undermined and is damaged when the main statute in this vital policy area is regularly questioned or ignored." Iraq War opponents stated that President Bush surpassed the initial authorization in continuing the war beyond Saddam's overthrow, but they have failed to repeal or alter the original authorization, to deny funding, or to set specific troop withdrawal time lines.[20] The arguments about the War Powers Resolution reinforce the premise that ambiguity is a useful weapon and notifying the enemy of our plans is detrimental to our mutual efforts and national security.

─12─

Connecting the Dots

THE PASSAGE OF TIME AND THE BENEFIT of contemporary history provide insight into the events that led to the horrific suicide truck bombings in Beirut on October 23, 1983. For one thing, the involvement of Hezbollah, which was suspected from the beginning, has become clear.

As mentioned earlier, on September 26, the same date that the September War's cease-fire became effective, the National Security Agency intercepted a diplomatic cable sent from Tehran to Hojjat ol-Eslam Ali-Akbar Mohtashemi-Pur, the Iranian ambassador to Damascus. Mohtashemi's nickname in Iran is Father of Hezbollah, since he created the organization. Sent from the Iranian intelligence organization, the Ministry of Information and Security, the cable ordered him to contact Husayn al-Musawi, the leader of the terrorist group Islamic Amal (the predecessor of what became Hezbollah), and to instruct him "to take a spectacular action against the American Marines." Both Hezbollah and Islamic Amal were under the direct control of the Iranian government.

THE TESTIMONY

This intercepted intelligence was revealed for the first time at the March 17, 2003, trial of *Deborah D. Peterson et al. v. the Islamic Republic of Iran et al.* Deborah Peterson is the sister of Lance Cpl. James C. Knipple, who was killed in the BLT bombing. Her civil action suit was filed under a 1996 U.S. law that allows Americans to sue nations that the Department of State considers sponsors of terrorism for damages suffered in terrorist attacks. Sworn testimony by several expert witnesses disclosed a treasure trove of intelligence and other information that left no doubt as to Iranian and Syrian involvement in this act of war. It was also divulged that the attacks could not have taken place without approval at the highest levels, specifically from President Akbar Hashemi Rafsanjani and the supreme leader of Iran, Ayatollah Ruhollah Khomeini.

The lead attorneys who filed the suit on behalf of the families and victims were Thomas Fortune Fay and Steven R. Perles. Judge Royce C. Lamberth, who presided over the case in the U.S. District Court for the District of Columbia, began the trial by determining that the plaintiffs had a right to obtain judicial relief from Iran.

I was called as the first witness and spent more than two hours on the stand answering queries about the security environment in Beirut during our mission, its rules of engagement, decisions I had made, and actions I had directed. I also explained the presence mission, which I noted was nebulous by design. I mentioned that during the investigations, I was criticized for "allowing" BIA to reopen even though I knew it increased our vulnerability. I explained that I had absolutely no vote in that decision; it was made by the president of Lebanon. I also pointed out that our mission was political and diplomatic, so normal tactical considerations took a back seat. I reviewed the day of the attack in considerable detail and the anguish associated with the rescue operation. I ended my testimony by clarifying one of the main reasons we were attacked: there were some positive initiatives that offered some hope to the war-ravaged country, but outside forces were not going to chance any success by the multinational force. Ironically, the opening day of the trial happened to be the twentieth anniversary of my assumption of command of the 24th MAU at Camp Lejeune.[1]

Later, Lt. Col. Larry Gerlach, the battalion commander, gave some enlightening and professional background on rules of engagement and responses made to the threats we faced. He recited in detail his severe injuries, paralysis, and fractures and his miraculous recovery. He reinforced the need that the litigation's focus should be on justice, accountability, and deterrence. His testimony reflected the same demeanor, professionalism, and dedication to his Marines that had marked his exceptional career.[2]

Family members who had suffered the loss of a loved one gave the most emotional, heartrending testimony. Their personal accounts told of their sorrow and heartbreak when they learned of the deaths, stories that were repeated 241 times all across America. Deborah Peterson recalled the agony of waiting to hear news about her brother's fate following the bombing and the reaction of their father, retired U.S. Navy captain John D. Knipple, when he first heard: "Debbie, our worst nightmare has been realized." It wasn't until November 8 that Lance Cpl. James C. Knipple's body was officially identified. He was buried at Arlington National Cemetery on November 10, the Marine Corps' 208th birthday. Captain Knipple was instrumental in having a Lebanon Cedar planted at Arlington in section 59, where his son and twenty other Beirut veterans are buried. Among the marble headstones of these fallen heroes and beneath the tree lies a granite stone with the words "Let Peace Take Root" chiseled at the top. It is not only an eternal reminder of Knipple's and the other men's sacrifice but also an expression of hope for the future.

Ms. Peterson also presented to the court a "Statement of the Families." It summarized their views and what the litigation represents (see appendix F).[3]

The personal pain and heartache were exemplified by the moving testimony of Lynn Smith Derbyshire, the sister of Capt. Vincent Smith, who perished in the bombing. Captain Smith, a talented aviator assigned as the air liaison officer to Battalion Landing Team 1/8, had all the tickets to enjoy a successful career. His father, Lt. Gen. Keith Smith, USMC (Ret.), was the commanding general of the 2nd Marine Aircraft Wing during our deployment in 1983. Mrs. Derbyshire recalled for the court Vincent in their youth in a family of nine children (she named her son Chandler Vincent in memory of her brother), his selection for the U.S. Naval Academy, and the news about the Beirut disaster as she left church on that Sunday morning. Then she spent two anguished weeks waiting and praying before learning of Vincent's death from her father, who called and said, "The waiting has come to an end. They have positively identified Vincent's remains. Come on home, honey." Later, she read a compilation of letters she had written to friends following the 9/11 attacks in New York and Washington, and the aborted attack in Pennsylvania. These attacks reopened old wounds after long years of grief, making her feel the loss all over again. The Smiths and the rest of the families sought justice and accountability by those who perpetrated this crime against the peacekeepers. The families' courage and solidarity reflected the same spirit and determination of those young men whose sacrifice will never be forgotten.[4]

The most striking testimony was provided by Adm. James "Ace" Lyons, USN (Ret.), who was the deputy chief of naval operations for plans, policy, and operations in 1983. He testified that the director of naval intelligence had given him the September 26 NSA intercept two days *after* the October 23 suicide truck bombings. He stated that similar copies were delivered to the CNO, Adm. James D. Watkins, and the Secretary of the Navy, John Lehman. Admiral Lyons described, in generic terms, the contents of the intercepted cable and gave the information to the court in a sealed envelope. He added, "If ever there was a 24-karat gold document, this was it." Judge Lamberth accepted the classified information under seal to protect the NSA's sources and methods, but he noted that the intercept was obtained nearly four full weeks before the suicide attacks. He wondered why no one took steps to protect the Marines or head off the attack.[5]

The intelligence was not passed on to individuals who could respond to the threat. DOD consultant and noted author Michael Ledeen testified that this failure to share intelligence "drove a change in the structure of the intelligence community. We should have seen it coming, we had enough information . . . but we didn't because of the compartmentalization of the various pieces of the intelligence community." He also said that this failure led CIA director William Casey to establish the Counterterrorist Center (CTC), a cross-discipline organization, whose primary purpose was to prevent terrorism and, when that failed, to fight back against the terrorists.[6] When I retired from the Marine Corps in 1986, I returned to the CIA and worked in the new CTC, which was then led by legendary spymaster Dewey Clarridge.

It is germane to recall that all key factions and the Lebanese government agreed upon the September 26 cease-fire, which ended the September Mountain War and laid the groundwork for the national reconciliation talks. That the NSA intercepted an Iranian intelligence services (MOIS) message from Tehran on the same date as the cease-fire clearly indicates that the decision makers in Tehran and Damascus had already decided to use direct, lethal terrorist attacks against the U.S. and French MNF to expedite our departure from Lebanon. I suggest that no matter how remote the chances for success were in the upcoming reconciliation talks, the attacks' timing indicates that both Iran and Syria seemed determined not to risk the possibility of any positive result. Using proxy Shiite terrorists for the attacks would provide them with plausible deniability to the United States and the international community. It worked.

In addition, the fact that the multi-confessional Lebanese Army had held together and performed well during some fierce battles in the September War had to be a cause for concern among the leaders of Iran and Syria. The fighting involved Syrian advisers, radical Palestinians based in Syria, the Druze, the Islamic Amal, and the Iranian Revolutionary Guard Corps. It was likely a combination of all these factors that led the terrorist states to reach the conclusion that conventional attacks would not produce their objectives—to derail the national reconciliation talks and to expedite the MNF's exit from Lebanon—soon enough. After the suicide truck bombings, the talks were doomed before they began, and the MNF was pulled out of Lebanon.

Several other revealing and enlightening gems of intelligence corroborated other sources and testimony. A videotape deposition provided by Mahmoud (a pseudonym), a former member of Hezbollah, confirmed that Iranian ambassador Mohtashemi made a telephone call during October 1983 from Damascus to Baalbek, the city in the Bekaa Valley where the IRGC had set up an operational base. The testimony disclosed that Mohtashemi told the IRGC's Iranian leaders to proceed with the planned attacks on the American Marines and French paratroopers. The Iranians went to Beirut, where they prepared the explosives for the attacks.[7]

Mahmoud's testimony also revealed that the driver of the suicide truck bomb was an Iranian national named Ismail Ascari.[8] Iranian leaders were taking no chances that Hezbollah, in its formative stages, would not cooperate, so they brought in an Iranian to drive the nineteen-ton stakebed truck bomb. It may also help explain why Iran, while denying any involvement in the attack, has erected a monument to commemorate the suicide bombing of the Marine barracks. Amid chants of "Death to America," the stone monument, which is located at Tehran's Behesht-e-Zahra cemetery, was unveiled in 2004 by a committee of the Commemoration of Martyrs of the Global Islamic Campaign. Some of the participants were dressed as suicide bombers while others claimed to have signed up more than twenty-five thousand martyrdom-seeking volunteers.[9]

FBI special agent Danny Defenbaugh, who headed the FBI's forensic operation at the bombing site, then provided a technical assessment of the bomb. PETN (pentaerythritol tetranitrate) was the high explosive used. Unconsumed particles of PETN were found, as they had been at the U.S. embassy bombing the previous April. According to forensics expert Defenbaugh, the discovery of unconsumed particles meant the PETN had not come from unused artillery shells but from a bulk source. PETN was not manufactured in Lebanon but is sold to government military sources in the region in bulk. The evidence pointed to a state-sponsored terrorist operation.

Special Agent Defenbaugh also identified several canisters of compressed butane that had been in the bed of the truck with the PETN. This enhancement of the explosive, which was also found at the earlier U.S. embassy attack, indicated the Iranians were trying to create a fuel-air explosive (FAE). An FAE creates a shock effect with a propagation wave that produces additional heat and uses the oxygen twice as fast. Although Defenbaugh wouldn't speculate, another expert who testified later stated that its use verified the attack's antipersonnel function. It also explained why so many victims suffered severe burns.[10]

In revealing computations and a technical assessment of the bomb, Defenbaugh explained the explosives' extreme shattering effect. He first cited the building's main support columns. He explained there were thirty-six concrete reinforcement bars (rebars) within each column of solid concrete. The rebars were very large in diameter—one and a half inches (normal are seven-eighths to an inch). There were four columns together that had a girth of just more than 15 feet, and these columns stretched and snapped like rubber bands.[11]

Another factor used in the damage assessment was the measurements of the crater created by the blast. It measured 39 feet by 29 feet, 6 inches in an oblong shape. The explosive force drove an approximate 4-by-8-foot reinforced-concrete foundation slab, 7 inches thick with a 1-inch marble facing, 8 feet, 8 inches into the ground.

In describing the bomb's destructive strength, Defenbaugh displayed an enlarged photograph showing a tree line where the first sergeant's guard area was located. It was about 125 yards away from the point of detonation. He noted that the trees were shredded and totally stripped of all foliage. He then pointed to an item, which was part of a metal locker door. It was wrapped around one of the trees *twice* before the tree was shredded and bent over.

The original estimate of the explosion's size was twelve thousand pounds of explosive equivalent yield of TNT, but the FBI admitted the estimate was very conservative. Later, the FBI gave the evidence and technical data to Sandia National Laboratories for further study and testing, which resulted in increasing the size of the blast estimate to approximately twenty-one thousand pounds. It was at least six times more powerful than the van bomb used to destroy the

U.S. embassy and was the largest nonnuclear explosion on record.[12] The science, physics, and technical information confirmed the unanimous opinion of all MNF commanders with boots on the ground in Beirut. This "game changing" tactic, by its sheer magnitude, made it virtually impossible to carry out the peacekeeping mission in the deteriorating environment.

This information verified publicly what the FBI and others told us privately: the bomb's immense power precluded the necessity of the truck reaching the building. Its size virtually assured success for Iran and Syria in achieving their objective. In fact, I was also informed that the truck bomb did not even have to leave the airport access road adjacent to the BLT building's western side to create similar devastation and casualties. The shock waves (air waves and ground waves) produced by the twenty-one thousand pounds of explosives were so powerful that they would have overwhelmed any defenses, even if it had been detonated off-site. That the blast shattered the windows of the BIA's air control tower more than a third of a mile away shows the enormous force of the bomb. A big factor for any defense against this type of threat is to have a setback distance and blast walls, which, as I've noted, were impossible in our case because of our location in the middle of an active international airport. I tried to explain during my testimony before the Long Commission and the congressional investigations that only an antitank defense could have realistically countered such an attack, but that was also out of the question owing to our location. We had little control of civilian traffic coming to and from the airport complex, and when you don't have control, you don't have security.

The forensic investigators and expert witnesses uncovered several other intriguing details. There was likely an accomplice, or accomplices, located off-site who supported the operation and possessed a command-initiated or radio-controlled device that served as a backup or override to ensure the device initiated. This pattern was a common modus operandi among Islamist terrorists who wanted to guarantee that a bomb would explode.

Given the explosion's size, it is plausible that we could have suffered heavier casualties that Sunday morning if the suicide terrorists had delayed the attack two or three hours. By stopping the truck bomb on the airport access road next to the BLT Headquarters during the Sunday brunch, they would have caught large numbers of MNF personnel in the open, as it was the site of the only MAU mess facility ashore and drew all hands at meal hours. Among others, this scenario highlights the vulnerability of our location, which presented the terrorists numerous options. We were in a loser's game, and the opposition controlled the time, place, and method of attack.

The carbon-copy attack on the French paratroopers' headquarters, which occurred approximately eight minutes after ours, was most intriguing. The paratroopers had just moved into their new headquarters in the West Beirut seafront neighborhood of Ramlet el-Baida. Among the reasons they had selected this site was it had the space to allow emplacement of barricades and other obstructions for protection and control. During the attack, the French defenders fired on, halted, and, it is believed, killed the sacrificial driver of the pickup truck bomb (which was estimated to have packed less than half the explosive power of the BLT truck bomb) before he could penetrate the nine-story structure. The truck was believed to have been halted about fifteen yards short of the building. After that, a noticeable amount of time—many seconds but less than a minute—passed before the device was initiated. It was the opinion of the FBI and other experts that someone in a nearby location and not the driver of the truck command-detonated the bomb. Large enough to level the headquarters, it killed fifty-eight paratroopers and wounded scores of others.[13]

THE JUDGMENT

On May 30, 2003, Judge Lamberth issued a ruling in favor of the families and survivors, stating that the truck bombing was carried out by the group Hezbollah with the approval and funding of Iran's senior government officials. The judge called it "the most deadly state-sponsored terrorist attack made against United States citizens before September 11, 2001." He further stated, "In the early morning hours of that day, 241 American servicemen were murdered in their sleep by a suicide bomber. On that day, an unspeakable horror invaded the lives of those who survived the attack and the family members whose loved ones had been stolen from them." Judge Lamberth said, "Based on the evidence presented by expert witnesses at trial, the court finds that it is beyond question that Hezbollah and its agents received massive material and technical support from the Iranian government."

As pointed out during the trial, the Marines were more restricted in their use of force than an ordinary U.S. citizen walking down a street in Washington, D.C. He continued,

There is little that the court can add to the eloquent words of these witnesses. No order from this court will restore any of the 241 lives that were stolen on October 23, 1983. Nor is this court able to heal the pain that has become a permanent part of the lives of their mothers and fathers, their spouses and siblings, and their sons and daughters. But the court can take steps that will punish the men who carried out this unspeakable attack, and in so doing, try to achieve some small measure of justice for its survivors, and for the family members of the 241 Americans who never came home.

Four years later, on September 7, 2007, Judge Lamberth reaffirmed this finding and ruled that Iran must pay the families $2.65 billion in compensation for the suffering that resulted from the heinous attack. He added that he hoped the sizable judgment will "sound an alarm to the defendants that their unlawful attacks on our citizens will not be tolerated."[14]

HISTORICAL PERSPECTIVE

To put the tragic suicide bombings that happened in Beirut in 1983 into some historical perspective, several factors need to be closely examined. Over the past quarter century, it has been revealing to investigate the conduct of the countries that sponsored this terrorism, their supporting organizations and infrastructure, as well as some key players who were directly involved in major events during the peacekeeping mission and where they are today.

IMAD FAYEZ MUGNIYAH

Born in Tyre, Lebanon, in 1962, Imad Fayez Mugniyah first gained attention when he joined Yasser Arafat's personal bodyguard unit, the elite Force 17, in the late 1970s. He reportedly was close to Arafat when the PLO was based in Beirut and earned the nickname Tha' Lab (The Fox). His notorious résumé of terrorist attacks reflected his well-earned reputation as one of the world's most dangerous terrorists. Many in the intelligence community (IC) considered him more diabolical than Osama bin Laden since he was, first and foremost, a brilliant operative who reveled in the carnage he wrought and the infamy that the terrorist attacks brought. He is credited with pioneering the widespread use of suicide bombers, which has since become the favored tactic of Islamist extremists.

Besides the Beirut bombings of the U.S. embassy, the Marine barracks, and the French paratroopers' headquarters, his rap sheet includes the hijacking of TWA Flight 847 (during which a U.S. Navy diver was killed); the kidnapping and murders of U.S. military, intelligence, academic, religious, and diplomatic personnel in Beirut; the bombing of the Israeli embassy in Buenos Aires in 1992, killing twenty-nine people; and the bombing of a Jewish cultural center there in 1994, killing eighty-six people. He was a prime suspect in the 1996 bombing of the Khobar Towers in Saudi Arabia, killing nineteen U.S. airmen. Mugniyah likely played a role in establishing Iranian ratlines into Iraq and in creating the Special Groups, which were built to resemble Hezbollah.

Mugniyah has been directly linked to the kidnappings and murders of Bill Buckley and Col. William "Rich" Higgins. A classified Defense Intelligence Agency report revealed that Mugniyah was in charge of Higgins's execution in 1990. The report showed grisly details from a videotape of his hanging, including images of Mugniyah directing the execution in a windowless room thought to be in an apartment building in West Beirut.[15]

Mugniyah had extensive links with the MOIS and was directly linked to al Qaeda, bin Laden, and the former al Qaeda in Iraq commander, Abu Musab al Zarqawi. He likely played a support role in al Qaeda's 9/11 attacks on the United States.[16] The 9/11 Commission Report was explicit about Iran's connections with al Qaeda: "The relationship between Al-Qaeda and Iran demonstrate that Sunni-Shia divisions do not necessarily pose an insurmountable barrier to cooperate in terrorist operations." The report also stated, "Al-Qaeda members received advice and training from Hizballah and many of Al-Qaeda's 9/11 hijackers transited through Iran."[17]

Hezbollah is essentially the Lebanese branch of Iran's Quds Force, of which Mugniyah was a senior leader. The Quds Force is the IRGC's elite Special Operations–type branch. The al Qaeda attacks on the U.S. embassies in East Africa on August 7, 1998, were directly modeled on Mugniyah's earlier attacks in Beirut in 1983.

Hezbollah's 1983 bombings of the U.S. embassy in Beirut and its follow-on attack on the Marine barracks were seminal events in the history of terrorism. They marked the first time Islamist suicide bombers had attacked significant American and French targets. Al Qaeda has since come to be known for coordinated suicide missions—namely, the simultaneous East Africa bombings and the four simultaneous airplane hijackings on September 11, 2001. As terrorism expert Rohan Gunaratna explains in *Inside Al Qaeda: Global Network of Terror,* al Qaeda took its inspiration for this modus operandi directly from Hezbollah. Before meeting Mugniyah, bin Laden and his agents did not have the expertise to carry out such attacks.

Mugniyah's long history of carnage was marked by his elusiveness and effectiveness. Nonetheless, he met his demise in an upscale, newly built suburb of Damascus called Kafar Soussa at 10:15 p.m. on February 12, 2008. It is ironic that his manner of death, by a remote-controlled car bomb, was one of his signature weapons of choice. Justice was belatedly served to this evil coward, twenty-four years, three months, and twenty days after the suicide attacks on the peacekeepers in Beirut. His days as an Iranian hit man have ended, none too soon. He was reportedly coming from a meeting with Iranians who had been celebrating the thirtieth anniversary of the Islamic Revolution in Iran. It has been speculated that his killers were Mossad agents or Syrian security personnel or members of a Hezbollah faction.

The responses to Mugniyah's death were revealing and sobering. After years of Hezbollah denying Mugniyah's very existence, Hezbollah's leader, Sayyed Hassan Nasrallah, eulogized him over a coffin decked out in Hezbollah's flag. Nasrallah's eulogy placed Mugniyah officially with Hezbollah's greatest martyrs but exposed the terrorists' use of lies and deception to serve their nefarious interests.

Hezbollah sent a subtle but grave message at Mugniyah's funeral that does not bode for positive changes. If Hezbollah was serious and determined to distance itself from terrorism, it would not have bestowed honors at the official funeral of one of the world's most wanted terrorists. Nor would Nasrallah threaten "open warfare" with Israel over Mugniyah's coffin. Mugniyah may be dead, but his diabolical imprint left behind will be seen and felt for many years to come.

HEZBOLLAH (PARTY OF GOD)

In response to the Israeli invasion of Lebanon on June 6, 1982, Iran's IRGC established Hezbollah. The IRGC was dispatched to Lebanon via Syria to project Iranian goals, which included the elimination of Israel and the "liberation" of Jerusalem. Its political leader, Secretary-General Sayed Hassan Nasrallah, is a radical

Shiite cleric under Iran's control, and its spiritual leader is Sheikh Mohammad Hussein Fadlallah. Hezbollah terrorist activities mirror those of Imad Mugniyah, who was the group's international branch chief.

Since Hezbollah's founding, Iran has poured hundreds of millions of dollars in financial aid, military training, weapons, explosives, and diplomatic support into the organization. Syria has given financial, political, diplomatic, and logistical support. Their joint investment has paid some high dividends, as shown by Hezbollah's position in the Middle East today. Its political wing holds 23 seats in Lebanon's 128-member parliament and 2 cabinet ministerial posts. It has also developed a large social welfare network and operates schools, orphanages, and hospitals to assist Lebanese Shiites. Shiites compose about one-third of the population and have developed into a political and military entity completely beholden to Iran and Syria.

In May 2008, Hezbollah demonstrated raw military power in the streets of Beirut, leaving scores dead while settling domestic political scores with Sunni prime minister Fouad Siniora and others. In effect, Hezbollah staged a de facto coup, making it—and by extension its supporters in Tehran and Damascus—the dominant force in Lebanon. This move provided Iran and Syria with more military options against Israel, while embarrassing the United States and intimidating such moderate Arab nations as Egypt, Jordan, and Saudi Arabia.

Hezbollah has evolved from being one of twenty-five militias to becoming Iran's state within a state that challenges the Lebanese government for control of the country. In 2004, UN Security Council Resolution 1559 demanded, among other things, that the GOL disarm the Hezbollah militia. The government has not or, more accurately, cannot achieve this goal. Thus, Hezbollah is free to unleash unbounded violence against Israel, and it threatens the legitimate authority of the GOL. Iran and Syria are pulling the strings of this surrogate state and have never suffered any consequences for sponsoring innumerable acts of terrorism.

After more than a quarter century since its founding by Iran, Hezbollah has grown into being Iran's proxy army in southern Lebanon against Israel and the execution unit in carrying out Iranian policy worldwide. It has a global reach and has cells with highly skilled operatives on every continent. The Revolutionary Guards and Quds Force remain the primary sources of Iranian funding, intelligence, arms, and training while Syria also continues to provide funding, intelligence, logistical and diplomatic support.

Hezbollah's international network utilizes these cells to raise money, to get ready for activation for operations, and to maintain a logistical infrastructure for future attacks. One intelligence estimate reports that Hezbollah has ten cells in the United States and an annual budget of about $400 million, including $100 million to $200 million annually from Iran. Hezbollah raised extensive funds in Canada until 2003 when the Canadian government banned the organization.

One Hezbollah cell operating in Charlotte, North Carolina, ran a cigarette-smuggling ring that sent millions of dollars back to Hezbollah in Lebanon. When it was broken up in 2000, several cell members were accused by law enforcement of sending technical materials to Lebanon, including computers, night vision goggles, global positioning systems, and digital photo equipment. The leader of the cell, Mohamad Youssif Hammoud, had come to the United States from the Shiite sector of Lebanon that is located adjacent to the Marines' 1983 positions at Beirut International Airport. He entered the United States on June 6, 1992, via Caracas, Venezuela, where he paid $200 for a counterfeit visa.

Border guards caught the fraud, but what followed could be a case study on how clever criminals and terrorists use the bureaucracy against us for their own benefit. In what one could call a typical ploy, Hammoud claimed political asylum on the dubious grounds that Israel's Lebanese allies were out to get him, and this fear was his justification for buying a fake U.S. visa. He was allowed entry. A year later, in December 1993, an immigration judge rejected his plea and ordered him deported. Hammoud appealed, which permitted him to remain longer. A year later, while awaiting a verdict, he married an American, giving him legal standing to apply for permanent residency. The Immigration and Naturalization Service (INS) investigated and found both the marriage certificate and the American woman's birth certificate were fraudulent, so in August 1996, Hammoud was again ordered deported, this time within a month.

Ever resourceful, Hammoud went underground. In May 1997, he married a second American. As a backup, he took a third American wife in September 1997, even though she was already married. The INS then mislaid its file on Hammoud's earlier marriage and granted him conditional residency in July 1998. Three months later, Hammoud divorced his second American wife.

The real danger of this saga lies in the fact that Hammoud was a member of Hezbollah and was committed to its extremist views and obsessive hatred of the

United States. He was not an immigrant but a radical jihadist operating an active cell in enemy territory.

On July 21, 2000, about 250 law enforcement officers swooped down and arrested the cell members, eleven Lebanese Muslims, and seven American citizens who took money in exchange for fraudulent marriage licenses. In the U.S. District Court in Charlotte, based on reports of six cooperating witnesses, five secret informants, and other sources, it was revealed that Hammoud had received military training in Hezbollah camps in Lebanon. Several witnesses described him as 100 percent Hezbollah and stated that he would not hesitate to commit terrorist acts in the United States. The cell had built up a sizable arsenal, including fully automatic AK-47 assault rifles, and the members had conducted paramilitary-style training at a remote rifle range east of Charlotte.

It is particularly ironic that Hezbollah, the terrorist organization responsible for the murder of 241 peacekeepers of the 24th MAU in Beirut on October 23, 1983, was operating an active cell in the United States less than a three-hour drive from the MAU's home base at Camp Lejeune. It makes one wonder whether this setup was a coincidence.

—13—

Iran, Syria, and Hezbollah

IRAN

BEGINNING IN 1985, THE DEPARTMENT OF STATE published an annual report called *Patterns of Global Terrorism,* which revealed a wealth of information regarding global trends supported by statistical data. The report evolved into a political football and was discontinued in 2005. Reading the trends, I noted that 2004 reflected the highest number of significant incidents of terrorism ever and the second highest number of loss of life in thirty-five years (2001 being the highest). One constant fact throughout the reports was their description of Iran as the world's most active state sponsor of terrorism. Syria's unrestrained support of terrorism worldwide also earned it a high place on this infamous list.

Each of these country's roles in the suicide truck bombings of October 23, 1983, has been highlighted earlier. Some Iran experts and terrorism analysts, including Robert Baer, a former CIA case officer in the Directorate of Operations; Dr. Patrick L. Clawson, deputy director for research at the Washington Institute for Near East Policy; and Dr. Michael Ledeen, the U.S. intelligence and diplomatic official who testified at the March 2003 trial *Peterson v. the Islamic Republic of Iran,* have unequivocally stated Hezbollah was a tool of Iran. These experts also asserted that Iranian material support and training were essential to executing such a sophisticated plan as the truck bombing. The intelligence community had compiled an all-sources damage assessment after the Marine barracks bombing, in which it studied signals intelligence, overhead intelligence, human intelligence—everything—and put it all together. The IC concluded the evidence was overpowering and that Iran had been behind it. Dr. Ledeen stated he knew of no one who looked at the information and came to any other conclusion.

In 2005, the radical president of Iran, Mahmoud Ahmadinejad, called for Israel to be "wiped off the map." He is the leading spokesman for an extremist government that is in relentless pursuit of producing nuclear weapons despite international disagreement and increasing sanctions from the U.N. Security Council.

In 2007, the United States designated the Islamic Revolutionary Guard Corps as a specially designated global terrorist (SDGT) organization, making it possible to seize its lucrative business assets, which are substantial. This action is long overdue. The IRGC is heavily involved in obtaining nuclear weapons technology and in directly supporting the killing and maiming of hundreds of U.S. servicemen and women in Iraq and Afghanistan.[1]

Iran continues unabated to export, support, and promote terrorism world-wide. An objective analysis of the Iranian mullahs' intentions shows their patience and chicanery in achieving their objectives. Reportedly, Ahmadinejad hosted a terrorist summit in January 2006 in Damascus that was attended by al Qaeda, Hamas, other radical Palestinians, and Imad Mugniyah. Speculation regarding some of their objectives included ensuring an unstable, Shiite-controlled Lebanon to divert the Israeli government from its unilateral disengagement with the Palestinians and to use the Lebanon crisis during the summer of 2006 as a distraction to consolidate its position vis-à-vis Iraq's Shia majority.[2] The Iranians were buying time to hide its nuclear weapons development program. In retrospect, the speculation appears to be an accurate assessment.

Prior to 9/11, Hezbollah boasted that it had killed more Americans than any other terrorist group. The CIA director and other intelligence officials have observed that the Iranian-backed Hezbollah is more capable and dangerous than al Qaeda.

The revelations that Iranian weapons are killing U.S. troops in Iraq and Afghanistan should surprise no one. Conclusive evidence disclosed that the IRGC's Quds Force has transported into Iraq roadside bombs utilizing armor-piercing, explosively formed penetrators (EFPs) that originated in Iran. Other advanced weaponry found in Iraq—all from the Iranian arsenal—includes RPG-29 launchers, 240mm rockets, and perhaps the most ominous, the Misagh-1, a portable surface-to-air missile that uses an infrared guidance system. This influx of sophisticated weapons has been coupled with intelligence that Iran has facilitated Iraqi insurgents' travel and training within its borders. U.S. intelligence officials stated that such Iranian complicity could not take place without approval at the highest levels of the Iranian government.

Among the terrorist groups that Shiite Iran supports are al Qaeda, Hezbollah, Hamas, and the Palestinian Islamic Jihad. Three of them are Sunni groups and are supported, among other reasons, to undercut the peace process between Israel and the Palestinians. This support and Iran's strategic relationship with the Sunni Wahhabi al Qaeda are especially interesting. An Iranian defector from the intelligence services has reported his presence at two meetings in Iran between "top Al-Qaeda operations and Iranian officials" only months before September 11, 2001.[3] Additionally, another report indicates that Imad Mugniyah traveled from Iran to Lebanon "to coordinate links between Hezbollah and Osama Bin Laden's Al-Qaeda terrorist network." This relationship between Iran and al Qaeda was confirmed by the 9/11 Commission. The commission's report highlighted Iran's involvement in the 1996 Khobar Towers bombing in Saudi Arabia, its training of al Qaeda for actions against Israel and the United States, and its offer of safe transport and safe havens for al Qaeda operatives.[4]

What continues to unfold is the debunking of the theory that the ideological separation between the Sunnis and Shiites precludes any cooperation in operations against a common enemy, such as the United States and its allies. The evidence substantiates the old adage that my enemy's enemy is my friend. In reality, Iran has been waging war against the United States for more than thirty years, from the 1979 hostage crisis to the Marine barracks bombing to providing sophisticated weaponry to Sunni and Shia insurgents in Iraq. The Iranian leadership has chosen to wage a radically aggressive campaign to create and accelerate instability throughout the region by using their proxies, many of whom are non-Shia. Some examples include:

- assisting Hamas to launch rocket attacks into Israeli villages from the Gaza Strip;
- continuing to arm Hezbollah to challenge the duly elected government of Lebanon and prepare for the inevitable next war with Israel;

- aiding their lone Arab client, Syria, in their incessant drive to further destabilize Lebanon and Iraq (at last count, Syrian operatives have assassinated eight prominent anti-Syrian Lebanese, including former prime minister Rafiq Hariri in February 2005, journalists, and members of parliament);
- supporting the Sunni Taliban in Afghanistan against NATO forces;
- using the Quds Force to train, equip, and finance Shiite and Sunni extremist militias fighting U.S., Iraqi Army, and Coalition forces in Iraq.

Recently, a partner of the Quds Force has emerged called Department 2800, which was created to support the training, arming, funding, and sometimes direction of the radical Shia militias. Intelligence has confirmed training has taken place inside Iran while facilitating weapons delivery and other sensitive operational support. Senator Joe Lieberman (D-CT) revealed that Iran is operating three training camps near Tehran and "training these people coming back into Iraq to kill our soldiers."[5] Gen. David Petraeus rightly divulged in September 2007 that Iran is one of the main contributors to the death and destruction in Iraq and publicly accused Iran's own ambassador in Baghdad, Hassan Kazemi-Qomi, of being a member of the militant Quds Force. This intelligence all reflects Iran's relentless drive and flexibility in expanding its successful Hezbollah proxy model, which it created in Lebanon in 1983 and has grown and flourished ever since.

Given its history, many analysts and scholars believe that Iran would use nuclear weapons if it acquires them. Iran has not demonstrated any restraint in using any weapon in its arsenal, and Hezbollah appears to be its chosen proxy for executing terrorist operations whenever and wherever Tehran selects the targets. This scenario has a familiar ring.

Iran has evolved as a major player in the Middle East with growing influence. Its proxy war with Israel, which many fail to see as only one front in the global war on terrorism, increases Iran's popularity across the Muslim world. Along with its control of Hezbollah in Lebanon, Iran has attained significant influence with Hamas in Gaza while being allied with Syria. The Iranian capability to orchestrate trouble for Israel on three fronts of its choosing does not promote confidence for the future of the peace process. Add the Quds Force's links to the Taliban and Iranian munitions being smuggled into Iraq and Afghanistan, and Iran has positioned itself to continue to wreak havoc while avoiding retribution.

BRIG. GEN. MASTAFA MOHAMMAD NAJJAR

In August 2005, Mastafa Mohammad Najjar was named the defense minister of Iran. This exalted position has taken on new importance during Iran's inexorable drive to develop nuclear weapons. His previous assignment as the senior commander of the Islamic Revolutionary Guard Corps earned him a reputation of ruthlessness and ideological loyalty. In 1983, he commanded the fifteen hundred–man IRGC expeditionary force sent to Lebanon's Bekaa Valley. As noted, this Iranian unit provided security, planning, training, and operational support for the dual suicide truck bombings on October 23, 1983. Najjar's success in these attacks, which are still celebrated in Tehran today, led to the withdrawal of the multinational peacekeeping force. Withdrawing the MNPF after the bombings, without the United States dispensing any retribution, became a turning point in the unbounded use of terrorism by radical Islamist fanatics worldwide. Under his command, Najjar's IRGC played a key role in the formation of Hezbollah and the education and training of its operations chief, Imad Fayez Mugniyah, who reportedly had lived in and operated out of Iran.

I have often wondered whether Najjar was among those members of the IRGC involved in the fighting at Suq el Garb during the September War of 1983. Whether he was present there is unknown, but his position as commander of the IRGC's detachment lends credence to the supposition that he would have wanted to participate. My guess is that he did.

As the Iranian defense minister, he was most certainly involved in global terrorist attacks and the acquisition of nuclear weaponry. It is more probable than possible that Iran will use its favorite proxy, Hezbollah, to carry out future attacks against the West, including the United States. Najjar's long association with Mugniyah also adds credence to this belief. We could find ourselves, in our own homeland, the victims of a weapon of mass destruction (WMD) in an attack planned and executed by some of the same players who carried out the Beirut barracks bombing in 1983. Some of these dots could very well connect.

BRIG. GEN. AHMAD VAHIDI

In 1983, when Ayatollah Khomeini ordered the IRGC to get more involved with Lebanon's internal affairs, Vahidi was one of the key leaders to be tasked with the formation and operations of the IRGC's Lebanon contingent. His previous assignment was as chief intelligence officer for the IRGC's Ballai Garrison in Turkey, which was a base for special operations abroad.

The Iranian mullahs recognized Vahidi's successful service in Lebanon, including the dual suicide truck bombings in Beirut in 1983. He was promoted in 1991 and assigned by Iran's supreme leader, Ayatollah Ali Khamenei, to establish the Quds Force for the IRGC, serving as its first commander until 1997. All terrorist operations carried out by the Ministry of Information and Security during this period were under his close supervision.

Currently, the deputy defense minister for armed forces logistics, Vahidi was listed by the European Union in June 2008 as a person linked to Iran's proliferation-sensitive nuclear activities and its development of nuclear weapon delivery systems. His primary task is to oversee the research and development of WMDs. Vahidi is another dot connected to the IRGC's Lebanon contingent who has risen to the highest levels of the Ministry of Defense.

Brig. Gen. Ahmad Kazemi

Shortly following Mohammad Najjar's ascent to the top of Iran's defense ministry, another close confidant of his from the IRGC's Lebanon contingent was appointed by Ayatollah Khamenei to head the IRGC's ground forces. During the ceremony marking General Kazemi's promotion, the commander of the IRGC, Maj. Gen. Yahya Rahim Safari, acknowledged and praised Kazemi's past activities in the guard's Lebanon force.

Kazemi's previous assignment was commander of the IRGC Air Force, where he was responsible for the production and development of the Shahab missile. He has been credited with developing solid-fuel technology for the Shahab, which increases the missiles' accuracy. Kazemi also oversaw the development of the Shahab-4 missile with the projected range of two thousand to three thousand kilometers, capable of carrying a nuclear warhead that could strike Israel or the heart of Western Europe.

On January 9, 2006, Kazemi was killed, along with a hundred others, when a decrepit military plane crashed in Iran after it was ordered to fly despite warnings by its pilot. It was a fitting end to an arrogant thug who rose to infamy on bloodshed and carnage. Kazemi is gone, but it makes one wonder how many other alumni from the IRGC's Lebanon contingent in the early 1980s have risen to the highest levels of today's Iranian Defense Ministry.

GEN. ALI-REZA ASGARI

A former Iranian deputy defense minister and founding member of the IRGC, General Asgari disappeared while on a personal visit to Istanbul on December 7, 2006. Whether he defected or was kidnapped remains to be determined as of this writing. He is another Beirut dot to be connected. Like his predecessor Najjar, Asgari was the commander of the IRGC in Lebanon in the 1980s and 1990s and, according to former CIA case officer Robert Baer, was a central figure in the kidnappings that became prevalent following the Marines' withdrawal from Lebanon, including that of Bill Buckley. Baer stated that Asgari undoubtedly took part in the planning of the 1983 suicide truck bombing of the Marine barracks in Beirut.[6] His long association with Defense Minister Najjar should provide further evidence that the bombings' key perpetrators have ascended to the Iranian Defense Ministry's highest positions. He was interrogated by Western intelligence services, which no doubt focused on Iranian plans to attack U.S. and Western interests.

SYRIA

In the byzantine world of Lebanese politics, one aspect is certain: Syria, while being predominately Sunni, has been one of the main beneficiaries of the Lebanese civil war. Syria's Sunni majority is dominated by the Alawites sect. Iran's creation of Hezbollah, the troop movements of the Iranian Revolutionary Guard Corps, and Iran's sustained military, financial, and logistical support of both groups could not have occurred without Syrian collusion and complicity. The main competing Lebanese groups—the Sunnis, the Shias led by Hezbollah, the Maronite Christians, and the Druze—can rely on Syrian (and Iranian) interference to fan the flames of discontent among their parties. Iran and Syria are still committed to destabilizing the government and maintaining control of Lebanon. Those factors were present in 1983 and have expanded significantly ever since. Syria and Iran use each other to pursue mutual goals. It seems a contest to determine who hates Israel the most to gain influence and popularity in the Arab world. After Syria lost its main benefactor after the collapse of the Soviet Union, Iran provides the financial support, along with military and operational backing to confront Israel and destabilize the western-supported GOL. (Who else would?) The recent Lebanese election supporting the western tilt is likely to increase Syrian/Iranian (through

Hezbollah) destabilization efforts. The pro-western Iraq government (albeit tentatively) on Syria's other border increases their need to prevent stability in Lebanon. Both will continue to use terrorism and subversion (via Hezbollah and other pro-Syrian factions inside Lebanon) to accomplish this. Iran has offered to fund, to the tune of $1 billion last year, new Syrian fighter jets, tanks and anti-ship missiles, and to aid Syria's nuclear and chemical weapons research programs. Syria reaps many benefits, political and strategical, to maintain a destabilized Lebanese government.[7]

Besides its implication in former Lebanese prime minister Hariri's assassination, Syria remains the prime suspect in several other murders in Lebanon. Syria and Iran have a marriage of convenience. Syria has allowed the IRGC to use its territory for massive shipments of weapons to Lebanon, while Hezbollah has become a wholly owned subsidiary of Iran. This relationship between Syria and Iran has grown and developed the past quarter century to such a degree that former secretary of state Condoleezza Rice called Syria "a way-station for Iranian arms that cross the Middle East."[8]

Syria has a broader role than just accommodating transshipment of arms from Iran to Hezbollah in Lebanon. Following the 2006 Israeli-Hezbollah conflict, intelligence revealed that Hezbollah possessed large numbers of sophisticated medium-range rockets manufactured by the Syrian munitions industry. Add the fact that many insurgents' attacks against American troops in Iraq originated in Syria, and it points to Syria's response to America's goal of fostering democracy. Syria's answer is to export death and destruction, securing its fully deserved place as one of the leading state sponsors of terrorism worldwide.

GEN. GHAZI KENAAN

The chief of Syrian intelligence in Beirut from 1982 to 2002, Gen. Ghazi Kenaan built a reputation for instilling fear in his opponents as well as his associates. He was a key member of the select Baathist clique close to President Hafez al-Assad and Assad's successor and son, Bashar. It has been reported that Kenaan had a boundless, greedy appetite for money and power. In 1983, he was a key player, if not *the* key player, in providing the infrastructure in Lebanon for transporting weapons and equipment and moving the IRGC contingent through Syria into Syrian-controlled territory in the Bekaa Valley.

In more recent times, Kenaan was widely suspected of organizing Hariri's assassination. As the UN investigation closed in on him, his financial assets in the United States were frozen. To no one's surprise, in late 2005, he was found shot dead in his office. The official Syrian report ruled it a suicide. A colleague of Kenaan's, Foreign Minister Farouk Al-Sharaa, also a veteran of the Assad clique, told reporters that "unjust and vague information had contributed to the killing"—whereupon he quickly corrected himself, "I mean, the suicide." It points to how Syria prefers to fix problems directly and quickly follow with a denial of any involvement. The final UN investigative report on Hariri's assassination has since been delayed.[9]

VICE PRESIDENT ABDUL HALIM KHADDAM

A close confidant of President Hafez al-Assad's since high school, Khaddam was the deputy prime minister, the minister of foreign affairs, and the chief negotiator for the cease-fire that ended the September War in 1983. He met often with U.S. special envoy Robert McFarlane and Saudi Arabian negotiator Rafiq Hariri. The 24th MAU aircraft flew the negotiators frequently during this period. After the Israelis' withdrawal in the late summer of 1983, Khaddam predicted to his Lebanese counterpart, Elie Salem, that the United States would withdraw after it had lost a few Marines.[10] Khaddam remained a principal power player in the Syrian ruling elite for nearly thirty years and remained a close adviser to Bashar Assad. He ultimately was advanced to vice president of Syria. As the Syrian primary diplomat in Lebanon through the years, he became friends and formed lucrative business partnerships with the Lebanese elite, particularly Hariri, who would become Lebanon's prime minister.

Following Hariri's assassination, Khaddam likely saw the handwriting on the wall and shortly thereafter announced his resignation from the government. He moved to Paris, allegedly to write his memoir. Within months, Khaddam broke his silence and disclosed that President Bashar al-Assad had harshly threatened Hariri not long before the assassination and that the operation could not have been carried out by Syrian intelligence officials without Assad's knowledge. He later called for the overthrow of the Assad regime.

Khaddam further revealed his deep convictions that Assad was responsible for the Hariri killing and indicated that he was also behind several subsequent assassinations in Lebanon of anti-Syrian opposition leaders. Khaddam has openly met with the UN investigators looking into Hariri's murder and reportedly has provided unique insight into Syria's role in this assassination.[11]

LEBANON

Lebanon's plight could easily be a case study of what can happen to a country that does not or, more appropriately, cannot control its own borders. Its small size and disparate population intensify the differences among the many conflicting parties. These multiple religious groups' disputes have often escalated into violent clashes internally and allowed foreign armies to use Lebanon as their battlefield.

The bombings of the U.S. embassy and the MNF peacekeepers' headquarters provided an early glimpse of Islamist fanaticism and its adherents' obsessive hatred of the West and what we represent. The experience also revealed their game book on how they plan to fight us and laid the framework for the current global war on terrorism.

RAFIQ HARIRI

Born in Sidon, Lebanon, in 1944, Rafiq Hariri was educated in Lebanon and moved to Saudi Arabia in 1965 after leaving Arab University in Beirut. He started his own construction business, which eventually grew to become the largest in the region, making him a billionaire. A Sunni who never forgot his Lebanese roots, Hariri stayed involved in his home country's economic and political life. In 1983, he returned as a key negotiator for Saudi Arabia, attaining the cease-fire that ended the September Mountain War. Later, Hariri became the primary instigator behind the National Reconciliation Conference that ended the Lebanese civil war in 1989. (Called the Taef Agreement, it also included the drafting of a new constitution for Lebanon.) A Lebanese patriot, he worked tirelessly toward Lebanese independence. Elected to the parliament, he later was appointed prime minister of Lebanon five times between 1992 and 2004.

In October 2004, Hariri resigned as prime minister to protest Syrian demands for a change to the Constitution that would extend the term of Lebanese president Emile Lahoud, a Syrian puppet. The Syrian-controlled Lebanese Parliament virtually assured passage of the change. Hariri was summoned to Damascus, where he was intimidated, humiliated, and threatened by Bashar Assad, according to the former Syrian vice president, Abdul Halim Khaddam.

On February 14, 2005, Hariri's high-security motorcade was driving midday through the fashionable hotel district, which Hariri had rebuilt after the civil war, when a massive truck bomb demolished the convoy. More than two thousand pounds of high explosives were packed in the Mitsubishi van, which had been stolen in Japan and driven to Lebanon from Damascus by a Syrian colonel. Hariri and seven of his bodyguards were instantly killed, with at least 14 bystanders killed and nearly 220 injured. The primary reason for his assassination was deemed to be Hariri's work behind the September 2004 adoption of UN Security Council Resolution 1559, which called for the withdrawal of all foreign forces from Lebanon. It is well to remember that this issue was the Syrians' main point of contention with the 1983 U.S.-sponsored Lebanese-Israeli Peace Accord (the May 17 Agreement) and repeated later at the national reconciliation talks in November 1983. Syrian pressure eventually forced President Gemayel of Lebanon to revoke the peace accord on February 17, 1984. Four Lebanese generals, top pro-Syrian security chiefs, were arrested and held since September 2005 for Hariri's murder. A judge of the special international tribunal investigating the assassination ordered them released in April 2009, saying it did not have enough evidence to indict them.

In the category of unintended consequences, it was precisely Syria's over-the-top, heinous assassination of Hariri, a Lebanese son and patriot, that ignited international pressure and demonstrations in Beirut. It launched the Cedar Revolution, which forced Assad to withdraw his army after almost thirty years of occupation. However, even though the Syrian Army departed, Syria's intensive efforts to destabilize Lebanon's elected government have not subsided. If Syria, along with Iranian-supported Hezbollah, is successful, the return of the Syrian Army to Beirut is virtually certain.

WALID JUMBLATT

As the leader of the Progressive Socialist Party and the Druze minority, Jumblatt was a fierce opponent of the Lebanese government and its Christian president Amin Gemayel in 1983. The Marine compound at Beirut International Airport was a frequent target of Druze artillery and Katyusha rockets fired from positions in the hills overlooking Beirut. Originally, this incoming was interpreted as spillover fire directed at the "real" target, an adjacent Lebanese Army training camp and

LAF artillery positions. As the danger escalated during the summer of 1983, Druze batteries in the hills would "walk" adjusted artillery and rocket fire into Marine positions. The game and their intentions were no longer hidden. To the wonder of many observers, Jumblatt was controlled and supported by Syria, whose agents were considered responsible for the murder of Walid's father, Kamal Jumblatt, in Lebanon in 1977.

Shortly after the Israelis announced their intention to withdraw to the Awali River, mortar, rocket, and artillery fires from Druze batteries rained on BIA, wounding three Marines and closing the airport. Jumblatt often used this barrage as an expression of protest to register his discontent with the Lebanese government and the Marines. Under Syrian pressure, on July 23, Jumblatt announced the formation of a National Salvation Front opposed to the May 17 Agreement.

Throughout August 1983, Jumblatt and President Gemayel publicly jockeyed for position. Gemayel announced that the Lebanese Army would enter the Shouf Mountains to fill the vacuum left when the Israelis abandoned their positions "because it is the only alternative to the armies of occupation." Jumblatt announced to the press in Damascus that the U.S. Marines in the MNF had "bluntly and directly" threatened the Druze. On August 28, following a Druze bombardment of BIA and the surrounding area, the Marines returned fire in self-defense. The next day, another Druze barrage of mortar rounds killed two Marines and wounded several others. The Marines' response this time was precise and lethal, silencing the Druze fire.

On September 1, during savage fighting in the Shia southern suburbs, Amal leader Nabih Berri stated that the Marines had "turned into a fighting force against Muslims in Lebanon." On the same day, Jumblatt said in Damascus that "the mere fact that the Marines are providing the Lebanese Factional Army with logistical support, expertise, and training is enough for us to consider them enemies."[12]

During the Mountain War, I did a satellite-feed interview with Ted Koppel of ABC's *Nightline*. Prior to the show, Koppel mentioned to me that he was also going to interview Walid Jumblatt for an opposing view. I was tempted to ask Koppel if he would ask Jumblatt why his militia was firing at the Marines at BIA since we were on a peacekeeping mission and in a defensive posture. I didn't have time to follow through with this request, but I later learned that Jumblatt said he did not believe we were a peacekeeping force because the Marines were helping the

Lebanese Armed Forces, which were shelling and killing his people. What Jumblatt did not mention was the Druze's indiscriminate shelling of Christian villages and East Beirut, causing untold civilian casualties. It was clear Jumblatt's total support was coming from Syria and that he was being used as a mouthpiece for Syrian propaganda.

It's taken some time, but apparently Jumblatt has had a change of heart. In December 2006, he depicted Syrian president Bashir Assad as a "serial killer." He has publicly accused Hezbollah, along with Syria, of being involved in some of the assassinations of prominent anti-Syrian opposition figures. He further asserted that there is political, security, and intelligence linkage between Hezbollah and Syria. Jumblatt told reporters that Hezbollah leader Sayyed Hassan Nasrallah is not a Lebanese leader, since he acts on instructions from Iran and Syria, and that Nasrallah's master instructor was Imad Mugniyah, who resided in Iran. Jumblatt can speak with some authority about Syrian and Hezbollah relationships. One wonders whether the crafty survivor has an ulterior motive or if this is a genuine change of heart, but in either case it may be too little and too late.

Pierre Gemayel

On November 21, 2006, just after attending church services in the Christian neighborhood of Jdeideh, Minister of Industry Pierre Gemayel was gunned down. He was the sixth anti-Syrian figure killed in two years. Gemayel, thirty-four, was the son of Amin Gemayel, who was president of Lebanon from 1982 to 1988 and during the multinational peacekeeping mission. Pierre's uncle, Bashir Gemayel, was the president-elect when he was assassinated by a massive bomb on September 14, 1982, which led to the Sabra and Shatila massacres and the return of the Marines for the presence mission.

The death of Pierre Gemayel, an outspoken opponent of the Syrian-allied Hezbollah and a supporter of the anti-Syrian faction, had Syrian fingerprints all over it. That his death came hours before the UN Security Council voted to endorse an agreement with Lebanon to create a tribunal and prosecute the pro-Syrian suspects in the Hariri assassination was no coincidence. It was the second time a Lebanese politician has been killed when the UN Security Council was meeting on Hariri's assassination. Syria, yet again, denied any involvement.

THE WORLD TODAY

The past quarter century has witnessed an enormous eruption of radical Islamist terrorism, which has evolved to become the most serious threat to our national security in the twenty-first century. The intense divisions among the Islamic ideologies of the Shiites, Sunnis, Alawites, Wahhabis, Salafists, and so forth have not been an impediment to their cooperating and coordinating mutual terrorist operations against a common enemy. They are united in their goal to subjugate the free world to the Islamic Sharia law and to destroy Western civilization.

Iran's close relationship with fellow state sponsor of terrorism, Syria, is a matter of record and a prime example that ideological differences do not hinder terrorist attacks on common enemies. Hamas in the Gaza Strip, al Qaeda worldwide, the Taliban in Afghanistan, and radical Shia and Sunni insurgents in Iraq are a few of the recipients of Shia Iranian overt and covert support. These actions have elevated Iran's stature throughout the Middle East while sending a not too subtle message to our Arab allies and their sizable Shia populations.

The primary vehicle Iran uses to execute its strategy is the Islamic Revolutionary Guard Corps and its Quds Force. The Hezbollah model, which has proven so successful in Lebanon since its inception in 1983, has appeared in Iraq to promote instability and to kill U.S. and Coalition forces. Few can argue with the fact that Iran's use of proxy forces has clearly advanced its goals while providing enough safe distance to avoid any direct retribution.

The unfolding Iranian strategy involving many activities across numerous fronts accomplishes several purposes with one overriding objective—the acquisition of nuclear weapons. The timing and intent of these activities are meant to create noise, divert attention, and buy the Iranians time to achieve their primary objective. Additionally, Iran is allegedly producing and stockpiling chemical weapons at several production sites. They are also suspected of having biological research laboratories and unknown quantities of biological agents and of having begun limited weaponization.[13] When one adds WMDs to Iran's current capabilities, the threat increases exponentially. These developments do not bode well for a peaceful future.

—14—

The War Comes Home

ON SEPTEMBER 11, 2001, I arose early to go into my office in Santa Barbara, California. Then the telephone calls started coming in. Like millions of Americans, I was mesmerized, watching and listening to the reports of the terrorist attacks on the World Trade Center and the Pentagon. My first thought was, The bastards have attacked our homeland almost exactly eighteen years after the Beirut suicide attacks. Even the modus operandi was similar: they used the simultaneous, co-ordinated suicide bombing model, only employing a different means of transporting the payloads to their targets.

It didn't take me long to realize the reason for these bold attacks on innocent Americans in our homeland. Since the suicide bombings of our U.S. embassy and peacekeepers in Beirut in 1983, we had never retaliated against those who have been murdering Americans. America had lost its sense of justice and its deterrence capability had lost any credibility. Our enemies smelled blood. I was watching the result of our passive response to these earlier acts of war.

I raced to my offices at Special Technologies Laboratory (STL) where I was the deputy director. The workforce comprised an exceptionally talented group of nuclear physicists, scientists, and engineers who created remarkable innovations under a Bechtel Nevada contract for the Department of Energy. I found the television sets were on, and everyone was closely monitoring the developments of this second Day of Infamy. When the hijacked American Airlines Flight 77 crashed into the Pentagon, it brought back some personal recollections. Just as many of my associates, I had visited the Pentagon on many occasions and have several Marine friends who have been stationed there through the years. My last assignment, before I left the CIA in 1990, was as the Counterterrorist Center's liaison officer to the Joint Chiefs of Staff. A month before 9/11, I had visited the Pentagon, specifically the renovated Wedge 1, which received the brunt of the suicide plane attack. STL had provided equipment and services as part of the facilities' upgrade contract.

As the day wore on, I received notification that STL was tasked to deploy a team to New York, and I was to be a member. STL had developed an impressive and effective ground-penetrating radar system that had been utilized worldwide primarily to search for survivors of natural disasters such as earthquakes. The Special Rescue Radar and Technical Support Team, led by Senior Engineer Rory McCarthy, and its equipment were put aboard a Bechtel executive jet that flew nonstop through the night. With all commercial flights grounded, it was strange to look out the aircraft's window and not see any aircraft in the air anywhere. We arrived at LaGuardia Airport at dawn and were whisked to the Javits Convention Center in Manhattan with a Connecticut State Police escort that had been called in to augment security.

For the next week, we operated out of the Javits Center and traveled to Ground Zero with other rescue teams searching for survivors. As we moved through the site, the utter devastation and massive recovery operation quickly brought me back to Beirut eighteen years earlier, provoking the same gut-wrenching feeling. Fortunately, we were not taking sniper fire at Ground Zero, but the same seething rage returned, which I later realized was inevitable.

The courageous, superhuman efforts of the New York City police officers, firefighters, and rescue teams mirrored the peacekeepers' performance in Beirut not that long ago. My father's family had lived in New York before moving to St. Louis in the 1920s, and Dad would tell us what a special place New York was. Those thoughts returned to me when our team was being transported from the Ground Zero site, many times late at night. The streets were lined with mostly young people, waving American flags and applauding. Volunteer chefs from some of the finest restaurants gave the rescue teams meals they'd cooked, and other volunteers passed out drinks, fruit, water, and snacks. This outpouring of patriotism was reflected in all Americans pulling together in a common cause. With politics set aside, a battered Old Glory flying in the midst of the ruins at

Ground Zero sent an inspirational message to freedom-loving people everywhere that America, reflecting a national defiance, would not waver before these heinous attacks and that the spirit of America lives on. These are memories I will never forget.

The search for survivors, despite enormous exertion from the rescue teams, soon gave way to reality. Hoping against hope, I began to have the same sinking feeling that I had experienced in Beirut. The Twin Towers' collapse literally pulverized everything and everyone within and around them. Adding to this destruction were the fires, perpetuated by the jet fuel, cremating whatever did remain. It was a level of absolute destruction that I had never seen before and hope never to witness again. Ground Zero in New York was Beirut on steroids in terms of devastation and loss of lives. The chances of finding anyone alive became more fleeting with each passing moment.

On the flight back to Santa Barbara, the realization hit me that we were officially at war with a fanatical enemy who uses extreme Islamic ideology to further its deranged attacks on free people. I also realized this war was not going to be short.

SUICIDE ATTACKS

The American spirit of solidarity after the 9/11 suicide attacks was something to behold. There was a national realization that the attacks were against all Americans and not just those victims in New York, Washington, and aboard a doomed flight that crashed into a field in Pennsylvania. Our freedoms, liberty, and way of life are threatened by Islamist jihadists who have stated and demonstrated their visceral hatred for Western civilization. This clash of modern-day civilizations cannot be wished away.

The introduction of suicide vehicle bombs as a tactic in Beirut in 1983 proved to be an effective, if heinous, tool. The bottom line is that it worked, and recent history has verified its ruthless efficiency and enormous cost in innocent lives. The suicide attacks on the U.S. and French peacekeepers were cynically planned to ensure success for the terrorists and to cause massive casualties. Today, a Beirut-type suicide truck bomb remains the biggest threat in Iraq and Afghanistan.

Maj. Gen. John F. Kelly, commanding general in Ramadi, Iraq, in 2008 related how this threat was drilled into all his Marines. He realized that this kind of attack was all the terrorists had left to really hurt them as they prepared to turn over Anbar Province to the Iraqis. Kelly had lost his best friend in the 1983 Beirut bombing.

On April 22, 2008, two Marines were assigned to guard the main gate of the Joint Security Station (JSS) Nasser in Ramadi. At dawn, they spotted a very large Mercedes truck—in fact, the same model used in the Beirut attack—as it turned down an alley from the main street and accelerated toward the facility, weaving through concrete barricades. The two Marines knew exactly what was happening. They immediately opened fire, one with an M-60 machine gun, the other with his M-16 rifle. The entire event as it appeared on the JSS security camera tape lasted about six seconds.

The Marines' accurate fire peppered the radiator and windshield; the truck slowed but kept rolling. A few dozen feet from the gate, the truck exploded. Both Marines were killed while still firing their weapons. An investigation later concluded that the truck, driven by a suicide bomber, carried a bomb with an estimated explosive weight of more than two thousand pounds. Three Marines were wounded as were eight Iraqi officers and twenty-four civilians. The attack was timed to cause maximum casualties. Because of an ongoing relief in place, more than fifty Marines were on site with a similar number of Iraqi police officers. Only because of the two Marines' bravery was a catastrophe averted. The investigators and survivors agreed that if the Marines had not stood their ground to their deaths, the truck bomb would have decimated the JSS and everyone in it.

On Friday, February 20, 2009, Navy Crosses were presented to the families of Lance Cpl. Jordan Haerter and Cpl. Jonathan Yale at the National Museum of the Marine Corps at Quantico. The parents of some of the Marines saved by Haerter and Yale attended the ceremony as a sign of respect and to express their gratitude to the families. In making the presentation, Navy secretary Donald Winter stated that Haerter and Yale earned "a place of legend in Marine Corps history for generations to come. Although not from the same unit, they acted as one in response to the threat."[1]

To further gain an appreciation of this threat, it is helpful to note not only the attacks but also the targets selected. In Iraq and elsewhere, targets have included headquarters of Iraq's parliament, mosques, girls' schools, police and military training and recruiting centers, marketplaces, financial centers, hospitals, trains, buses, funerals, wedding receptions in hotels, student gatherings, restaurants, and Internet cafés. The attacks' intimidation factor is as clear as their global scope. The Islamist extremists fully understand the impact these attacks have on civilized societies and focus on targets that are essential and revered by free people.

Beyond the carnage, suicide bombings provide grand theater via the international media coverage. Since their genesis in Beirut in 1983, suicide attacks have become a weapon of choice of the Shia and Sunni alike. This insidious tactic carries a profound psychological message of fear and subjugation. Humiliation and hate are constant companions. Such attacks are very difficult to deter, and their increased usage reflects the terrorists' desire for the spectacular hysteria and cruel depiction of the chaos they create.

TODAY'S CHALLENGE

America and the rest of Western civilization are facing a formidable threat unlike any other we have ever faced. This enemy has no regard for the rules of warfare, wears no uniform, plots secret attacks on vulnerable civilian targets, and rejoices in the carnage it wreaks. Its extreme ideology forbids freedom of conscience, rejects any tolerance, and demands total adherence to dictatorial orders. Such beliefs can only be imposed through force, fear, and intimidation. Those who object are brutalized or killed.

One of the terrorists' prime objectives, since the 1983 Beirut bombing, is to end American and Western influence in the Middle East. Their ultimate goal is to establish an Islamic empire encompassing a region from Spain, across North Africa, through the Middle East and South Asia, all the way around to Indonesia. Their ambitions include arming themselves with weapons of mass destruction, destroying Israel, and causing mass casualties among Americans and our Western allies. In order to prevent such attacks, we must stay on the offensive, taking proactive measures with our allies to disrupt their plans and attacks. President George W. Bush rightly pointed out that terrorist states and their proxies do not reveal these threats in formal declarations and that responding to such enemies only after an attack is not self-defense—it is suicide.

Terrorism is a tactic with strategic goals that Islamist extremists use to advance their cause and intimidate free democracies. The 9/11 Commission produced many recommendations, including the legislation that created the Office of the

Director of National Intelligence. One of the commission's most important recommendations was to recognize the enemy's nature and sources of hatred and to realize that we must deal with these issues. In addition to being militarily proactive in using deadly force against organized terrorists, we must address the source of the resentment and hostility.

What was once a proud culture among the world's civilizations, Islam today finds many of its adherents living in a level of poverty that feeds their rage, frustrations, and loathing. Many Muslim countries, such as Pakistan, Egypt, and Indonesia, urgently need help building schools that teach reading and arithmetic instead of sending their children to the madrassas, which instill hatred of America and our allies. Currently, the latter is often their only option.

As a member of the 9/11 Commission, former secretary of the navy John Lehman pointed out that America must take just as vigorous and as proactive a role in the war of ideas as we do in the military war against the Islamist terrorists. In conjunction with our military, we must halt the source of this hatred by fighting and winning the war of ideas.

Currently, we are seeing debates over such controversial subjects as rendition, interceptions of terrorists' phone and Internet traffic, the prison at Guantánamo Bay, the definition of torture, and deliberate leaks of national security information to the media. All attempt to answer the key question, how should we fight this battle? Those holding positions of responsibility would do well to think through the implications of a successful WMD attack on a U.S. city. One likely result would bring much heavier restrictions on our personal freedoms and privacy to increase the level of security that the American people would demand.

The Islamist jihadists attacked us in Beirut, but they have also struck in New York, Washington, London, Madrid, Tel Aviv, Bali, Kabul, and numerous other locations around the world. Their indiscriminate targeting of civilians and brutality reflect their fear and hatred of liberty and freedom. We must pursue victory over this scourge of mankind, not only for our own security, but also to honor the valor and sacrifice of our finest and most dedicated warriors, those who go into harm's way to protect the freedoms we all cherish.

Appendix A.
Responses

NONLETHAL RESPONSE: AUDIO-VISUAL AND ELECTRONIC SIGNALS

Activate alert conditions four through one

Scramble helicopters to ships

Activate counter-mortar/counter-battery radars

Lay 81mm mortars on threat azimuth

Lay M-198 155mm howitzers on threat azimuth

Move TOW vehicles within perimeter to direct-fire position

Move M60A1 tanks within perimeter to direct-fire position

Move NGF ships to fire support area (FSA) appropriate to threat

Launch section of AH-1T Cobras to battle positions over Green Beach

Electronic countermeasures

SEMILETHAL RESPONSE: AUDIO-VISUAL SIGNALS

Fire red star cluster from TOW/tank

Fire platoon one of 81mm mortar illumination rounds over target

Fire battery one of 155mm howitzer illumination rounds over target

Fire anti-SAM flare from AH-1T Cobra over Green Beach

Fire two battery, single salvo of NGF illumination rounds over target

LETHAL RESPONSE: DIRECT FIRE

Direct fire .50-caliber machine gun

Direct fire 105mm tank main gun

Direct fire Dragon missile/TOW missile (range and target dependent)

Direct fire M-198 155mm howitzer

Direct fire from 3-inch/50 naval gun

Direct fire from 5-inch/54 naval gun

Direct fire from AH-1T (choice of system dependent on pilot's judgment, target, and threat range). Order of priority:
>20mm cannon
>5-inch Zuni rocket
>TOW missile

LETHAL RESPONSE: INDIRECT FIRE
>81mm mortar
>155mm howitzer
>AH-1T Cobra 2.75 rocket
>5-inch/54 naval gun
>Fixed-wing aircraft

This formalization of our response schedule would be evaluated each step for applicability in each situation and its effect upon the attacking forces. There was no fixed time period between each step, and many of them could be simultaneous. Some could be skipped if they were considered inappropriate for a particular situation. All, however, would be considered. Close coordination would be maintained with higher headquarters during the process. The *primary* purpose of this schedule is to convey my intent to limit our response to the lowest level possible.

Appendix B.
Edward Hickey's Message to the White House

CONFIDENTIAL

WHITE HOUSE SITUATION ROOM

5/4/95

PAGE 01 OF 05   EDWARD V. HICKEY JR 0003   DTG: 271727Z OCT 83   SN: 07347
SIT761   AN010312   TOR: 300/19432

DISTRIBUTION: MCF DEAV BAKE /005
WHSR COMMENT: BAKER DEAVER MCFARLANE

OP IMMED
ZCZCSAM003
DE WTE33 +0003 3001727
O 271727Z OCT 83
FM EDWARD V. HICKEY JR.

TO THE WHITE HOUSE FOR BAKER, DEAVER, MCFARLANE

CONFIDENTIAL / DELIVER IMMEDIATELY

THE FOLLOWING MAY HELP THE PRESIDENT IN HIS ADDRESS TONIGHT.

WHAT I WITNESSED IN THE PAST THREE DAYS IS AN UNBELIEVEABLE

TESTIMONY TO THE ARMED FORCES.   THE SCENES WILL REMAIN WITH

ME FOREVER.   THE AIRMEN REVERENTLY UNLOADING CASKETS, LATE

AT NIGHT ON A COLD RUNWAY, AIR FORCE CREWS AND MEDEVAC

PERSONNEL WORKING FEVERISHLY, LOVINGLY AND AROUND THE CLOCK.

ARMY DOCTORS AND NURSES WHOSE SKILL RESULTED IN MEDICAL

MIRACLES.   SAILORS FROM EVERY SHIP IN THE FLEET, INCLUDING

THE NEW JERSEY, VOLUNTEERING TO COME ASHORE TO DIG FOR

SURVIVORS, AND THOSE MARINES-WORDS SIMPLY CANNOT DESCRIBE

WHITE HOUSE SITUATION ROOM

PAGE 02 OF 05   EDWARD V. HICKEY JR 0003   DTG: 271727Z OCT 83   PSN: 073473

THEM: A CRITICALLY INJURED MARINE IN AN INTENSIVE CARE

WARD LABORIOUSLY SCRIBBLING "SEMPER FIDELIS".   SENIOR

MARINES, INCLUDING THEIR COMMANDANT, WITNESSING

THE EVENT CRYING OPENLY; MARINES WHO HAD NOT SLEPT FOR

36 HOURS SEARCHING FOR THEIR FRIENDS IN THE RUBBLE.   THE

MARINE WE BROUGHT OUT WITH US, SITTING IN THE BACK OF OUR

DARKENED PLANE, TEARS STREAMING DOWN HIS FACE, CLUTCHING

A PICTURE OF HIS BROTHER WHO WAS KILLED - AND A SENIOR AIDE

TO THE COMMANDANT WITH HIS ARM AROUND HIM, AND TEARS STREAM-

ING DOWN HIS FACE TOO.   AND, THE MARINES, ALL OF THEM

EXHAUSTED, RETURNING TO THEIR POSTS WITH GREATER RESOLVE

THAN EVER.   AFTER WITNESSING THESE SCENES AND OTHERS WHICH

I WOULD NOT BELIEVE IF I DIDN'T WITNESS, MY ONLY

THOUGHT OVER AND OVER WAS WHERE IN GOD'S NAME DO WE FIND

SUCH MEN AND WOMEN.

ONE MEMORY I SHALL CHERISH A LIFETIME IS A NAVY JEWISH

CHAPLAIN WORKING IN THE RUBBLE, CONSOLING AND INSPIRING THE

RESCUE WORKERS, WEARING A ROUND PIECE OF CAMOUFLAGE CLOTH

CONFIDENTIAL

WHITE HOUSE SITUATION ROOM

PAGE 03 OF 05   EDWARD V. HICKEY JR 0003   DTG: 271727Z OCT 83   PSN: 073473

IN PLACE OF A YAMAKA.

ON FRIDAY PRECEDING THE TRAGEDY THE RABBI HELD A MEMORIAL SERVICE FOR A MARINE. HE ASKED THE PROTESTANT AND CATHOLIC CHAPLAINS TO JOIN HANDS AND READ THE 23RD PSALMS IN UNISON. HIS PURPOSE WAS TO SYMBOLIZE WHAT WE, AS AMERICANS, WERE TRYING TO ACCOMPLISH.

HE TOLD THE ASSEMBLED BATTALION OF MARINES, MANY OF WHOM WOULD BE IN THAT BUILDING ON SUNDAY, THAT IF WE WERE SUCCESSFUL., SOMEDAY CHRISTIANS, MOSLEMS AND JEWS IN THAT TROUBLED PART OF THE WORLD WOULD BE ABLE TO JOIN HANDS - AND WHEN THAT DAY ARRIVES LEBANESE CHILDREN WOULD BE ABLE TO GROW UP IN A SOCIETY LIKE OURS - LIKE THE SOCIETY IN WHICH THOSE YOUNG MARINES GREW UP - ONE OF SECURITY, PEACE AND FREEDOM.

THE MORNING OF THE EXPLOSION THE PROTESTANT CHAPLIN WAS IN THE BUILDING AND TRAPPED UNDER DEBRIS. THE RABBI AND PRIEST, SHARING A ROOM IN A BUILDING ABOUT 50 METERS AWAY RUSHED TO THE SCENE. THE PROTESTANT CHAPLAIN WAS ONE OF THE FIRST THEY

CONFIDENTIAL

WHITE HOUSE SITUATION ROOM

PAGE 04 OF 05   EDWARD V. HICKEY JR 0003   DTG: 271727Z OCT 83   PSN: 073473

CAME ACROSS.   IGNORING THE POSSIBILITY OF SECONDARY EXPLOSIONS

AND WITHIN EASY AIM OF SNIPERS DUE TO FIRES WHICH LIT THE AREA,

THEY MANAGED TO EXTRACT THE INJURED CHAPLAIN FROM THE WRECKAGE

AND CARRIED HIM TO SAFETY.   THE RABBI AND PRIEST RETURNED

TO THE RUBBLE AND CONTINUED TO WORK.   THE PRIEST DID WHAT HE COULD

TO RELIEVE THE INJURIES AND ANNOINTED OVER TWE HUNDRED -

EVERY ONE OF THE CASUALTIES.   THE RABBI PRAYED OVER EACH VICTIM,

AS HE DID SO HE USED PARTS OF HIS JACKET AND UNDERSHIRT TO

WIPE THE BLOOD OFF FACES OF THE MARINES.   AFTER USING UP HIS JACKET

AND UNDERSHIRT, HE USED HIS YAMAKA TO WIPE THE FACE OF AN INJURED

MARINE.   TWO DAYS LATER HE SAT UTTERLY EXHAUSTED WHEN A MARINE

WALKED UP TO HIM WITH A SQUARE PIECE OF CLOTH WHICH HE HAD CUT FROM

HIS UTILITY HAT AND FASHIONED INTO A YAMAKA.   THIS MORNING I SAW THE

RABBI IN A HOSPITAL CONSOLING THE WOUNDED, HE STILL WORE THE

YAMAKA - HE TOLD ME IT WAS THE GREATEST HONOR EVER BESTOWED

UPON HIM.

 I WOULD PREFER THE SOURCE OF THE ABOVE TO BE ANONYMOUS.

IF IT HELPS THE PRESIDENT HOWEVER, FOR THE SOURCE TO BE IDENTIFIED

CONFIDENTIAL

WHITE HOUSE SITUATION ROOM

PAGE 05 OF 05   EDWARD V. HICKEY JR 0003   DTG: 271727Z OCT 83   PSN: 073473

AS AN ASSISTANT TO THE PRESIDENT WHO HE SENT TO LEBANON TO PROVIDE

AN ASSESSMENT AS THE FATHER OF A MARINE-WHO TONIGHT IS IN GRENADA AND

WHO IS SCHEDULED FOR DUTY IN LEBANON - IT'S OK.

Appendix C.
White House Situation Report

WHITE HOUSE SITUATION ROOM

PAGE 02 OF 03   BEIRUT 1728   DTG: 230807Z OCT 83   PSN: 064222

E.O. 12356: DECL: OADR
TAGS: PINS, ASEC, MOPS, LE, FR, US
SUBJECT: MAJOR BOMB ATTACK ON US AND FRENCH MNF
CONTINGENT - SITUATION AS OF 0830 LOCAL

1.   (C—ENTIRE TEXT).

2.   AT 0622 LOCAL SUNDAY MORNING, OCTOBER 23, A VEHICLE
LOADED WITH EXPLOSIVES DEMOLISHED THE HEADQUARTERS OF
THE USMNF BATTALION LANDING TEAM AT THE BEIRUT
INTERENATIONAL AIRPORT (BIA).   THE USMNF HEADQUARTERS
ESTIMATES THAT AT LEAST TWO HUNDRED PEOPLE WERE IN THE
BUILDING, WHICH SERVES ALSO AS BARRACKS, AT THE TIME.
THEY BELIEVE MOST OF THE PERSONNEL IN THE BUILDING ARE
NOW DEAD.   (SIMULTANEOUSLY, A FRENCH MNF SUBORDINATE
HEADQUARTERS BUILDING WAS SEVERELY DAMAGED BY AN
EXPLOSION IN AN ADJACENT BUILDING IN THE RAMLET AL BAYDA
AREA.   WE HAVE FEW DETAILS AT THIS TIME, BUT WE
UNDERSTAND THAT THERE ARE AT LEAST 10 DEAD AND MANY MORE
WOUNDED).

3.   THE US MARINE BLT IS A SUBORDINATE UNIT TO THE
24TH MARINE AMPHIBIOUS UNIT WHICH MAKES UP THE USMNF
PRESENCE IN BEIRUT.   THE COMMANDER OF THE 24TH MAU,
COL. TIMOTHY GERAGHTY,   IS UNHURT AND IN CONTROL OF
THE SITUATION.   HIS HEADQUARTERS, IN A NEARBY BUILDING
CONTINUES TO FUNCTION EFFECTIVELY.   SURVIVORS AND
BODIES ARE STILL BEING EVACUATED FROM THE RUINS OF THE
BLT BUILDING.   RED CROSS AND OTHER LEBANESE DISASTER
RELIEF PERSONNEL ARE ON THE SCENE, AND HEAVY EQUIPMENT
IS BEING USED TO CLEAR THE WRECKAGE.   WOUNDED
PERSONNEL ARE BEING EVACUATED TO THE ITALIAN MNF FIELD
HOSPITAL NEAR SABRA/SHATILA REFUGEE CAMP, TO US NAVY
SHIPS OFFSHORE, AND PROBABLY TO LOCAL HOSPITALS AS WELL.
FRENCH WOUNDED ARE ALSO BEING SENT TO THE ITALIAN HOS-

WHITE HOUSE SITUATION ROOM

PAGE 03 OF 03   BEIRUT 1728   DTG: 230807Z OCT 83   PSN: 064222

PITAL AND TO LOCAL HOSPITALS. LEBANESE ARMED FORCES
ARE ON THE SCENE PROVIDING ASSISTANCE.

4.   AS THE USMNF CONTINGENT RECONSTRUCTS THE INCIDENT
A TRUCK LOADED WITH EXPLOSIVES WAS DRIVEN INTO AN
AIRPORT PARKING LOT IMMEDIATELY SOUTH OF THE BLT
BUILDING. IT CRASHED THROUGH A METAL GATE, PAST
MARINE DEFENSIVE POSITIONS AND INTO THE LOBBY OF THE
BUILDING. THE BUILDING IS ABOUT 50 METERS NORTH OF THE
EDGE OF THE PARKING LOT. THE LOBBY EXTENDED THE
FULL HEIGHT OF THE 4 OR 5 STORY BUILDING, AND THE
TRUCK APPARENTLY EXPLODED IN THE CENTER OF THE BUILDING,
PEELING IT OUTWARD IN ALL DIRECTIONS.

5.   CODEL HUMPHREY, WHICH HAD ARRIVED IN BEIRUT THE
PREVIOUS EVENING, HAD SPENT THE NIGHT ON BOARD THE
USS I-WO JIMA OFFSHORE AND HAD NOT COME ASHORE. THE
EMBASSY IS ADVISING THE SENATOR TO REMAIN ON BOARD
SHIP UNTIL THE SITUATION HAS CLARIFIED.

6.   AMBASSADOR BARTHOLOMEW WILL BE VISITING THE
SCENE SHORTLY.
BARTHOLOMEW
BT

Appendix D.
Congressional Letters

RONALD V. DELLUMS, CALIF.
PATRICIA SCHROEDER, COLO.
ABRAHAM KAZEN, JR., TEX.
ANTONIO B. WON PAT, GUAM
LARRY P. McDONALD, GA.
BEVERLY B. BYRON, MD.
NICHOLAS MAVROULES, MASS.
EARL HUTTO, FLA.
IKE SKELTON, MO.
MARVIN LEATH, TEX.
DAVE McCURDY, OKLA.
THOMAS M. FOGLIETTA, PA.
ROY DYSON, MD.
DENNIS M. HERTEL, MICH.
MARILYN LLOYD, TENN.
NORMAN SISISKY, VA.
RICHARD RAY, GA.
JOHN M. SPRATT, JR., S.C.
FRANK McCLOSKEY, IND.
C. ROBIN BRITT, N.C.
SOLOMON P. ORTIZ, TEX.
RONALD D. COLEMAN, TEX.

ROBERT E. BADHAM, CALIF.
BOB STUMP, ARIZ.
JIM COURTER, N.J.
LARRY J. HOPKINS, KY.
ROBERT W. DAVIS, MICH.
KEN KRAMER, COLO.
DUNCAN L. HUNTER, CALIF.
THOMAS F. HARTNETT, S.C.
DANIEL B. CRANE, ILL.
DAVID O'B. MARTIN, N.Y.
JOHN R. KASICH, OHIO

JOHN J. FORD, STAFF DIRECTOR

U.S. House of Representatives
COMMITTEE ON ARMED SERVICES
Washington, D.C. 20515

NINETY-EIGHTH CONGRESS

MELVIN PRICE (ILL.), CHAIRMAN
September 30, 1983

Dear Colonel Geraghty:

On behalf of the Armed Services Committee delegation that visited your command in Lebanon last Saturday, I want to thank you for the opportunity to meet with you and your men and for your very frank discussion of the situation faced by the Marines there.

After hearing your remarks, surveying the surrounding countryside from atop your headquarters, and talking to many of your men, we felt we had a much better grasp of the situation. When we returned to Washington, we reported to the Armed Services Committee and to the House (see attachment). Portions of our report were included in the resolution that passed the House on September 28.

I hope that what we succeeded in including in the resolution will help to dispel any uneasiness your men may have about the Congress' continuing concern for their welfare. The revised resolution requires the executive branch to submit a report to Congress every 60 days on the situation in Lebanon--to include a detailed accounting of the status of the Marine contingent. Congress, in turn, is preparing to use the required reports and other means to monitor your situation on a continuing basis.

Colonel Geraghty, the most lasting impression we experienced during our trip was the heartening feeling that a very capable group of young Americans led by dedicated officers is performing outstandingly in one of the most demanding situations military men can be called on to face. Our delegation received inspiration from the manner in which the Marines in Lebanon are demonstrating daily what it means to be an American.

Best wishes to you and your men. We were especially pleased to learn of the achievement of a cease-fire the morning after we left Lebanon. That is great news, and we certainly hope it will hold.

Sincerely,

Samuel S. Stratton
Head of Delegation

Attachment

Col. Tim Geraghty, USMC
Commander, 24th MAU
FPO New York 09502

We were most impressed by your cool leadership!

BILL NICHOLS
3RD DISTRICT, ALABAMA

2407 RAYBURN BUILDING
WASHINGTON, D.C. 20515
PHONE: (202) 225-3261

COUNTIES:

AUTAUGA   LEE
CALHOUN   MACON
CHAMBERS   RANDOLPH
CLAY   RUSSELL
CLEBURNE   TALLADEGA
COOSA   TALLAPOOSA
ELMORE

COMMITTEE ON
ARMED SERVICES

DISTRICT OFFICES:

104 FEDERAL BUILDING
POST OFFICE BOX 2042
ANNISTON, ALABAMA 36202
PHONE: 236-5655

107 FEDERAL BUILDING
OPELIKA, ALABAMA 36801
PHONE: 745-5222

115 EAST NORTH SIDE
TUSKEGEE, ALABAMA 36083
PHONE: 727-6490

Congress of the United States
House of Representatives
Washington, D.C. 20515

September 28, 1983

Colonel Timothy J. Geraghty
Commander 24 MAU
Headquarters
24 MAU Det. M
FPO New York, New York 09502

Dear Colonel Geraghty:

As a member of the House Armed Services delegation who visited your headquarters over the weekend, I want to take this occasion to express my appreciation for the many courtesies which you rendered to this Member of Congress.

As an old soldier from World War II, I perhaps more than many deeply appreciate the job which you and our other Marines are performing in the Beirut area. Your task is not easy and the dedication I observed in talking with your officers, non-commissioned officers and men typifies all of the fine qualities which have been displayed over the years by your branch of service.

My continued best wishes as you command this important Marine Amphibious Unit.

Sincerely,

Bill Nichols, M. C.

BN/j

Appendix E.
Addendum to National Security Decision Directive 103, September 10, 1983

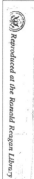

~~SECRET~~

SYSTEM II
91075 Add-On

THE WHITE HOUSE

WASHINGTON

September 11, 1983

Addendum to NSDD 103 On Lebanon of September 10, 1983

~~SECRET~~

It has been determined that occupation of the dominant terrain in the vicinity of SUQ-AL-GHARB by hostile forces will endanger Marine positions. Therefore, successful LAF defense of the area of SUQ-AL-GHARB is vital to the safety of US personnel (USMNF, other US military personnel in Beirut, and the US diplomatic presence). As a consequence, when the US ground commander determines that SUQ-AL-GHARB is in danger of falling as a result of attack involving non-Lebanese forces and if requested by the host government, appropriate US military assistance in defense of SUQ-AL-GHARB is authorized. Assistance for this specific objective may include naval gun fire support and, if deemed necessary, tactical air strikes, but shall exclude ground forces. (S)

I further direct that the Secretary of State immediately inform and consult with other MNF contributor governments and appropriate Congressional leadership on this directive. (S)

Ronald Reagan

DECLASSIFIED
Authority S. Tilley NSC (F87-035) 5/17/99
BY _____, NARA, Date 8/56/99

~~SECRET~~
Declassify on: OADR

COPY _____ OF 2 COPIES

CHRON FILE

~~SECRET~~

Source: Reagan Library

Appendix F.
Statement of the Families

Printed verbatim from Trial Transcript, March 7, 2003.

ON OCTOBER 23RD, 1983, the Marine barracks building at the Beirut International Airport was attacked by a suicide terrorist bomber driving a Mercedes truck with a gas-enhanced explosive device equal to 21,000 pounds of explosives. It was the largest non-nuclear explosion ever detonated on the face of the earth. It killed 241 Marines and other Servicemen and wounded countless others. Others have died since from their wounds.

This horrible act of terrorism, carried out by a terrorist group called Hezbollah, was sponsored, condoned, facilitated and financed by the Iranian government. The Beirut families and survivors who have chosen to participate have filed this lawsuit against the Iranian government in the hope of creating a deterrent for future acts of state-sponsored terrorism and also to exact a small measure of justice that has not yet been realized by our still grieving families.

Since it is unlikely that Iran will give up the terrorists responsible—in fact, they continue to harbor them—a lawsuit seemed to be the answer to our prayers for, at least, justice.

The Marines and Sailors and Soldiers serving in Beirut were called Peacekeepers because they were sent in a gesture of good faith for our commitment to peace in the Middle East. Their mission was to provide a presence in Beirut, but not to interfere. They served with honor, valor, courage and restraint.

The motto of the Beirut Veterans of America is, "Our first duty is to remember." We have never forgotten our heroes of Beirut, that they paid the ultimate price for a chance for peace. They came in peace and they were murdered in their sleep.

We the families of the Beirut Peacekeepers, in their memory and in their honor, want to join the fight against terrorism. The courtroom is our battlefield. This is where the war on terrorism will be fought and won. We want to write the last chapter on the Peacekeepers in Beirut and establish the legacy they deserve.

Our hope is that their legacy will be that through their sacrifice, the first of many, peace was realized and terrorism was defeated.

Holding terrorist nations responsible for their crimes is the best deterrent to terrorism. There will never be peace until we first have justice. Let no other family ever feel the pain of grief so strong and the despair of injustice so deep that we have lived with since their deaths. The memory of the Peacekeepers of Beirut, our sons and brothers, fathers and husbands, are our conscience and our guide in our quest for justice.

We must hold Iran responsible and accountable for this act of terrorism. Then and only then will we make clear to them that sponsoring terrorism will cost them billions. We must make it hurt.

The U.S. Government must allow the Beirut families to attach any judgment from this court to the frozen Iranian assets held by the U.S. Government since the seizure of the U.S. Embassy in Tehran in 1979 when 52 Americans were held captive for 444 days.

Instead of the Marine barracks bombing being a blip on the war on terrorism or the American conscience, this horrific act should be recognized for what it really was—a turning point in Iranian and U.S. relations that made it undeniably clear to Iran that they could not get away with kidnapping and murder.

Since the bombing in Beirut, we have watched in horror the continued use of terrorism as a political tool. Terrorism has grown like a cancer on humanity and has gone time and time again unchallenged and unchecked. It is time for justice, it is time to take a stand, it is time to stop terrorism by any means available, it is time to do the right thing for all victims of terrorism.

We challenge the White House, the Department of Justice and the State Department to support us in obtaining the justice we deserve, the justice that the heroes of Beirut demand.

Notes

Chapter 1. The Beginning

1. Eric Hammel, *The Root: The Marines in Beirut, August 1982–February 1984* (San Diego: Harcourt Brace Jovanovich, 1985), 4–9.
2. Benis M. Frank, *U.S. Marines in Lebanon, 1982–1984* (Washington, D.C.: Headquarters Marine Corps, 1987), 9.
3. Richard Reeves, *President Reagan: The Triumph of Imagination* (New York: Simon & Shuster, 2005), 123–24.
4. George P. Shultz, *Turmoil and Triumph: My Years as Secretary of State* (New York: Macmillan, 1993), 103.
5. Robert C. McFarlane with Zofia Smardz, *Special Trust* (New York: Cadell and Davies, 1994), 210–11.
6. Shultz, *Turmoil and Triumph*, 102.
7. Ibid., 103.
8. Ibid., 105–7.
9. Department of Defense (DOD) Commission Report on BIA Terrorist Attack, October 23, 1983, 35–36.
10. Hammel, *The Root*, 60–61.
11. Frank, *U.S. Marines in Lebanon*, 56.

Chapter 2. Preparation and Deployment

1. Robert Baer, *See No Evil: The True Story of a Ground Soldier in the CIA's War on Terrorism* (New York: Three Rivers Press, 2002), 67.
2. Frank, *U.S. Marines in Lebanon*, 61.
3. Ibid., 68–69.
4. DOD Commission Report on BIA Terrorist Attack, 30.
5. Caspar W. Weinberger, *Fighting for Peace: Seven Critical Years in the Pentagon* (New York: Warner, 1990), 155–56.
6. Shultz, *Turmoil and Triumph*, 221.

Chapter 6. The Predictable War

1. Tom Clancy with Gen. Carl Stiner and Tony Koltz, *Shadow Warriors: Inside the Special Forces* (New York: Putnam's Sons, 2002), 242–43.
2. McFarlane, *Special Trust*, 250–51.
3. Clancy, *Shadow Warriors*, 246.
4. Thomas L. Friedman, *From Beirut to Jerusalem* (New York: Farrar, Straus and Giroux, 1989), 77.

Chapter 8. Suicide Bombings and Aftermath

1. Hammel, *The Root*, 372–75.
2. General P. X. Kelley's speech at the dedication of the Beirut Memorial, Camp Lejeune, North Carolina, October 23, 1986.
3. Frank, *U.S. Marines in Lebanon*, 101.

Chapter 9. Warriors' Compassion

1. Personal Notes of Col. Gerry Turley, USMC (Retired), April 5, 2007.

Chapter 10. Investigations

1. DOD Commission Report on BIA Terrorist Attack, 74–5.
2. Ibid., 90–141.
3. House Armed Services Committee (HASC) Report on Adequacy of U.S. Marine Corps Security in Beirut, December 19, 1983, 41–42.
4. Ibid., 27.
5. Ibid., 29.
6. Ibid., 46–47
7. Ibid., 76–78
8. Ibid., 35
9. Ibid., 48
10. Long Commision Report, 92.
11. Lou Cannon, *President Reagan: The Role of a Lifetime* (New York: Touchstone, 1991), 396.
12. Weinberger, *Fighting for Peace*, 165.

Chapter 11. Lessons Learned

1. Larry Pintak, *Beirut Outtakes: A TV Correspondent's Portrait of America's Encounter with Terror* (Lexington, MA: Lexington Books, 1988), 92–93 and 171.
2. Shultz, *Turmoil and Triumph*, 220–21.
3. Cannon, *President Reagan*, 361.
4. Thomas L. Friedman, "Fair Game," *New York Times/Life and Times*, October 1993.
5. Shultz, *Turmoil and Triumph*, 103–5.
6. Ibid., 107.
7. Ibid., 110.
8. Timothy Naftali, *Blind Spot: The Secret History of American Counterterrorism* (New York: Basic Books, 2005), 131–34.
9. Weinberger, *Fighting for Peace*, 161–62.
10. Naftali, *Blind Spot*, 134.
11. Ronald Reagan, *An American Life* (New York: Simon & Schuster, 1990), 464.
12. Naftali, *Blind Spot*, 134.
13. Weinberger, *Fighting for Peace,* 162.
14. John F. Lehman, Jr., *Command of the Seas* (New York: Charles Scribner's Sons, 1988), 326.
15. Ibid., 329–37.
16. Robert F. Turner, "The War Powers Resolution: Its Implementation in Theory and Practice," *Foreign Policy Research Institute* (Philadelphia, 1983), 108–9.
17. Shultz, *Turmoil and Triumph*, 226.
18. Gen. P. X. Kelley, Testimony before Congress, September 13, 1983.
19. *Washington Post*, October 23, 1994, C2.

20. Karen DeYoung, "Ex-Secretaries Suggest New War Powers Policy," *Washington Post*, July 9, 2008.

Chapter 12. Connecting the Dots
1. Transcript of trial: *Peterson et al. v. Islamic Republic of Iran* (March 17, 2003), 20–47.
2. Ibid., 167–79.
3. Ibid., 201–13.
4. Ibid., 213–25.
5. Ibid., 48–57.
6. Ibid., 234–35.
7. Ibid., 13.
8. Ibid., 5.
9. Reuters, "Iran Hard-Liners Mark 1983 Attack on U.S. Marines," December 2, 2004.
10. Transcript, *Peterson et al. v. Islamic Republic of Iran et al.*, 138–42.
11. Ibid., 126–27.
12. Ibid., 120–46.
13. Ibid., 142–45.
14. Joseph Klein, "Judgments Against Iran," *FrontPageMagazine.com*, September 10, 2007.
15. Sara Carter and Bill Gertz, "One of the Most Dangerous Terrorists Killed in Syria," *Washington Times*, February 18, 2008.
16. Kevin Peraino, "The Fox Is Hunted Down," *Newsweek*, February 25, 2008.
17. Thomas Joscelyn, "Death by Car Bomb in Damascus," *Weekly Standard*, February 15, 2008.

Chapter 13. Iran, Syria, and Hezbollah
1. "Serial Killers of Americans," *Washington Times*, August 16, 2007.
2. Peraino, "The Fox is Hunted Down."
3. Andrew McCarthy, "Negotiate with Iran?" *National Review Online*, December 8, 2006.
4. Joscelyn, "Death by Car Bomb in Damascus."
5. Joseph Lieberman, "Iran's Proxy War," *Wall Street Journal*, July 6, 2007.
6. Ivan Watson, "Understanding the Case of Ali Reza Askari," *All Things Considered*, National Public Radio, April 2, 2007.
7. JoshuaPundit.blogspot.com, July 21, 2007.
8. "Full Nelson for Syria's Assad," *Investor's Business Daily*, December 14, 2006; Condoleezza Rice interview published in Israeli newpaper *Maariv*.
9. This Week Section, *National Review*, November 7, 2005.
10. Cannon, *President Reagan*, 362.
11. Gary C. Gambill, "Dossier: Abdul Halim Khaddam," *Mideast Monitor*, February 2006.
12. Cannon, *President Reagan*, 366.
13. Peter Crail, James Martin Center for Nonproliferation Studies, January 4, 2007.

Chapter 14. The War Comes Home
1. Tony Perry, *L.A. Times*, February 20, 2009.

Glossary

AAV	Amphibious assault vehicle (also called AMTRAC)
AK-47	Soviet-designed 7.62mm assault rifle, also known as a Kalashnikov
ALO	Air liaison officer
Amal	Shiite militia
ANGLICO	Air-Naval Gunfire Liaison Company
APC	Armored personnel carrier
AT	Antiterrorism or antitank
AUB	American University of Beirut
BIA	Beirut International Airport
BLT	Battalion landing team; also refers to the battalion headquarters building
C-4	Composition 4 (a plastic explosive)
CH-46E	U.S. Marine/Navy medium helicopter (Sea Knight)
CH-53E	Marine heavy assault helicopter (Super Sea Stallion)
CIA	Central Intelligence Agency
CINCEUR	U.S. commander in chief, European Command
CINCUSNAVEUR	Commander in chief, U.S. Naval Forces, Europe
CJCS	Chairman, Joint Chiefs of Staff
CMC	Commandant of the Marine Corps
CO	Commanding officer
Cobra	AH-1T gunship helicopter
COC	Combat operations center or change of command
Comm	Communications
COMSIXTHFLT	Commander, Sixth Fleet
CP	Command post; also combat post; also checkpoint
CTC	Counterterrorist Center, within the Central Intelligence Agency
CTF	Commander, task force
CTF 60	Commander, Task Force 60: Adm. Jerry Tuttle, Carrier Battle Group
CTF 61	Commander, Task Force 61: Commodore Rick France, Amphibious Squadron 8 (PHIBRON 8)
CTF 62	Commander, Task Force 62: Col. Tim Geraghty, commanding officer, 24th Marine Amphibious Unit (24th MAU)
DIA	Defense Intelligence Agency
DOD	Department of Defense
DOS	Department of State
Dragon	Wire-guided antitank missile
Druze	Muslim sect; also Progressive Socialist Party (PSP) led by Walid Jumblatt

EOD	Explosive ordnance disposal
EXO	Executive officer
FAC	Forward air controller
FAE	Fuel air explosive, or gases used to enhance destructive effect
FASTAB	Field Artillery School's target acquisition battery (U.S. Army)
FMFLANT	Fleet Marine Force, Atlantic
GOL	Government of Lebanon
Grunt	Marine infantryman
Gunner	Marine commissioned warrant officer
Gunny	Gunnery sergeant
HASC	House Armed Services Committee
Head	Lavatory
Helo	Helicopter
Hezbollah	"Party of God," a radical Shiite organization founded by Iran in 1983 that played a major role in suicide attacks against the multinational peacekeeping force
HMM	Marine medium helicopter squadron
Hooterville	Nickname that Beirut Marines gave to an adjacent slum, Hay-al-Sellum
HST	Helicopter support team
Huey	UH-1 utility helicopter
IC	Intelligence community
IDF	Israel Defense Force
Illume	Illumination
Incoming	Incoming fire
IR	Infrared
IRGC	Islamic Revolutionary Guard Corps, which is also called Pasdaran
JCS	Joint Chiefs of Staff
JP-5	Jet propulsion (grade 5); jet fuel
Katyusha	122mm Soviet-built artillery rocket
KIA	Killed in action
LAAW	Light antitank assault weapon
LAF	Lebanese Armed Forces, the official armed forces of the Lebanese government
LCU	Landing craft, utility; also called U-boat
LF	Lebanese Forces, the major Christian militia built around the Phalange Party
LF6F	Landing Force Sixth Fleet
LFORM	Landing Force Operational Reserve Material
LHA	Combination well-deck ship and helicopter carrier with large troop carrying capacity; also used by VSTOL (AV-8) aircraft (vertical/short takeoff and landing)
LNO	Liaison officer
LPD	Landing platform, dock; a well-deck ship with a helicopter platform
LPH	Landing platform, helicopter (an amphibious assault ship); e.g., flagship USS *Iwo Jima*
LS	Landing site
LSD	Landing ship, dock; a well-deck ship with a helicopter platform

LST	Landing ship, tank; large landing craft with bow-opening doors for off-loading tracked and wheeled vehicles
LZ	Landing zone
M-16	U.S. 5.56mm assault rifle
M-60	U.S. 7.62mm machine gun
M-60A1	U.S. battle tank
M-198	U.S. 155mm towed howitzer
MAB	Marine amphibious brigade
MAF	Marine amphibious force, or the largest MAGTF
MAGTF	Marine air-ground task force
MARG	Mediterranean Amphibious Ready Group
Maronite	Largest Christian sect in Lebanon
MAU	Marine amphibious unit; the smallest MAGTF, built around a BLT, HMM, and MSSG and typically numbering about eighteen hundred personnel
MEA	Middle East Airlines, a privately owned, Lebanese-flagged passenger airline
Medevac	Medical evacuation
MNF	Multinational force
MNPF	Multinational Peacekeeping Force
MOS	Military occupational specialty
MRE	Meal, ready to eat; or standard military rations
MSR	Main supply route, a road used to support a force logistically to sustain its capability
MSSG	MAU Service Support Group
MTT	Mobile training team of U.S. military members assigned to train foreign military personnel in specific skills
NCO	Noncommissioned officer
NCOIC	Noncommissioned officer in charge
NEO	Noncombatant evacuation operation
NET	Communications network
NRO	National Reconnaissance Office
NSA	National Security Agency
OMC	Office of Military Cooperation, which coordinates and facilitates providing U.S. military equipment, training, and supplies to the armed forces of another country
OPS	Operations
OPSEC	Operational security
PETN	Pentaerythritol tetranitrate, a high explosive used by terrorists in the suicide truck bombings of U.S. and French MNF on October 23, 1983
Phalange	Lebanese Christian faction founded in 1936 by Pierre Gemayel, who also was father of Lebanese president Amin Gemayel (1982–88)
PHIBRON	Amphibious squadron of normally three to five ships designed to transport and land Marines
PLA	Palestinian Liberation Army; Syrian supported
PLO	Palestinian Liberation Organization
PSP	Progressive Socialist Party, or the main party of Druze providing military and social service as well as political representation

Quds Force	A secretive Iranian paramilitary unit of the IRGC whose primary mission is international terrorism planning and operations; "Quds" means Jerusalem in both Persian and Arabic Recon Reconnaissance
ROE	Rules of engagement, or rules that lay out the limitations and circumstances under which U.S. forces may initiate combat
Root, The	Marine name for the city of Beirut
RPG	Rocket-propelled grenade; Soviet-made antiarmor weapon
S-1	Personnel and Administration Section
S-2	Intelligence Section
S-3	Operations Section
S-4	Logistics and Supply Section
SA-7	A handheld SAM
SAM	Surface-to-air missile
SEALs	U.S. Navy's elite sea, air, and land special operations unit
SECNAV	Secretary of the Navy
Semtex	A plastic explosive
Shiite	Muslim sect; also known as Shia
SNCO	Staff noncommissioned officer
SRB	Service record book; individual Marine's personal information
Sunni	Muslim sect
TAB	Target acquisition battery
TARPS	Tactical aerial reconnaissance pod system
TMA	Trans Mediterranean Airways, a Lebanese-flagged, cargo-carrying, privately owned airline
TNT	Trinitrotoluene, a powerful explosive
TOW	Tube-launched, optically guided, wire-controlled missile
WIA	Wounded in action
WO	Warrant officer
Zuni	A type of air-to-ground or air-to-air rocket

Bibliography

Baer, Robert. *See No Evil: The True Story of a Ground Soldier in the CIA's War on Terrorism.* New York: Three Rivers Press, 2002.

Cannon, Lou. *President Reagan: The Role of a Lifetime.* New York: Touchstone, 1991.

Clancy, Tom, with Gen. Carl Stiner and Tony Koltz. *Shadow Warriors: Inside the Special Forces.* New York: G. P. Putnam's Sons, 2002.

Dolphin, Glenn E. *24 MAU, 1983: A Marine Looks Back at the Peacekeeping Mission to Beirut, Lebanon.* Baltimore: Publish America, 2005.

Frank, Benis M. *U.S. Marines in Lebanon, 1982-1984.* Washington, D.C.: Headquarters Marine Corps, 1987.

Friedman, Thomas L. *From Beirut to Jerusalem.* New York: Farrar, Straus and Giroux, 1989.

Gunaratna, Rohan. *Inside Al-Qaeda: Global Network of Terror.* New York: Columbia University Press, 2002.

Hammel, Eric. *The Root: The Marines in Beirut, August 1982-February 1984.* San Diego: Harcourt Brace Jovanovich, 1985.

Lehman, John F., Jr. *Command of the Seas.* New York: Charles Scribner's Sons, 1988.

Martin, David C., and John Walcott. *Best Laid Plans: The Inside Story of America's War against Terrorism.* New York: Touchstone, 1988.

McFarlane, Robert C., with Zofia Smardz *Special Trust.* New York: Cadell and Davies, 1994.

Naftali, Timothy. *Blind Spot: The Secret History of American Counterterrorism.* New York: Basic Books, 2005.

Pintak, Larry. *Beirut Outtakes: A TV Correspondent's Portrait of America's Encounter with Terror.* Lexington, MA: Lexington Books, 1988.

Pugh, Robert L. *Policy Aspects of the Deployment of U.S. Marines to Lebanon, 1982-1984: A Case Study.* Washington, D.C.: Department of State, Foreign Service Institute, 1984-85.

Reagan, Ronald. *An American Life.* New York: Simon & Schuster, 1990.

Reeves, Richard. *President Reagan: The Triumph of Imagination.* New York: Simon & Schuster, 2005.

Shultz, George P. *Turmoil and Triumph: My Years as Secretary of State.* New York: Macmillan, 1993.

Timberg, Robert. *The Nightingale's Song.* New York: Touchstone, 1995.

Turner, Robert F. *The War Powers Resolution: Its Implementation in Theory and Practice.* Philadelphia: Foreign Policy Research Institute, 1983.

Weinberger, Caspar W. *Fighting for Peace: Seven Critical Years in the Pentagon.* New York: Warner Books, 1990.

Wilson, George C. *Supercarrier: An Inside Account Aboard the World's Most Powerful Ship, the USS John F. Kennedy.* New York: Macmillan, 1988.

Index

About the Author

COL. TIMOTHY J. GERAGHTY was born and raised in St. Louis, Missouri. He was a career Marine officer who commanded a reconnaissance company in Vietnam and while a lieutenant colonel served in a special assignment with the Central Intelligence Agency's Special Operations Group. As a colonel, he commanded the 24th Marine Amphibious Unit in Beirut, Lebanon, in 1983 as part of the Multinational Peacekeeping Force. Upon retirement from the Corps, he returned to the CIA to serve in the Counterterrorist Center and later worked in private industry. He resides in Phoenix, Arizona.